Bernice L. H

CHANGING

SEX

TRANSSEXUALISM,

TECHNOLOGY,

AND THE IDEA

OF GENDER

DUKE UNIVERSITY PRESS   Durham and London 1995

CONTENTS

PREFACE

I fell into this project sideways. In the summer of 1990, I had just passed my comprehensive examinations and was beginning work on a dissertation concerning the idea of identity in feminist theory. It was a topic I had been thinking about for some time and it seemed a natural for a theory-minded feminist graduate student like myself. But no matter how much I applied myself to the task, most of my thoughts on the issue seemed uninspired, boring, even obvious. By October, that project clearly had no future and I was fishing around for another one. I was also relatively homebound, with acute tendinitis in one foot. In a rather despairing mood, I began reading — and this book started to happen to me.

The idea of transvestism was kicking around feminist literary criticism at the time, and when I finally got to the library to look for primary source material, I inadvertently found texts that dealt with transsexualism. Now that was really fascinating. For about six months I read anything and everything I could find about cross-dressing and sex change. I attended a national conference for transvestites and transsexuals. I started to write critiques of the existent feminist treatments of transsexualism. The possibilities for understanding the construction of "gender" through an analysis of transsexualism seemed enormous and there wasn't a lot of critical material out there. But it wasn't until the following summer, in a seminar on "Theorizing the Body," that I found my "hook," my way into the project.

It was very simple, really. In thinking about technologies of the body, I realized that certain technologies were essential for the material practices known as "sex change." After all, without endocrinology and plastic surgery, there could be no hormonal treatments or genital surgery. I hypothesized that transsexualism emerged in the twentieth century at least in part due to advances in medical technologies that made physical "sex change" possible.

The essay that I wrote for the seminar was supposed to be the first chapter of my dissertation but instead provided an outline for the entire text. During my research I discovered that the use of the term "gender" as a reference for the social aspects of sex identity first occurred in the context of research on intersexuality (hermaphroditism) in the 1950s. Clinicians developing protocols for the treatment of intersexuality needed a theory to help them decide what sex to place their subjects in. After all, for the first time in history, doctors could "fix" intersexuality with the relatively new sciences of endocrinology and plastic surgery. "Gender" was a concept that helped physicians and psychologists theorize the experience of subjects who needed medicine to determine what sex they should be, as well as the experience of those who were manifestly one sex but wanted to be the other. In this way, a project that initially suggested that studying transsexualism was a way to investigate the operation of gender in culture became one that suggested how gender was produced as a named concept in the first place.

Thus, while this book has a theoretical purpose and focus, it is also necessarily historical. At the broadest level, my work participates in what may be called the "Foucauldian paradigm," which I understand to involve the analysis of shifts in epistemological paradigms as a way of interpreting and marking the emergence of new forms of being human. In this sense, Foucault's work on madness, on the emergence of clinical medicine, on the development of prison systems in the nineteenth century, and (most famously) on the history of sexuality are foundational to the enterprise I undertake in this book. In each of his projects, Foucault endeavored to examine the discourses of a particular institutional context in order to determine the conditions that made its emergence possible. Foucault also elaborated a methodology that refused to see power as emanating from a source outside the subject in order to repress or inhibit the actions of that subject. Rather, he conceptualized power as, essentially, an enabling aspect in the formation of subjectivities. Since power circulates in discourses, it is through the analysis of discursive formations that one can trace the conditions of possibility for the emergence of new subjectivities—new ways, that is, of being human.

Foucault's emphasis on the analysis of discourse as a method of "doing history" has deeply influenced my own approach to the cultural study of medicine and of the phenomenon of transsexuality. In this book, I focus narrowly on the "official discourses" of transsexualism—those produced both by medical personnel and by transsexuals—in order to ascertain the discursive conditions that made the emergence of the demand for sex change and its recognition within medicine possible in the twentieth century. As I noted above, I argue that these discourses themselves depend upon specific technical practices within medicine—endocrinology and plastic surgery—that developed in the late nineteenth and early twentieth centuries. The discursive conditions of possibility for the emergence of transsexualism, therefore, are contingent upon certain *material* conditions that make the technology of sex change possible.

It was the work of Roland Barthes, not of Foucault, however, that helped me theorize the impact of the term "gender" on the semiotic economy of "sex." I began to think about this when I realized that although most people adhered to a distinction between "sex" and "gender" that relegates the first term to nature and the second to culture, some were beginning to use "gender" to refer to both realms. Instead of "sex discrimination" people used the term "gender discrimination"; on some affirmative action forms, applicants were asked to enter their gender—male or female. Thus, although "gender" originally was used by researchers to refer to social attributes of sexed identity, it was beginning to dominate popular discourses to such an extent that its older usage—as a direct substitute for the word "sex"—was being revived. Gender was taking over the semiotics of sex.

Barthes's book *Mythologies* helped me to think through this issue by showing me how a concept (such as gender) comes to overdetermine a signifying field. I use Barthes's theory of myth because it works with this set of materials. Conceptualizing gender as myth helps to explain why (almost) no one knows its history as a concept, even though gender is one of the most important categories of critical analysis to be theorized in the twentieth century. Using Barthes's work in *Mythologies* also helps to explain why many feminists tend to relegate sex to the realm of the "natural" and therefore the untheorizable in feminist terms. "Myth," in Barthes's conception, radically erases the semiotic conditions of its own existence; as a secondary semiotic chain, it obscures the significance of a prior semiosis that is its "ground." Gender, I argue, does this with sex.

I explain and elaborate this material in detail in chapter 6, "Semiotics of Sex, Gender, and the Body." While the other chapters work to establish the largely historical and interpretive arguments of the book (the development of endocrinology and plastic surgery as necessary both technically and ideologically to the emergence of transsexualism, the crucial theorization of gender in the creation of treatment protocols for intersexuality, the emergence of the demand for sex change as the central symptom of the disorder, the effacement of technology in the autobiographies of "official transsexuals"), chapter 6 attempts to articulate the relationship of these arguments to debates in critical theory today. Thus, chapter 6 is necessarily different from the other chapters; it is more densely theoretical and more embedded in the discourses of critical theory because in it I lay out the theoretical premises of my analysis and make my argument concerning the effect of "gender" in contemporary discourse and society. This book makes a crucial connection between the history of the concept of gender and its theoretical elaborations; chapter 6 theorizes that connection.

In revising my dissertation into a book—a project which took about a year and which substantially altered the text—I have tried to make the book as reader-friendly as possible because I anticipate a multidisciplinary reading audience. The readers for Duke University Press, Suzanne Kessler and Julia Epstein, helped me to rewrite the text for a broader audience than the dissertation anticipated. Reynolds Smith, my editor at Duke, was also crucial to this endeavor. Other helpful advice came from Anne Fausto-Sterling, Nancy Cervetti, Karen Richman, Anne Bartlett, Alice Adams, members of the Lesbian/Gay Studies and Feminist Workshops at the University of Chicago, and audiences at the annual conferences for the Society for Literature and Science in 1992 and 1994. Katherine Hayles taught the seminar where I first conceptualized the basic argument of my thesis. Dallas Denny, editor of *Chrysalis Quarterly*, provided much-needed materials on short notice. Jill Fishman offered valuable, last-minute technical support. And Clair James, as always, helped with editing, indexing, and proofing.

Herman Rapaport, my dissertation advisor, deserves a round of applause for his support of this unorthodox project and his unfailing help to get me a job that would allow me to continue my research. He consistently pushed me to theorize this project and helped me to respond to commentary on my manuscript. I couldn't ask for a mentor more generous with his time and expertise. An Iowa Fellowship and teaching support from the English department at the University of Iowa allowed me to conduct most of the original research. A position as a Mellon Instructor in the Humanities at the University of Chicago made it possible for me to revise the manuscript for publication, just as a Mellon dissertation fellowship enabled me to spend one year "just writing" the original text.

My parents ask me so many questions about my work that I sometimes have to tell them to stop. Their interest in my scholarship and their challenging interrogation of it continue to motivate me to make my ideas a little clearer, a bit more precise. They are perhaps my toughest audience, but also my most loving.

I was pregnant for most of the year that I revised this manuscript; I am perhaps one of few expectant mothers who worry that they will give birth to a hermaphrodite. At four months, I sat in front of my computer rewriting my chapter on intersexuality, thinking that I knew more about congenital anomalies of sex than any pregnant woman should know. Rachel waited until I sent the manuscript off to Duke before making her way into this world; I thank her for her patience.

Clair James makes possible what I think of as "my life." While his son Joshua first taught me about what it means to be subject to demands, it is Clair who serves as a constant springboard for my ideas, who listens to me go on and on about problems with my work, who entertains our daughter while I write this preface. There is no other person more important to my well-being.

In a roundabout fashion, this book ended up being about identity after all. It is not, however, about people. This book addresses questions about discourses, technologies, and narratives of identity. While in the end I am critical of the phenomenon of transsexualism, I hope it is clear that I do not (cannot) condemn transsexuals themselves. Transsexuals and nontranssexuals alike live in a world of discourse that structures and supports the narratives of identity defining our existence. We are all implicated in the discursive scenarios I outline in this book.

I would like to thank the members of the International Foundation for Gender Education and Iowa Artistry who spoke with me about their experiences in 1991 and 1992. I hope that this book helps to illuminate heretofore uninterpreted aspects of those experiences, as it has helped me to differently understand many of my own.

Portions of the book were published previously by the University of Chicago Press in "Demanding Subjectivity: Transsexualism, Medicine, and the Technologies of Gender," *Journal of the History of Sexuality* 3, no. 2 (October 1992): 270–302.

Indeed, the bond that in every individual connects the physiological life and the psychic life—or better the relation existing between the contingence of an individual and the free spirit that assumes it—is the deepest enigma implied by the condition of being human.

—Simone de Beauvoir, *The Second Sex*

Take advantage of old pre-existing cabling by converting it for use in new applications at a fraction of the cost of new cabling. Lyben Gender Changers will end frustrating cable gender mismatch problems by allowing you to connect to cables with the same gender. Gender Changers transform virtually any cable . . . to its gender counterpart—male or female. So if you need to join two male connectors, simply plug each one into a single Female to Female gender changer. Lyben Gender Changers come in two sizes, a standard size measuring 2.25″ thick (suitable for most applications) and a Mini size measuring just 6mm in thickness for compact and inconspicuous connections. Both models connect all wires.

—*Lyben Computer Systems* (1992–93 Fall–Winter Edition)

CHANGING SEX

INTRODUCTION:

TRANSSEXUALISM, TECHNOLOGY,

AND THE IDEA OF GENDER

In 1958, a young woman named Agnes appeared at the Department of Psychiatry of the University of California, Los Angeles, seeking plastic surgery to remedy an apparent endocrine abnormality.[1] At the time, a group at the medical center was involved in a study of intersexed patients.[2] By all accounts, Agnes was a "feminine" woman with predictably female secondary sex characteristics: developed breasts, wide hips and small waist, long hair, smooth skin.[3] Nevertheless, rather than a vagina, labia, and clitoris, she had a fully developed penis and atrophic scrotum. She had no female internal organs; a laparotomy demonstrated "the presence of all male anatomic structures."[4] She had been brought up as a boy but insisted that she had always felt female. During puberty, she claimed, her female secondary sex characteristics developed spontaneously.

Clearly disturbed by this "natural mistake," Agnes sought corrective plastic surgery. The UCLA researchers, including psychoanalyst Robert Stoller, sociologist Harold Garfinkel, and psychologist Alexander Rosen, worked with Agnes to determine the cause of her abnormality and to investigate its effects upon her gender role and personal management skills.[5] The medical team found no physiological reason for the genital aberration but hypothesized that Agnes suffered from "testicular feminization syndrome, that is, extreme feminization of the male body (breasts, no-body and facial hair, feminine skin and subcutaneous fat distribution) due to œstrogens produced by the testes."[6] This diagnosis seemed to be confirmed after surgical removal of the penis and testes: Agnes experienced menopausal symptoms postoperatively.[7] The specific cause of her feminization remained in doubt, however, since the evidence was circumstantial: only signs of the effects of testicular feminization syndrome were present, and the supposed originating condition was read back from them. There was no absolute evidence that Agnes's testes were producing estrogen. After the surgery, Agnes was given estrogen replacement therapy, since the (alleged) source of estrogen—her testes—had been excised and she began to experience symptoms of menopause.[8]

To the chagrin of Robert Stoller, Harold Garfinkel, and others involved with the case, five years after she obtained a surgical sex change (and eight years after she originally appeared at the UCLA clinic) Agnes revealed that she had not spontaneously developed female secondary sex characteristics during adolescence, as she had maintained, but that at the age of twelve she began taking her mother's Stilbestrol, a synthetic estrogen used in estrogen replacement therapy.[9] Agnes's "passing" from man to woman turns out to have been based on another kind of "passing" altogether. Agnes fooled the doctors into believing that she was intersexual when in fact she was a "male transsexual, a biologically normal male who nonetheless feels himself to be a female and who wishes to be transformed into a female."[10] The current official definition of transsexualism, as presented in the *Diagnostic and Statistical Manual of Mental Disorders* (third edition, revised), includes the following: "The essential features of this disorder are a persistent discomfort and sense of inappropriateness about one's assigned sex in a person who has reached puberty. In addition, there is a persistent preoccupation, for at least two years, with getting rid of one's primary and secondary sex characteristics and acquiring the sex characteristics of the other sex. . . . Invariably there is the wish to live as a member of the other sex."[11]

In this book I examine the discourses and technical practices that made "sex change" an option for Agnes and others like her. In the twentieth century, it became possible for human subjects to alter certain aspects of their sexual physiology, to become "authentic" representatives of the "other sex." For intersexual subjects, medicine considers these interventions into bodily sex legitimate (albeit not routine) measures by which people without a singular sexual physiology may obtain one. Transsexuals' access to these same medical procedures is considerably more circumscribed by medical protocols concerning interference with "normally functioning" organs. Nevertheless, in the latter half of this century, transsexuals have established themselves as a population deserving of social and medical "sex reassignment."[12]

The emergence of transsexualism in the mid-twentieth century depended on developments in endocrinology and plastic surgery as technological and discursive practices. This would seem to be a self-evident claim, insofar as "sex change" is impossible without the technological and ideological support provided by medical practitioners and the medical establishment. However, these links between medical technology, medical practice, and the advent of "sex change" in the twentieth century have been ignored by most scholars who study the subject, who more usually understand transsexualism as representative of a transhistorical desire of some human subjects to be the other sex.[13]

In contrast to this view, I argue that developments in medical technology and practice were central to the establishment of the necessary conditions for the emergence of the demand for sex change, which was understood as the most important indicator of transsexual subjectivity.

Traditionally, both cultural critics and clinicians have downplayed the impact of medical technologies on transsexual subjectivity and the demand for sex change. For example, Vern Bullough (one of the most important contemporary historians of sex and gender variations) portrays transsexualism as an ahistorical and universal disorder of human sexuality that finally, in the twentieth century, has found relief.[14] By arguing that transsexualism is a twentieth-century phenomenon that should be read against specific technological advances in medical science, I am suggesting that, like homosexuality, transsexuality is a category of experience and identity that can be read as a result of specific social and cultural conditions.[15]

Homosexuality, as studied in the academy by gay affirmative scholars, has become the focus of a vital intellectual project that both facilitates the discovery (or reconstruction) of gay sensibilities and experiences in history and theorizes the emergence of what we now think of as "homosexuality" in the modern world. Gay and lesbian studies clearly form one significant foundation for my work on transsexualism, especially insofar as the idea of an emergent (as opposed to universal) subjectivity is central to my arguments.[16] Transsexuality, I will argue, is not *analogous* to homosexuality—either as a sexuality, as an object of study, or as an experience of being a sexual minority (although it is this latter experience of transsexuals that most closely resembles homosexual life in the modern world).[17] It is transsexualism's special *conceptual* and *material* relation to medical discourse and practice that distinguishes it from homosexuality.

Thus, while transsexuals suffer from many public and private indignities that make their social position like that of lesbians and gays in important ways—with regard to housing and job discrimination, living in a "closet," passing, being subject to violent attacks, etc.—transsexuals must seek and obtain medical treatment in order to be recognized *as transsexuals*.[18] Their subject position depends upon a necessary relation to the medical establishment and its discourses. Much of the discussion in chapter 4 traces transsexuals' agency in establishing their "condition" as a legitimate diagnostic category within medical language and, significantly, within clinical practice. Indeed, after the category of homosexuality was removed from the *Diagnostic and Statistical Manual of Mental Disorders*, in 1980, the category transsexualism made it in, as 302.5x, a gender identity disorder.[19] That is, transsexuals *entered* the DSM series as a "legitimate" object of medical scrutiny and intervention after gays and lesbians successfully argued themselves *out* of that supervised space. It is precisely this difference from lesbian and gay subjectivity that distinguishes transsexuality and suggests its unique relation to the *authorizing* discourses and practices of medicine.

Because of this relation to the medical institution, it seems appropriate to concentrate on the official discourses of transsexualism within medicine. In gay and lesbian studies, it has become problematic to attribute too much power to the medical profession in naming, identifying, and thereby constructing gay subjectivity.[20] However, transsexuals distinguished themselves as a separate population within medicine by differentiating themselves from homosexuals (as well as transvestites), and they did this at least in part by asserting that their special problem was not "sexual deviance" but a condition rectifiable by available medical technology. It is only by analyzing the alliance between transsexuals and their clinicians—and at a larger level the dialectical relation between "sex change" technology and the demand for sex change—that we can understand how transsexualism was accepted into at least some mainstream medical discourses, a condition essential to its emergence as a public form of identity.

Thus, while homosexuality can (and should) be understood outside of a medical context, I argue that transsexualism necessarily depends upon a relation to developing medical discourses and practices. However, it is also true that it is only in relation to existing medical discourses on homosexuality that transsexualism accrued meaning within medical practice—transsexuality was decidedly *not* homosexuality, in the eyes of both the doctors and those identifying themselves as transsexuals.[21] This fact demonstrates the homophobia central to the official medical understanding of transsexual subjectivity. The homophobia is also evident in the treatment of intersexuality, as we can readily see in the case of Agnes.

Agnes's access to medical intervention depended on her ability to represent convincingly a feminine demeanor entitled to female reproductive organs. In the first published article documenting her case, "Passing and the Maintenance of Sexual Identification in an Intersexed Patient," the authors evaluate Agnes's appearance:

> The most remarkable thing about the patient's appearance when she was first seen by us was that it was not possible for any of the observers, including those who knew of her anatomic state, to identify her as anything but a young woman. . . . Her hair, which was long, fine, and pulled back from her face across her ears, was touched a blonde-brown from its normal brown. . . . There was no facial hair. Her eyebrows were subtly plucked. . . . The only trace of masculinity in her face (and this would go unnoticed if one were not alert to the problem of intersexuality) was a jaw and mouth a little larger than usually found in pretty women and

only noticeable if one looked upward into the patient's face rather than downward from above. . . .

She was dressed in a manner indistinguishable from that of any other typical girl of her age in this culture. There was nothing garish, outstanding, or abnormally exhibitionistic in her attire, nor was there any hint of poor taste or that the patient was ill at ease in her clothes (as is seen so frequently in transvestites and in women with disturbances of sexual identification). All of her mannerisms seemed appropriately feminine, though there was a touch of awkwardness about her reminiscent of a gawky adolescent who had not yet developed the full, subtle, feminine control of her body that would come in later years.

Her voice was rich, soft, pitched at an alto level, *and with a lisp similar to that affected by feminine-appearing male homosexuals.*[22]

I have quoted at length from the clinicians' description because the contrast between their acceptance of the representation of "true" femininity and their identification of Agnes's lisp with the "affectations" of feminine homosexual men is so startling. This demonstrates the doctors' belief that they can detect "true" and "illusory" representations of femininity, the latter understood as those "affectations" taken up (or on) by nonfemale subjects. The comment about Agnes's lisp is made at the end of this long series of descriptions of her perfect (or near-perfect) femininity, and it serves to unsettle, but not *destabilize*, the doctors' perception of her as a deserving female person.

However, this comment about the lisp resonates later in Garfinkel's discussion of Agnes's boyfriend Bill:

[Agnes's] feelings . . . that she was an inferior female, were accompanied at first by the repelling thought that perhaps Bill was "abnormal." . . . She dismissed this by recalling that Bill had fallen in love with her before he knew about her condition. . . . At different times in the course of our conversations she insisted that there was nothing in his manner, appearance, character, treatments of her and other women, and treatments of men that "resembled homosexuals." By homosexuals she meant effeminate appearing men who dressed like women. . . . Following the operation we obtained an account of Bill's appearance and manner from the urological intern and resident who had attended her case. . . . The resident reported that he was struck with Bill's small stature, fine dark features, and swishy manner. In leaving the room Bill batted his eyes at the resident from which the resident took the message, "You and I know what's in there." We were reluctant to credit the resident's account since his dislike for Agnes was evident on other scores. He was firmly opposed to the decision to operate, stating that the operation was neither necessary nor ethical. It was his conviction that there had been anal intercourse, a conviction he held because of the flabbiness of the anal sphincter. With respect to the unknown source of estrogens, he preferred the hypothesis that Agnes . . . had for many years obtained them from an exogenous source.[23]

Agnes was not the only one concerned about the possibility that Bill was homosexual, and Garfinkel's decision to include the intern's description of Bill, despite his sense of its unreliability, suggests his (Garfinkel's) own uncertainty about Bill's sexuality. That the intern was correct about the source of Agnes's estrogens only complicates a story that implies that heterosexual couples do not engage in anal intercourse. For Agnes and Bill, of course, anal intercourse would have been one of two forms of intercourse (although not the only form of sexual activity) available to them.[24] That it might have been preferable to them anyway was not an admission either was likely to make to Agnes's doctors or the researchers involved in her case. Evidently, the doctors and others were constantly on the alert for signs of incipient homosexuality in their patient. Agnes's apparent heterosexuality was an essential component of her convincing self-representation as a woman: Harold Garfinkel spends a significant portion of his chapter on Agnes in *Studies in Ethnomethodology* discussing Agnes's "management" of Bill and his sexual demands. Indeed, Garfinkel presents Agnes's initial approach of the doctors at the UCLA Medical Center as a result of Bill's continued desire for physical intimacy, even after Agnes had disclosed to him the nature of her anatomy.[25]

Clearly, Agnes felt it was in her best interest to discuss Bill as much as possible: in her Saturday morning talks with Harold Garfinkel, "Bill was discussed in every conversation."[26] Interestingly, when listing the areas in which the clinicians could obtain no information from Agnes, Garfinkel includes (among other categories) "what her penis had been used for besides urination," "how she sexually satisfied herself and others and most particularly her boyfriend both before and after the disclosure," and "the nature of any homosexual feelings, fears, thoughts, and activities."[27] Agnes's silence on these matters is telling. She accurately perceived that passing as a woman necessitated passing as a heterosexual woman, and the responses of the doctors and other clinicians, as evidenced in these documents, only corroborate that decision as the right one.

The heterosexist bias in the medical constructions of intersexuality and transsexualism will become increasingly evident throughout the progress of this book. As Robert Stoller notes in *Sex and Gender*, "Those of us who have worked with these patients have been struck by the fact that all transsexuals and many transvestites (but by no means all) insist that they are not homosexuals."[28] This articulation on the part of transsexuals demonstrates their insistence on their distinctness from other sexological "conditions" recognized by the medical establishment—to be recognized as homosexual would inhibit the accomplishment of their goal of sex change. However, any strategic intention in this denial of homosexuality inevitably supports homophobia through its repeated use in public pronouncements by transsexuals.[29] In recognizing and accepting this denial, physicians and other clinicians demonstrate the homophobic prejudice that grounds the practices of sex change in a desire to see bodies that are sexed in accordance with social categories of appropriate gender performance. As we shall see, this prejudice is a central component in the establishment of treatment protocols for intersexual subjects, developed by John Money and colleagues at Johns Hopkins Hospital in the mid-1950s, protocols in which "gender" was first introduced into medical discourse to signify the social performance indicative of an internal sexed identity.

The main thrust of my argument is that the development of certain medical technologies made the advent of transsexualism possible; an essential corollary argument is that these technologies also made possible the contemporary use of the word "gender." As endocrinology and plastic surgery developed, doctors could be more active in their treatment of intersexual subjects; clinicians could intervene at the level of anatomy and physiology to enable their patients to simulate one or the other sex. This ability presented an ethical problem to attending physicians: if medical science had the power to enable an intersexual person to become a male or female person, what factors should the physician take into account in deciding which sex the subject should become? Increasingly, physicians depended upon the patient's *sense* of him or herself as a sex. As I will show, the idea of a psychosocial identity in sex was codified in the 1950s as "gender" and that term subsequently developed the signification so powerfully expanded and enriched by feminists of the second wave.

The different entries for "gender" in the two editions of the *Oxford English Dictionary* suggest these developments. In the first edition, published in 1933, there is no entry for "gender" that encompasses this sense of the psychosocial articulation of, or counterpart to, "natural sex." The closest entry is "3. *transf.* Sex. Now only *jocular.*"[30] The examples included for this definition range from the fourteenth to the nineteenth centuries, and all use "gender" as a direct substitute for "sex." In the second edition of the *OED*, however, there is a "b" section appended to the main entry: "In mod. (esp. feminist) use, a euphemism for the sex of a human being, often intended to emphasize the social and cultural, as opposed to the biological, distinctions between the sexes. Freq. *attrib.*"[31] The examples used to demonstrate this usage include examples from feminist scholarship, as well as the clinical literature on gender role/identity that develops from the intersex research in the 1950s (see chapter 3).

The point here is very simple: something happened after 1933 and before 1989 to introduce into the English language a new way of using the word "gender" to refer to sex. I have marked its emergence in the mid-1950s. "Gender" was first articulated (in this particular sense) as part of a medical lexicon that had as its object the treatment of a specific (and small) set of patients—those born with sexually indeterminate genitalia and/or reproductive organs.[32] "Gender," however, has not remained within the medical context in which it was first uttered; nor did its inaugurators intend it to. Part of the appeal of gender identity theory is its contention that all of us have a gender identity and that it is somehow detachable from our sex. "Normal development" is defined as congruent sexual anatomy and gender identity. To be gendered in opposition to one's sex is therefore a problem, despite the fact that sex and gender are, in the context of this theory, analytically distinct.

Feminist theorists picked up on the distinction between "sex" and "gender" and used it to develop theories of women's oppression that examined the ways in which biological sex (a possibly neutral complementarity) became social gender (a system of unequal social stratification).[33] In this context, "gender" became the target of feminist critique, as "sex" seemed to represent a fixed set of biological characteristics (or limitations) that remained outside the realm of feminism's social crusade. As Elizabeth Grosz writes, "Presuming that biology or sex is a fixed category, feminists have tended to focus on transformations at the level of gender. Their project has been to minimize biological differences and to provide them with different cultural meanings and values."[34] There exist, of course, feminist critiques of the articulations of "sex" in scientific discourse, and these became more and more important through the 1980s and early 1990s as feminist theory both tired of its onslaught on "gender" and recognized the rich arena of "science" for critical analysis.[35] However, the hegemony of "gender" as feminism's category of analysis cannot be denied, as its use has allowed feminists to claim the social construction of women's inequality (and therefore the possibility of its social rectification).

Donna Haraway examines the development of the concept of gender in her suggestive essay "Gender for a Marxist Dictionary," where she argues that "the ongoing tactical usefulness of the sex/gender distinction in the life and social sciences has had dire consequences for much of feminist theory, tying it to a literal and functionalist paradigm despite repeated efforts to transcend those limits in a fully politicized and historicized concept of gender."[36] She offers a brief glimpse of the scenario that I investigate in detail in this book and identifies the origins of the gender identity paradigm in "an instinctualist reading of Freud; the focus on sexual somatic- and psychopathology by the great nineteenth-century sexologists (Krafft-Ebing, Havelock Ellis) and their followers; the ongoing development of biochemical and physiobiology of sex differences growing out of comparative psychology; proliferating hypotheses of hormonal, chromosomal, and neural sexual dimorphism converging in the late 1950s; and the first gender reassignment surgeries around 1960."[37] As part of a larger "reformulation of life and the social sciences in the post-Second World War" era, Haraway argues that the idea of gender facilitated the emergence of a feminist scholarship inattentive to the "'passive' categories of sex or nature," largely through an inattentiveness to the *discursive* aspects of science's construction of its objects of knowledge (the body, for example).[38]

Haraway's historical understanding of the concept of gender in Western discourse is relatively unique in feminist theorizing. Indeed, the analysis I offer will both verify and complicate the claims Haraway makes in "Gender for a Marxist Dictionary." As I am particularly interested in how the idea of gender was introduced in relation to and consequently operates within medical discourses concerning "sex change," I focus on the conceptual emergence of "gender" in relation to developing medical technologies and the clinical practices made possible by those technologies. This narrowness of focus allows me to explore in great depth the extent to which the commonsense understanding of transsexualism as a "disorder of gender identity" is a cover-up for the potentially more threatening idea that transsexuals are subjects who choose to engineer themselves. In the chapters that follow, I will show the extent to which the advent of transsexualism was dependent upon the development and use of specific medical technologies within the discursive parameters of medicine, as well as the extent to which transsexuals' and transsexual advocates' discourses mask that dependence by strategically maneuvering within the discourses of gender. That is, I will argue that the story of gender subsumes the story of technology in the transformation of transsexual subjects from one sex to the other.

Feminist accounts have routinely ignored or argued against the significance of technology in the "transsexual phenomenon."[39] The few feminist assessments of transsexualism published in the late 1970s and early 1980s tend to be harshly critical of those who surgically and hormonally alter the physiological signifiers of sex. These examinations are informed by theories of cultural feminism, insofar as they take "woman" as a self-evident category (the cultural significance of which is based on a biological capacity or identity), value concepts such as authenticity and integrity (as descriptive of experience or identity), and perceive the danger of transsexualism to lie in its threat to women as a group.[40] Janice Raymond is the foremost architect of this position; Marcia Yudkin and Margrit Eichler follow most of her points.[41]

One point common to these particular feminist critiques of transsexualism is the idea that transsexuals represent the extreme, but logical, result of Western culture's rigid gender codes. They are also, in this analysis, its victims. As part of this critique, cultural feminists see male-to-female transsexuals as producing stereotypical images of femininity that degrade women. Opting for feminine (self-)representations that highlight traditional femininity, male-to-female transsexuals demonstrate that they only reproduce "a man's idea of a woman." [42]

Cultural feminists portray transsexual behavior (adherence to socially defined gender roles and insistence on surgical and hormonal "sex change" as necessary to live "as a woman or man") as buying into society's gender norms instead of rebelling against them. Implicit in this analysis is the assumption that transsexuals should take their cues from feminists, who, in Raymond's words, have "at least demonstrated that women can break the bonds of 'core' gender identity with the recognition that 'the personal is indeed political.' " [43] Transsexuals, in this analysis, do not acknowledge the social dimension of their oppression and need to look to feminists, who *as women* overcame the cultural coding of their situation as "personal" to achieve liberation as a group. [44]

Yudkin follows Raymond in considering female-to-male transsexuals as tokens. For both authors, the essential reality of the transsexual phenomenon is represented in male-to-female transsexualism. The medical institution, as Raymond describes it, operates on women who wish to become men only in order to make it seem as if the syndrome affects men and women equally. In reality, these theorists believe, transsexualism is about men producing women that more adequately fit male stereotypes of femininity. Transsexualism in this sense represents a backlash against feminism, and female-to-male transsexuals are tolerated because they provide a smokescreen for the truth of the transsexual phenomenon. [45]

These feminists also criticize the medical institution for endorsing a medical-therapeutic model of healing that simply perpetuates rigid gender codes and therefore, the phenomenon of transsexualism. [46] Raymond presents the most extensive critique of the medical institution's role in the "transsexual empire." She writes that "transsexualism has become a favorite child of the medical psychiatric specialists." [47] In her view, clinicians discourage transsexuals from considering their situation politically, and as possible to remedy on grounds other than medical. [48]

A most significant aspect of these cultural feminist critiques of transsexualism is their nostalgia for the "natural" or "original" female body. [49] Later feminist critics of transsexualism expunge such nostalgia from their work. In the late 1980s and early 1990s, feminist treatments of transsexualism were less invested in theories of cultural feminism and more interested in what we may broadly consider cultural studies and poststructuralist analysis. These later essays investigate transsexualism in order to say something about a broader *theoretical* concern: the social construction of sexed subjectivity, the naturalization of social differences between the sexes, the deployment of sex *as* gender, or the forcing of the body into institutionalized and binary modes of being its sex. Yet despite their conceptual divergences, the feminist cultural studies arguments and the cultural feminist arguments share two important themes.

First, none of the cultural studies articles displaces the major argument of the cultural feminist theorists: transsexuals continue to be construed as the exemplary adherents of a gender system that literally causes their disorder. While Marjorie Garber states that transsexualism is not about (biological) sex, she affirms that it is about gender: "[I]t is to transsexuals and transvestites that we need to look if we want to understand what gender categories mean." [50] Judith Shapiro treats "transsexualism as a point of departure for examining the paradoxical relationship between sex and gender," and suggests that transsexualism may well be the exception that proves the rule(s), demonstrating that "the ability of traditional gender systems to absorb, *or even require*, such forms of gender crossing as transsexualism leads us to a more sophisticated appreciation of the power of gender as a principle of social and cultural order." [51] Central to both Garber's and Shapiro's comments is the belief that studying transsexualism will shed light on the *operation* of gender in culture. What I will argue is that while transsexualism certainly does this, an investigation of the transsexual phenomenon *also* (and more significantly) leads us to analyze the *production* of the concept of gender in Western culture.

Second, the feminist cultural studies essays are able to present transsexualism solely as an effect of the gender system precisely because they avoid engaging with the significance of technology in the constitution of transsexual subjectivity. The cultural feminist essays explicitly denounce what they term the medical institution and its technologies as tools of the patriarchy's continued exploitation and degradation of women, presenting what amounts to a patriarchal conspiracy theory concerning transsexuals' relation to medical technologies. The cultural studies feminists, on the other hand, can only locate the technologies within an ideological system that overdetermines all material effects. [52]

Susan Birrell and Cheryl Cole, in a detailed and finely argued piece on Renée Richards and the "naturalization of sexual difference in the world of sport," twice remark that two different levels, or "dimensions," of construction were involved in the making of Renée Richards: a technical one, having to do with the literal making of a female body, and an ideological one, having to do with discourse. Each time they mention these, they assert that their analysis will concern the second kind of construction: the technology of gender, not of sex reassignment. [53] The technology of surgery is presented as private, while the ideological discourses they analyze they consider public. In this distinction, Birrell and Cole separate technology from the ideological field; implicit in this is the assumption either that technology is completely subsumed within ideology, or that a consideration of it is immaterial to their arguments. The technologies that they do mention—the famous Barr body test that Renée Richards initially refused to take and Richards's hormone therapy—are not considered with regard to their material effects, but only insofar as they represent specific ideological constructions of the female body.

To use one of these as an example of the value of a serious account of the material technologies of sex, Richards's refusal to submit to a Barr body test was based on her argument that it is not scientifically reliable. The Barr body test is a buccal smear. Cells from the interior of the cheek are stained and examined in order to indicate sex chromatin. In a cell with two X chromosomes, one will ball up and concentrate the chromatin stain: this is the Barr body. In a cell with an X and a Y chromosome, this does not occur. Thus, a "positive" text supposedly verifies genetic femaleness, while a "negative" test, genetic maleness. The Barr body test is not infallible, however; as Richards points out, it is a test that some "real women" would fail. This could be possible due to the test's inherent inaccuracy, or the fact that not all individuals raised as women have an XX chromosomal distribution.[54] In addition, the use of the Barr body test in the sports world as the definitive test of sex attests to the value ascribed to the chromosomes as the supposedly undeniable signifiers of physiological sex. That Birrell and Cole do not discuss this issue, significant as it has been in the recent sports world, reveals their own reluctance to acknowledge that technology impinges on the constitution of "women" as well as transsexuals.[55]

Technology figures prominently in Carole-Anne Tyler's essay, "The Supreme Sacrifice?: TV, 'TV,' and the Renée Richards Story," in the form of an analysis of television, the medium she examines to argue her case.[56] She argues that television is a primary technology through which people learn about transvestism and transsexualism. Tyler argues that television as a technology elicits a fetishistic gaze and naturalizes the narratives that it produces. For Tyler, television represents a technology of gender in Teresa de Lauretis's sense, a technology of representation that constructs "gender" as an effect.[57]

One of the most significant aspects of television talk show representations of transsexualism is, however, the very erasure of medical technology as an aspect of transsexual experience. The representational technologies of television obscure the narratives of medical intervention that are essential in the construction of the subjects who "bare their souls" in front of live audiences. In other words, the stories available through television talk shows perpetuate a blindness to the technological construction of the subject at work in the phenomenon of transsexualism. They participate in the cover-up of the very scene I investigate in this book.[58] Tyler would argue that this "other scene" is really constituted by castration anxiety and fetishistic denial. While I do not deny that a scene of such proportions may be involved in transsexual scenarios, I would suggest that such an interpretation is bound up in a refusal to accord technology its place as a signifier of ideological and material proportions. That Tyler's essay purports to be about "televisual transvestism" underscores this

point: using "The Renée Richards Story" as her primary text, Tyler denies the
specificity of the technological interventions that make Renée Richards different from transvestites (cross-dressers who do not seek surgical and hormonal
sex change). In her analysis, both transvestism and transsexualism stand in for
the same "other scene."

In the introduction to their anthology *Body Guards: The Cultural Politics of Gender Ambiguity,* Julia Epstein and Kristina Straub acknowledge that the relatively
new phenomenon of surgical sex change has contributed to the emergence
of transsexual subjectivity; however they subsume this idea within the larger
history of transvestism and "gender dysphoria."[59] This suggests that transsexualism is simply the twentieth-century outgrowth of earlier historical variants
of cross-gender tendencies. Epstein and Straub write that

> gender blurrings have a long pre-twentieth-century history and a wide
> cultural distribution, and have attracted a variety of different explana-
> tions, or explanatory narratives. Surgical possibilities for "gender re-
> assignment" have only opened in a late modern period (and what is more
> *postmodern* than transsexualism?), but there is indeed nothing remotely new
> about transvestism or "gender dysphoria" except the official profession-
> alizing and medicalization of the terms.[60]

However, I would point out that transvestism, gender dysphoria, and transsexualism are all terms introduced in the twentieth century to designate certain
behaviors and particular subjects. The issue is not just that surgical technologies
make sex change possible, as Epstein and Straub indicate, but that these technologies have affected the distinctions between sexological categories—transvestism, gender dysphoria, and transsexualism (as well as homosexuality)—
and thus who can claim an identity under their signs. If we consistently read
back through the categories of the contemporary period, we are bound to miss
the specificity of what it meant for historically dissimilar subjects to represent
(in a variety of modes) the "other sex."[61]

The cultural studies feminists' refusal to consider the significance of medical
technologies to the emergence of transsexual subjectivity in the twentieth century is an oversight that is connected to their dependence on the gender system
as the primary cause of transsexualism. The belief that only gender ideology
produces the phenomenon supports the deferral of an engaged critique of
the technology instrumental to its existence. The cultural feminists, who were
much more interested in a critique of technology, could only construe it as an
effect of male domination. The fact that medical technologies are intimately
involved with transsexualism supports their argument that the medical institution, as a male-dominated power structure, wants to produce women who
will enact traditional sex role stereotypes. Thus, for the cultural feminists, the

technology is merely a paradigmatic example of (masculine) ideology at work.

We cannot know the relation between technology and the contemporary Western gender system unless we are willing to grant to the technology a relative autonomy from what are known as gender ideologies. The same technological practices involved in sex change are engaged in other situations and many were developed outside the context of transsexual research and treatment. Many of the same technologies benefit women. To argue that technology suffers from being an inevitable effect of gender ideologies is to ignore its internal differences and diverse local circulations. To argue that technology does not influence ideological constructions of the body because the influence is always the other way around represents antitechnological thinking at its most reductive. Rather, developments in technology make new discursive situations possible, open up new subject positions. We need to take account of the significance of the body as a semiotic economy constrained by the ideology of gender, but we also need to recognize the body as a system that asserts a certain resistance to (or constraint upon) the ideological system regulating it. Medical technologies directly address this resistance of the body and, by changing the body's capacity to signify sex, affect the potential relation of the body to what are known as gender ideologies.

Each of the feminist theorists discussed above asserts a facticity to gender, although with differing emphasis. For each, gender is something opposed to sex but also dependent on sex—even if only in an artificial and contingent way. Gender then, is not only a self-evident category of analysis for these theorists, it makes a consideration of the semiotics of the body unnecessary. The semiotics of gender, as described by these theorists, is totalizing. Their omission of technology as a crucial player in the phenomenon of transsexualism demonstrates the dangers of automatically prioritizing an analysis of the gender system and thereby occluding discontinuities between concepts of gender and the idea of sexual difference. These feminist critiques remain within a socially intelligible, conventional, attitude toward gender—one that, we shall see, is apparent in the mainstream medical discourses about transsexualism.

Teresa de Lauretis has published a compelling account of gender's relation to technology, or rather, of gender as a technology: Technologies of Gender: Essays on Theory, Film, and Fiction. In the introductory essay, "The Technology of Gender," she argues that gender is "the product of various social technologies, such as cinema, as well as institutional discourses, epistemologies, and critical practices." [62] This second sense of technology relies on the metaphor of scientific or industrial techniques in order to support the claim that representational forms are technologies and that gender is one effect of the intersection of such technologies with ideological systems. Other effects might be labeled race, class, or sexual orientation. De Lauretis's use of the term "technology" is borrowed from Michel Foucault's work on sexuality, where it signifies the power/knowledge synthesis that, through institutions and discourses, produces sex.[63]

This use of the term "technology" allows a shift from repression to production in the constitution of sex and sexuality. That is, technologies are understood to produce things, as opposed to powers that have only negating oppressiveness attributed to them, that only repress. Foucault uses the term to underscore the productive element of the discourses concerning sex, in order to upset the conventional understanding that those discourses are singularly oppressive to sex, itself understood as some thing outside the discourses. "Technology" thus signifies through a metaphoric slippage from the realm of applied science to that of cultural production. In this sense, gender as a technology is understood to produce the cultural objects that it is said to describe. And "technology," as a term, becomes useful for de Lauretis insofar as it divests itself of its relationship to scientific practices and accrues meaning as a measure of cultural construction.

I understand and use the term in both senses defined above: as a specific technical practice within a given field and as a social practice of representation. Both kinds of technology are engaged in the production of subjectivities, and both are instrumental to the phenomenon of transsexualism as we know it today. De Lauretis's essay "The Technology of Gender" attempts to deploy the second notion of technology in order to displace sexual difference as the natural basis of the social construction of gender.[64] She argues that insofar as gender is constituted as or by representations, it can also be reconstituted because it is constantly in the process of production. The problem here is that the material "technologies of gender" never receive any attention: technology is always metaphoric, never understood in its literal, denotative sense. Thus, "gender" as the product of material technologies (especially those related to the body and its functions), not only as one effect of ideological production, disappears as a possible object of feminist investigation.

Yet, the material technologies of gender are crucial to those who depend on them to be a sex. And they are the object of the demand for sex change, which most frequently is enunciated as a demand for sex change surgery. To demonstrate the necessity of investigating the emergence of transsexualism in relation to the technologies of medicine, I would like to consider another case history in which the relations of body, sex, and a demanding subjectivity are centrally significant.

In 1930, a Danish painter named Einar Wegener traveled through Europe seeking a resolution to his physical pain and psychological malaise. He suffered from abdominal pain and periodic nosebleeds, as well as the compulsion to dress and act as a female persona, "Lili." Originally, Wegener dressed as a woman when his artist wife's model failed to come to a sitting; "Lili" eventually became a companion to his wife and an escape from masculinity for Wegener himself. One night, encouraged by a friend, he subjected himself to an examination by a German doctor who said that he could operate and give Wegener "new and strong ovaries. This operation will remove the stoppage in your development which occurred at the age of puberty." When the doctor told Wegener that he could be freed from his male body and initiated into femininity, he added, "it is fortunate that you have such a pronounced feminine feeling. That's why I think I shall be able to help you." The scene implies that Wegener was a hermaphrodite, although with no externally visible signs of intersexuality. Thus, what entitled him to surgical intervention was the diagnosis of an aberration of physiological sex, the existence of a pair of rudimentary ovaries supposedly stunted through x-ray treatments a year earlier, as well as a pronounced feminine "disposition." [65]

The chronology of Wegener's approach to doctors and the development of his demand for surgical intervention is somewhat unclear in *Man into Woman: An Authentic Record of a Change of Sex,* Wegener's pseudonymous autobiography, written primarily in the third person and published after Lili's death under the name of its editor, Niels Hoyer (another pseudonym). Wegener's "problem" is introduced as "of the strangest kind." He sought the help of doctors for ill-described physical pain. One practitioner of x-ray therapy (then called Roentgen rays) "had nearly killed [Wegener]." Another doctor (a friend of Eugen Steinach, the famous sex hormone researcher and colleague of Magnus Hirschfeld) "pointed in the right direction," whereupon Wegener sought out three surgeons. Only then does the text reveal that the cause of Wegener's search for a doctor was that he "believed that in reality he was not a *man* but a *woman.*" [66]

Wegener could pass as Lili without surgical intervention, as could Agnes pass as a woman, and in each case the rationale for surgery was based on a diagnosis of intersexuality. In addition, in each case the markedly feminine demeanor of the subject was taken as an indicator of an interior female physiology. However, these cases are markedly dissimilar with regard to endocrine technology. Einar Wegener did not have synthetic estrogens available to regulate his endocrinological sex, and therefore his secondary sex characteristics. In order to effect hormonal "sex change," he subjected himself to the major abdominal surgery required for ovarian grafts, a state-of-the-art endocrine therapy available in the early 1930s. Agnes, on the other hand, used synthetic hormones in tablet form that she obtained from her mother in order to present herself as intersexual and therefore as a candidate *biologically* entitled to sex reassignment surgery.

The difference between these two cases is not merely that Lili needed major abdominal surgery in order to introduce estrogens into her body, but that Agnes was able to simulate the hormonal levels and effects of the other sex without the mediation of a doctor or other professional. Agnes independently produced the adequate signifiers of an intersexual condition, representing her sex as a self-contradictory semiotic system so that she could obtain the sex conversion surgery that she desired. In her specific case, the hormones were available because her mother was prescribed estrogen replacement therapy following a panhysterectomy, but there are always avenues to obtain prescription drugs without a doctor's note. What allowed Agnes to produce the secondary sex characteristics common to human females in a seemingly spontaneous manner were developments in scientific and clinical endocrinology in the twentieth century.

For both Agnes and Lili, sex change was an attempt to resituate themselves symbolically in the other sex category, to live, speak, and breathe "as women." To do so, they had to invest heavily in traditional representations of femininity, to make themselves recognizable icons of femaleness. They also had to present themselves in the context of intersexuality, so that their bodies would be understood as the contested sites of physiological sex badly in need of unifying transformations. For both of them, given the contemporary discursive situation of sexology and sexological medicine, the way to the other sex lay through the convincing presentation of an intersexual physiology. The doctors, stewards of the technologies necessary for sex change, recognized in their subjects the sign of woman and acted accordingly.

Einar Wegener underwent a castration operation in order to be admitted to his doctor's clinic for women in Dresden. Clinically, castration is removal of the testes, not the penis. The relation between the gonads and identity are made clear in the following passage from *Man into Woman*, Wegener's edited autobiography:

> Punctual to the minute he called on Professor Arns.
>
> "Since I saw you yesterday I have been talking to Professor Kreutz [Wegener's doctor]. We are both agreed that a young colleague here, a surgeon of repute, ought to treat you first. When that is over, there will no longer be any obstacle to your reception in the Professor's clinic. *That means, it is not you who will be received there.*"
>
> "Not I?"
>
> "Kreutz runs a women's clinic. Your case"—the Professor then laughed a little—"is somewhat unusual, even for us doctors. This means, therefore, that when the surgeon here dismisses you, *you will no longer be Andreas Sparre* [Einar Wegener], but—"
>
> "Lili!"[67]

Andreas/Einar without testicles became Lili. But Wegener's body allegedly carried two sets of gonads, one male and the other female: the purpose of the ovary graft was to stimulate his "diminished" ovaries. What allowed Lili to come alive permanently, as it were, were medical assessments of Wegener's masculinity/femininity ratio, carried out by a "blood specialist" and a sexual psychologist. The choice of which set of gonads to excise, in other words, was made based on Wegener's alleged psychosexual and hormonal constitution. Professor Arns told Wegener that "Hardenfeld [the sexual psychologist] has told me that he too regards the masculine element in you as by far the least considerable part of your being, which, in his opinion from the emotional standpoint, reveals between eighty and one hundred per cent of feminine characteristics. The examination of your blood has yielded a similar result."[68]

As we shall see in chapter 1, this indexing of sexual characteristics (mental and emotional) in alignment with hormonal indicators characterizes the "glandular thesis" at its best. The thesis also involved the notion that those who did not represent the ideal of either sex category necessarily housed inadequate organs of internal secretion. These subjects were deviants. Wegener established his innate and "normal" femininity by expressing his disgust for those who represented intermediary types. In the waiting room of Professor Arns, he sat among

> a group of abnormal persons [who] seemed to be holding a meeting — women who appeared to be dressed up as men, and men of whom one could scarcely believe that they were men. The manner in which they were conversing disgusted him; their movements, their voices, the way in which they were attired, produced a feeling of nausea.[69]

What differentiated Wegener from the "men of whom one could scarcely believe that they were men" was a femininity that did not merely mask his original masculinity, but superseded it precisely because it represented an "authentic" condition. If one believes the autobiography, Wegener's presentations of himself as Lili were consistently met with disbelief upon their unveiling (even in the case of his own mother). Lili always convinced her viewers of her femininity: it was, in fact, never in doubt. She embodied a "natural" femininity, as opposed to effeminacy, which her doctors believed demonstrated the physiological origin of her cross-sex behavior. This connection between the verisimilar presentation of a sex and the idea that such a convincing presentation must be caused by hormonal or other physiological processes was evident in Agnes's case, and we shall see its development within endocrinology in chapter 1.

Like Agnes, Lili was able to convince her doctors of an innate femininity, but she was unlucky in her surgical results. Although vaginoplasty was, by the 1930s, an accomplished (although not routine) procedure, Lili did not survive: "Paralysis of the heart put an end to her short young woman's life." She came into physical being in the spring of 1930, and died the following year, appar-

ently as a result of a final operation, the purpose of which was to provide her
with a vagina ("I have now returned to Dresden for the last operation to effect
a natural outlet from the womb"). She had gone back to her doctor with this
question: "Tell me, Professor, do you think that I am now strong enough for
another operation, for I want so much to become a mother."[70]

The demand for surgery is characteristic of transsexuals since the widespread publicity surrounding Christine Jorgensen's transformation in 1952, but
in the case of Lili Elbe, the demand for surgical sex change developed out of
Einar Wegener's search for a physician who could appropriately diagnose and
treat his vague "illness." The demand arose in the context of the doctor-patient
relationship, in which the patient sought to alleviate what is represented as a
sexual aberration and the doctor had at his disposal new, experimental, medical technologies.[71]

Thus, Lili Elbe represents the emergence of a certain position in relation
to medical technology out of which modern transsexualism developed. At its
point of emergence, the demand for surgical sex change was not as strong or
specific as it became following the Jorgensen transformation, and it needed
both the suggestion of physicians and the claims to physiologic intersexuality
to help spur it into existence. Yet even in the context of Wegener's autobiography Lili's relation to technology shifted when she went back to her doctor
and asked for a vagina. Although consistently submissive when in the presence of her doctor, she was able to rouse herself to make the assertive request quoted above.[72] She demanded access to that paradigmatic experience of
women (motherhood) by means of the intervention of medical technology.

1

GLANDS, HORMONES, AND

PERSONALITY

In 1946, William Heinemann Medical Books released *Self: A Study in Ethics and Endocrinology*, by Michael Dillon. *Self* included the first sustained argument for technologically mediated sex change in the twentieth century, based on recent developments in endocrinology and the study of sex hormones. Dillon claimed that cross-sex behaviors could, in certain cases, be indicative of an abnormal endocrine physiology. In these cases, he argued, the adult subject should be free to decide his or her course of action: "If . . . there is an incompatability between the mind and the body, either the body must be made to fit the mind . . . or the mind be made to fit the body; and that is for the patient himself to judge if he be of age."[1] Dillon used the terms homosexuality and hermaphroditism to define the condition we would now call transsexualism; many of the themes he brought up in *Self* became central to theories of both intersexual and transsexual personality that emerged in the mid- to late-1950s. Most significant to the arguments of this chapter are Dillon's pleas for the recognition of the "natural mistake" that relegated many to the wrong sex category, and for the use of available medical technologies to repair "nature's error."

Written in a detached tone, yet compassionate in the focus of its ethical argument, *Self* was an attempt to address the philosophical and moral issues that emerged with the development of endocrinology as a medical specialty and technical practice. Dillon urged his readers to take a more sympathetic attitude toward those whose (endocrine-imbalanced) bodies caused them both suffering and ridicule. He presented himself as an ordinary male citizen who took it upon himself to consider the role of heredity and environment in human behavior and to educate the public about recent advances in medicine, as well as the social and philosophical implications of those advances. For these reasons alone *Self* constitutes a significant example of the impact of endocrinology in Britain during the first half of the twentieth century. Yet the book has added attributes in the context of my analysis—written by a person in the process of passing from the categorical status of a woman to that of a man, the book's arguments exemplify how popularizations of endocrine theory (as well as the science on which they are based) came to enable the emergence of transsexualism in this century.

Dillon began *Self* while employed as a garage attendant during World War II and during the period of his transformation from Laura Maud Dillon to Lawrence Michael Dillon. He obtained testosterone tablets from a doctor, and later, at the suggestion of a plastic surgeon, voluntarily underwent a bilateral mastectomy. He reregistered his birth sex as male.[2] Apparently, the physicians at the hospitals he attended believed he was a genetic male with a developmental abnormality.[3] Sir Harold Gillies, the surgeon who eventually took on the task of constructing an artificial penis and scrotum for Dillon, agreed to "put [him] down as an acute hypospadias," meaning that he would present Dillon's case as one of mistaken sex assignment at birth, not sex change.[4] *Self* was published prior to Dillon's reconstructive surgeries but while he received testosterone treatments, as he began attending Trinity College, Dublin, as a male medical student.

The general reader would know nothing of Dillon's sex status; the author argued insistently but abstractly in favor of sympathetic public judgment for homosexuals and hermaphrodites. In many ways, *Self* resembles the spate of other texts published between 1920 and 1950 that address the general reader and try to educate him or her about the "new science" of endocrinology. A few relevant titles include *The Tides of Life: Endocrine Glands in Bodily Adjustment, The Glands Regulating Personality, Our Mysterious Life Glands; And How They Affect Us, How We Become Personalities: The Glands of Health, Virility, and Success,* and *What We Are and Why: A Study with Illustrations, of the Relation of the Endocrine Glands to Human Conduct and Dispositional Traits, with Special Reference to the Influence of Gland Derangements on Behavior.*[5] Some of these books (and the others like them) were written by doctors, some by medical journalists. Dillon's *Self*, like the other texts, sets out to educate the public about endocrinology and its significance in the everyday life of modern men and women: "Here then is an attempt to put simply to the average reader the nature of certain parts of his body, the seven endocrine organs, parts which are somehow closely connected with his character, temperament and personality, so closely connected, in fact, that injuries to, or diseases of these glands may transform a man from a respectable citizen into a degenerate or criminal."[6] Comparing Dillon's introductory remarks with those of the other texts just mentioned reveals a striking commonality of purpose:

The object of this book is to present the latest knowledge of the glands and their secretions in a popular but strictly scientific manner, free from exaggeration, fanciful guesses, unsupported hypotheses, reckless sensationalism or biased commercialism. . . . We need a simple honest book dealing with our glands.[7]

It is the present assumption that study of the variation in glandular activities and reactions will bring us to a better understanding of the causes which underlie human behavior and of the variations in personality. . . . The ultimate and defensible postulate is that in them [endocrine glands] are to be found the roots of human behavior—that their control extends to the emotional as well as the physical centers.[8]

It is the purpose of this volume to present the essential facts about these endocrine glands. . . . [E]ven a limited knowledge enables one to turn to practical account the essential things for directing the mental and physical development that begins at birth and persists to the closing years of life. Now, for the first time in human history, we know the underlying causes of the quality called "personality," and possess the practical means of shaping and directing it.[9]

In this chapter, I look at the ways in which endocrinology, as a field of scientific knowledge and as a practice of clinical medicine, contributed to the emergence of transsexualism. The books quoted above represent and reiterate the theories of endocrinology found in texts published exclusively for medical audiences, crossing the discursive boundary that often separates medicine from the public sphere. The endocrine theories promoted in them make up what I call the "glandular thesis"—the underlying strata of claims concerning the regulating power of the endocrine glands in human life. This mirroring of discourses across the medical/public boundary is crucial to the emergence of transsexualism, since the publication of numerous popularizations of the glandular thesis guaranteed that individuals had access to the discursive apparatus of medical endocrinology.[10]

Public knowledge about medical advances and technological capabilities produces a situation in which individuals can name themselves as the appropriate subjects of particular medical interventions, and thereby participate in the construction of themselves as patients. This process is especially true with regard to elective surgical procedures, such as cosmetic surgery, where the demand for medical attention is made possible by public knowledge of its existence and probable success.[11] Knowledge about glandular or hormonal influence on personality became central to the self-understanding of the first subjects who asked physicians for medically mediated sex change. Two of the most important physicians advocating sex change for those subjects requesting it were endocrinologists (Harry Benjamin and Christian Hamburger). They

were educated in the initial period of endocrinology's popular efflorescence—
the first half of the twentieth century—and their backgrounds in glandular medicine clearly influenced the eventual theorization of transsexualism in
the 1950s.[12]

I will not argue that the similarity of public and medical discourses concerning endocrinology demonstrates the extent to which endocrinology as a science is bounded by ideological bias; rather, I want to demonstrate how powerful endocrinology became as a *cultural* discourse in the first half of this century.
This distinction is not insignificant. In my view, all sciences are bounded by
ideological bias, since to bring one's observations into meaningful discourse
with others one must articulate those observations in *language*, which necessarily means making them subject to ideology. Nevertheless, science, and in
that term I include the medical sciences, has a commitment to describing the
world *as it seems to be given*. Scientists try to bring into discourse the very things
that seem to escape discursivity, what poststructuralists have come to call "the
real." Therefore, the codes created by scientific endeavor have a different relation to "the real" than other kinds of codes. After Roland Barthes, I call the
descriptive code of medical science a "terminological" system or code.[13]

Medical science uses terminological codes to describe the human body.
These descriptive discourses underlie and support the material practices physicians engage to heal the body. Medicine, like other scientific disciplines, has
a certain investment in denying the ideological character of the codes it both
produces and uses in everyday practice. Yet demonstrating the ideological commitments of medicine and other sciences—not a particularly difficult thing
to do—does not directly address the sociocultural *effects* of medical progress
and knowledge production. In this chapter, while I discuss the ways in which
endocrine discourses reiterate the ideological commitments of traditional perceptions of sexual difference, I focus the argument on the ways in which the
production of the glandular thesis in the first half of the twentieth century
facilitated the emergence of transsexualism at mid-century. That is, I emphasize the cultural effects of the glandular thesis over the cultural bias inherent
within it.

In an essay concerning the relationship between social institutions and the
organization of scientific research, Nelly Oudshoorn writes:

> In analyzing the relationship between gender and science, most scholars
> in women's studies tend to conceptualize gender bias as something that
> comes from "outside." This conceptualization is based on the assumption
> that in science there exists an "inside" and an "outside"—a social/cultural
> context, and, apart from this, science itself. From this point of view, gen-

der bias is located in the social context, or "society," and then must be transferred into the "realms of science." [14]

Oudshoorn goes on to claim that "gender bias is an integral part of the whole fabric of science," especially in relation to the organization of research materials in the study of sex hormones. [15]

Oudshoorn's argument concerns the development of research on sex hormones in relation to three institutional sites of research—clinical gynecology, laboratory science, and pharmaceutical firms. She persuasively demonstrates that the early and continuing interest in female sex hormones had to do with women's greater involvement in medical institutions *as patients*: "The differences in the institutionalization of research on male and female reproduction not only led to bias in the access of research materials derived from the male and the female body: the existence of gynaecological clinics also provided an available and established clientele for the products of research on female sex hormones." [16] The development of sex hormone research, in her analysis, was intimately connected to the medical institution's greater interest in women as reproductive subjects: "Knowledge claims linking men with reproduction could not be stabilized simply because there did not exist an institutional context for the study of the process of reproduction in men." [17] Thus, the materials that scientists use to produce the terminological codes that make up scientific discourses affect scientific results or outcomes at the level of data collection and assessment: science depends upon, indeed is constituted by, an intimate relation to social institutions and beliefs.

In a culture where scientific discourses hold a significant amount of rhetorical power, however, any new developments that seem to promise a breakthrough understanding of "human nature" or a sure path to healthy living will themselves have discursive effects on the social. Thus, while Oudshoorn's work demonstrates the complicity of scientific endeavors with the structure of social institutions, it does not address how new forms of scientific knowledge reconfigure the social formation. If "the social" is always already "inside" science, then isn't science also "inside" the social? What are the social effects of discursive transformations in science; how do new concepts affect established ideas about humanity, the being of people and their social organizations?

It is my contention that advances in medical technologies and the discourses that surround and support the use of those technologies make possible new forms of being human. To take transsexualism as a form of being human that emerges in the twentieth century is to suggest that something happened historically to facilitate its emergence and codify its existence. Endocrinology, as the scientific study of the glands of internal secretion, was an essential discipline for the incipient development of what might be called "transsexual subjectivity"—understood as involving the demand for sex change through hormonal treatment and plastic genital surgery. In order to understand the impact of endocrinology on the emergence of transsexualism, we must examine both medical theories of the endocrine regulation of personality *and* those discourses produced for "public" consumption. Distinguishing between these discourses will not be as important for this analysis as demonstrating their points of convergence, since it is the public dissemination of scientific knowledge of the human endocrine system that will help us understand how certain human subjects in the twentieth century came to understand themselves as members of the "other" sex.

The development of germ theory in the late nineteenth century and the discovery of sulfa drugs and later antibiotics in the mid-twentieth century perhaps overshadow the development of endocrinology as a medical specialty. The realization that many diseases are spread through germs—bacteria and viruses—and the subsequent development of antiseptic procedures, vaccines, and sulfa and antibiotic drugs was instrumental in the transformation of medicine into a scientific service profession able to identify and treat contagious diseases. Endocrinology, on the other hand, concerned itself with diseases occurring within the human organism that were not caused by the invasion of germs or by carcinogens. Like vitamin deficiency diseases, some endocrine disorders are the effects of a lack—but unlike vitamins, endocrine secretions are produced in the body itself. Other endocrine diseases are caused by glandular overproduction.

Many people consider endocrinological diseases "mistakes of nature," since they have no specific social cause (such as contagion). In this sense, hormonal disorders represent errors in what people think of as "nature's grand design." Thus, endocrinologists' ability to rectify diseases of the internal secretory system can be perceived as victories against a randomly cruel natural force, victories for the ideal of humanity, victories for normality.[18] With the tools that endocrinological technology makes available, doctors can offer those who suffer from disfiguring or discomfiting endocrine disorders a place in the world of the physiologically and physically normal.

Charles-Edouard Brown-Séquard (1817–1894) is credited with the discovery that extracts made of glandular material can have therapeutic effects.[19] Often considered the "seminal" figure in modern endocrinology (a term that is, as we shall see, more appropriate than not), Brown-Séquard was also the originator of organotherapy, a precursor science that quickly became a fad in late nineteenth-century America. An elderly man in 1889, he subcutaneously self-injected extracts of canine testicular tissue and observed a rejuvenating effect. While the results of his experiment were contested, the principle was of immense importance to the development of endocrinology, as it suggested that endocrine glands affect the physiology of the body by secreting potent substances directly into the bloodstream, and not through the mediation of the nervous system. In addition, Brown-Séquard's work stimulated others to experiment with rejuvenating technologies. In the twentieth century, French physician Serge Voronoff experimented with transplants of monkey testes, and German researcher Eugen Steinach with a variation of vasectomy, both in order to restore youthfulness to elderly men.[20]

The first medical applications of endocrinology were made with gland extracts—from the thyroid, the pituitary, the testicles, and the ovaries, to name a few. Even after 1905, when British scientist Ernest Henry Starling introduced the term "hormone" as a name for the chemical secretion, glandular medicine was largely confined to the use of gland extracts to replace lost or defective glands in the body. Sometimes gland transplants would be attempted, but transplant technology was not well developed and human bodies tended to reject transplanted tissues. One chief complaint of Voronoff's monkey gland grafts was that the effects were temporary: often, the body would simply absorb the transplanted tissue. In addition, transplants or grafts necessitated surgery, which, although greatly improved through advances in anesthesiology and antisepsis, was still a risky procedure in the first quarter of the twentieth century.[21]

Since its inception in the late nineteenth century, endocrinology participated in the development of a medical vision that privileges an ideally functioning body, harmoniously regulated by a system of internal secretions (the hormones). Within its purview the ideal became conflated with the normal, or statistically average, and was espoused by doctors as a possibility available to all subjects during the life span. This fundamental perspective of endocrinological theory and its applications contributed to the development of the "glandular thesis," which held that the endocrine glands "regulate personality." In 1928, Louis Berman, an endocrinologist, wrote *The Glands Regulating Personality*, a popularization of endocrinology, in which he elaborated the glandular thesis in impressive detail. Berman presented endocrine glands as fundamental to the emotional regulation of the subject and the root cause of his/her behaviors. He explained that the internal secretions are "the real arbiters of instincts and dispositions, emotions and reactions, characters and temperaments, good and bad." Human beings, in this scenario, are "by-product[s] of a number of cell factories."[22] Another popular writer of the 1920s proclaimed the endocrine system the origin of political extremism and antisocial behaviors.[23] With these ideas, endocrinology—as the scientific discourse of the glandular thesis—supported itself on the earlier popularity of neurology and its paradigmatic disorder, neurasthenia. If the endocrinological system was weakened or out of balance, the body was more prone to disease. Significantly, it was also thought to be more prone to aberrant or antisocial behaviors, paralleling the earlier neurasthenic discourse.[24]

In the first three decades of the twentieth century, glandular therapy consisted of chemicals extracted or derived from either human or nonhuman endocrine glands, injected to make up for the loss of such a gland or an abnormality in its secretory processes. Later, synthetic hormones took the place of gland extracts and provided physicians with more exact methods of endocrine regulation. Nevertheless, whether the extracts came from nonhuman animals or the hormones were synthesized in the laboratory of a pharmaceuticals company, the therapy involved chemicals naturally found in the human body. Thus, organic chemicals "at home" in the human body constituted the cure for endocrine disorders and the appeal of endocrinology rested, at least partially, on the idea that the medical intervention was natural because it merely involved reintroducing a chemical that already should have been present in the body.

This aspect of glandular medicine became significant with regard to the management of intersexuality (hermaphroditism), as well as to later claims that endocrine imbalances caused transsexualism. If cross-sex proclivities were caused by hormonal aberrations, but the treatments were thought to restore a "natural balance" with "natural chemicals," then endocrine therapies could be used with equanimity by doctors wishing to alleviate their patients' suffering. Moreover, concurrent developments in embryology suggested that such a subject's apparent sex might be a deviation from his/her intended sex due to hormonal fluctuations in utero.[25] This combination of theoretical speculations enabled physicians to experiment with hormonal treatments for patients with extreme cases of cross-sex identification, without feeling that they were treating the patients unethically or otherwise compromising their treatment protocols.[26]

In establishing endocrinology as the appropriate medical specialty in the treatment of so-called sexual disorders, proponents of the glandular thesis confronted the growing popularity of psychoanalysis. Over the course of his lifetime, Sigmund Freud periodically gestured toward the possibility that future medical science would discover a more concretely somatic interpretation of human behavior than his own. This occurred specifically in the context of discussions concerning the development of human sexuality and the apparent human resistance to therapeutic recovery.[27] Because of Freud's insistence on the psychical mechanisms of physical symptom formation in certain illnesses, however, psychoanalysis's relation to the medical sciences, predictably, has been ambivalent at best and contentious at worst. In the 1920s, 1930s, and 1940s, endocrinology—especially as the popularized glandular thesis—challenged some psychoanalytic explanations of human behavior.

Some proponents of the glandular thesis used endocrinology both to support and rebuff Freud's pronouncements. Louis Berman wrote:

There has grown up, contemporaneously with the teachings of Freud, a body of discoveries and knowledge in biochemistry, concerning these factors, which is like a long sword of light illuminating a pitch-black spot in the night. The dark places in human nature seem to have become the sole monopoly of the Freudians and their psychology. But only seemingly. For all this time the biochemist has been working. . . . Not that the Freudian fundamentals will be scrapped completely. But they will have to fit into the great synthesis which must form the basis of any control of the future of human nature. The future belongs to the biochemist.[28]

Other writers were not so generous to psychoanalysis. Some proponents of the glandular thesis asserted that the emotions were the by-products of chemical reactions in the body, stimulated by glandular secretions. These researchers and writers believed that anger, irritation, depression, and lassitude (among other emotional states) were the result of glandular imbalances rather than repressed experiences. One writer advised people to have endocrine work-ups rather than sessions with an analyst, claiming that the problem was not in their minds, but their glands.[29]

These critics and scientists claimed that endocrinology offered a somatic explanation for problems contemporaneously described by psychoanalysis as mental.[30] This response reveals the skepticism about psychoanalysis's alleged lack of empirical foundations. In a short article in *Scientific Monthly*, Dr. Edwin Slosson wrote:

Both [glandular science and psychoanalysis] have a certain foundation in fact, and promise much for the future though neither can fulfill the anticipation of the public at present. But *the scientific basis of the glandular idea is much more solid and substantial.* An emotional complex is after all a figment of the imagination, but when you get out a chemical compound, extracted, purified, and identified, you have something tangible and when you put it back into the patient you can regulate the dose and record the reaction.[31]

Journalist Edward Smith and neuropathologist Max Schlapp similarly took aim at psychoanalysis, which in their eyes dealt with metaphysics instead of physics, symptomatology instead of etiology, and had as its most "deadly symptom" the production of a new vocabulary that "resort[s] to [the] most doubtful symbolism and most fearsome locutions. This is one of the fatal stigmata of metaphysics, this absence of lucidity and employment of exotic and sesquipedalian words."[32] (Of course, they did not comment upon the endocrinologists' penchant for coming up with odd names for all the hormones they were discovering; this was a problem particularly in relation to the "female" sex hormone estrogen, which for a time had three names—"estrin," "folliculin," and "theelin.")

Some physicians and sexologists tried to integrate psychoanalysis with the glandular thesis. André Tridon, author of numerous books about psychoanalysis and a practicing analyst himself, argued for the integration of endocrinology and psychoanalysis, since the views of both the endocrinologists (who believed that "personality lies in the glands") and of the psychoanalysts (who ignored the glands) "are only half-truths, and the solution lies in the thorough comprehension of the reciprocal influence exerted by the mind on the glands and the glands on the mind."[33] However, the half-century's two most influential sexologists—Havelock Ellis and Magnus Hirschfeld—both retreated from psychoanalytic theory to argue that sexual development, and therefore the development of "sexual inversion" or homosexuality, depended upon the glands of internal secretion.[34]

The glandular thesis was more inviting to many than psychoanalysis because it offered practical methods of regulating human behavior through attention to the body's physiology. The glandular thesis proposed that with careful personal and medical management, people could establish a calm serenity that would guarantee the harmony of their internal secretory systems, which would in turn maintain that desired state. Stressful situations and periodic outbursts were thought to encourage glands to habitually overproduce, inducing a glandular imbalance that subsequently overrode the intellectual reasoning that characteristically held deportment in check. Doctors and journalists announced that taking care of the body would result in increased mental stability and emotional security. Popularizers of the glandular thesis reminded the reading public that prisons and political groups were full of people with endocrine disorders that had motivated them to criminal, antigovernmental, or merely reform-oriented activities. To take care of the human body was also to take care of the social body, to insure its continued normal functioning.[35]

The glandular thesis offered a concrete, "scientific" rationale for perceived abnormal social behaviors and did not suggest the stigma (of guilt, of psychological responsibility) that psychoanalytic explanations of such behavior might encourage. Further, the idea of a constitutional homosexuality or inversion caused by a hormonal aberration and resistant to psychoanalysis had significant implications for the later treatment of transsexualism, which very early gained a reputation for being "intransigent" to psychotherapy. Dwight Billings and Thomas Urban claim that psychoanalysts first led the "attack" against the Johns Hopkins gender reassignment program in the late 1960s; the analysts argued that physicians providing treatment for so-called transsexualism were collaborating in their patients' psychoses.[36] The psychoanalytic position has always

been a contentious one in the context of organized allopathic medicine, however, since it advocates psychotherapeutic treatment (i.e., the "talking cure") in
lieu of more traditional medicinal treatment practices based on the administration of drugs. The development of the glandular thesis as an explanation for
perceived antisocial behaviors and socially aberrant sexual tendencies, on the
other hand, facilitated the development of glandular and hormonal treatments
for such behaviors and tendencies.

The idea that glandular imbalance was at the root of both physiological and
psychological illnesses motivated research and production by pharmaceutical
companies, who in turn advertised their products to physicians in all fields of
practice. Between 1939 and 1951, the Ciba Corporation published a journal for
physicans entitled *Ciba Symposia*. On the inside front cover of the first issue, the
editors introduced their journal in the following words:

> With pleasure and pride, "Ciba Symposia," . . . is henceforth to be pre-
> sented to members of the medical profession by Ciba Pharmaceuticals
> Products, Inc. Each month, and in a literary and scientific manner, "Ciba
> Symposia" will treat a pertinent subject chosen from the fields of anthro-
> pology, ethmology [sic], medical history, education, art, and the like.
> Avoiding the heat of debate and omitting techniques of commerce, it is
> our aim that "Ciba Symposia" bring enjoyable and constructive diversion
> to the physician whose interest is our primary concern.[37]

While *Ciba Symposia* omitted the "techniques of commerce" insofar as it did not
advertise other companies' products, each issue did include a few ads for Ciba
products, including "Nupercainal" (for relief from sunburn and hemhorroids,
among other complaints), antispasmodic preparations, throat lozenges, vaginal
suppositories, and decongestants.[38] Advertisements for hormonal preparations,
specifically sex hormone preparations, are among the most prevalent ads.

Figures 1 through 6 present a selection of *Ciba Symposia's* advertisements for
androgenic and estrogenic hormone preparations. Figures 1 and 2 demonstrate
the perceived efficacy of "male" hormone preparations for psychological problems, specifically those psychological problems associated with impotence.
The male figures in these ads are downcast or clearly distressed: the solution
to their difficulties lies in hormonal therapy — Perandren, a synthetic testosterone — rather than in psychotherapy. The "psychic trauma" of aging is not really
a *psychological* problem; rather, it is presented as a physiological problem with a
psychological symptom.

Figures 3 and 4 advertise "female hormonal substances": figure 3 presents
Di-Ovocyclin as "provid[ing] the *feeling of well-being* not offered by metabolic
breakdown products or exogenous synthetic drugs" [emphasis added]. Another
advertisement, not shown, states that "an injection of 1 mg. of Di-Ovocyclin

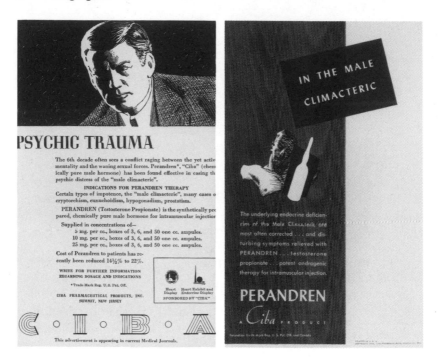

Figure 1. Source: *Ciba Symposia* 1, no. 2 (May 1939).
Figure 2. Source: *Ciba Symposia* 6, no. 8 (November 1944).

every 10–14 days will keep most patients symptom-free *and produce the gratifying euphoria associated with the administration of the natural female hormone and its derivatives."* [39] The female figures in the "Endocrine Excellence" advertisement exude this euphoric sensibility, especially the central figure, whose lack of national adornment and whose Caucasian features demonstrate that she is the "American" woman. Her "well-being," however, pales in comparison to the woman in figure 3 who is elevated in the night sky as a result of her hormonal treatment. This idea that the administration of estrogens produces a "euphoria" repeats itself in male-to-female transsexuals' discourse, and is a corollary to their oft-stated notion that the testosterone in their bodies is a "poison." [40]

The final two figures (5 and 6) represent two other significant impacts of the glandular thesis and its pharmaceutical support: the production of sex hormone preparations in tablet form and the attempt to bring more people under the regulation of glandular therapy. (The latter ploy was even more prevalent in the discourses of cosmetic surgery, as we shall see in the following chapter.) The advent of hormonal treatments in tablet form meant that obtaining and taking hormones became easier—both for those with a prescription and for those without one. [41] As we saw in the introduction, "Agnes" was able to facili-

Figure 3. Source: *Ciba Symposia* 9, nos. 1–2 (April/May 1947).
Figure 4. Source: *Ciba Symposia* 1, no. 6 (September 1939).

tate her sex change by taking her mother's Stilbestrol—obviously, this would have been impossible if Agnes's mother had had to take the synthetic estrogen by injection at the doctor's office. The development and dissemination of hormone pills enabled those who self-diagnosed themselves as "in the wrong body" to administer their own endocrine treatment, outside the supervision of professional medicine.

While figure 6 suggests that just as many women may need hormone therapy as men, in the context of the glandular thesis, women became the endocrinological subjects *par excellence*. Women's exemplary status as medical subjects is hardly unique to the first half of the twentieth century, but the glandular thesis raised their physiological value to new heights. Menopause especially presented physicians with a seemingly anomalous event: the cessation of a natural endocrine secretion. Almost all other such incidents represent malfunctions of the endocrine system.[42] Doctors thus had a tendency to see menopause as a malfunction, rather than a change in function or the cessation of an unnecessary function. Of course, many women experience physical discomfort during menopause, and physicians sought (and still seek) to alleviate their patients' suffering. But in the 1920s, 1930s, and 1940s they also saw menopause as contributing to nervous disorders, and believed that endocrine treatments for

Figure 5. Source: *Ciba Symposia* 7, nos. 5–6 (August/September 1945).
Figure 6. Source: *Ciba Symposia* 8, no. 9 (December 1946).

postmenopausal women could inhibit these as well.[43] Significantly, physicians believed that endocrine therapies would maintain their patients' femininity: the administration of gland extracts, and later hormones, could stop the passage of time that virilized women by depriving them of estrogen, the "female" sex hormone.

Early twentieth-century endocrinologists and gland theorists both challenged and upheld Virchow's famous nineteenth-century pronouncement that "woman is a woman because of her ovaries."[44] While many qualified their reduction of woman to her "sex glands" with statements that suggest man's dependence on his, most emphasized (or implied) that woman was more dependent on the two, slightly flat, ovoid bodies in her abdomen than man was on the ovoid bodies hanging below his penis. For example, William Berkeley wrote, in *The Principles and Practice of Endocrine Medicine*, that

> the student of the physiology of the sex hormones sees their influence beneficially pervading the body and brain of man and woman in a thousand ways. *Woman, particularly, is largely under the sway of her sex hormones, and reaches perfect physical and mental development only after she has borne a child.* Man is hardly less dependent.[45]

If, however, man is "hardly less dependent" on his testes than woman is on her ovaries, why is she "particularly . . . under the sway of her sex hormones"? Other authors demonstrated their agreement with Virchow's pronouncement through the differing amount of space they devoted to female or male gonadal dysfunction and their relation to cross-sex or antisocial behaviors. Herman Rubin included the following comments in his *Glands, Sex, and Personality*:

> Let us suppose that you are a captivating male; we must also presuppose, in this happy instance, that your strength and manliness, generosity and kindness, stem to a great extent from vigorous gonadal functioning. Undersexed males, as a rule, are notoriously petty, selfish, and old-womanish—attributes that are often spoken of as facets of personality, as indeed they are, but resting on factors of greater biochemical depth.
>
> Similarly, the female sex glands contribute most to your feminine grace and beauty, if you are a woman. It may seem absurd to state that a woman's sweetness of disposition and alluringly feminine traits depend greatly upon two small, oval bits of tissue, her ovaries. Yet the hormones of the ovaries have as profound effects upon personality as they do upon the soft and rounded contours of the body and feminine voice quality. Physical beauty alone does not insure 'good' personality; the icy beauty is far less attractive than the less beautiful woman who has winning eyes and a kindly smile—both unlikely in the absence of good ovarian function.
>
> . . . This wretched state of lack of charm is often indicative of endocrine disorder, and personality reconstruction may well begin with appropriate hormones. . . . Much can be done by stimulating the deficient glands, especially if the patient's mental outlook is also bolstered. Where the glandular causes are properly identified and treated, striking transformations from ugly ducklings to glamorous personalities have been wrought.[46]

This sort of exaggerated attention to women's "gonadal functioning" belies any rhetorical commitment to endocrine equality between the sexes.

Still other physicians simply made stereotypical comments concerning behavioral differences between men and women that, in the context of medical texts on endocrinology and glandular influence, imply their adherence to Virchow's view—or at least the extension of that view in light of the elaborations of twentieth-century endocrinology. In Weil's *The Internal Secretions: For the Use of Students and Physicians* we find the following commentary:

> Are the intellectual differences between men and women also parallel to the differences in their germ glands? Is it for this reason that "Woman is woman precisely through her ovaries?" In attempting to answer this

question we may be in danger of leaving the safe ground of facts established by experiment and observation, and of wandering into the region of philosophical speculation. However, it is a fact that during the past two decades experimental psychology has accumulated a rich supply of material which suffices to reveal mental differences existing in the two sexes in regard to many matters concerning which measurable differences in response to stimuli could be determined. It has been found, for example, that men distinguish sound and pitch better than women. Among older school children boys excel girls in mathematics, in critical and logical handling of formal problems, in gymnastics exercises. The color sense is better developed in women, and school girls excel school boys in memory and in ability to perform delicate handwork. The mental life of man is more occupied with abstract considerations, and with creative activities. Woman is more concrete, and has more shades of feeling; she is more suggestible, and her interests are personal; her fantasy is permitted freer play. . . . Even if . . . many differences be attributed to cultural influences, educational methods, and suggestions from the environment, there still remain certain differences not to be explained by these factors.[47]

The question Weil poses at the beginning of this passage is only weakly affirmed at the end, but the implication of his argument cannot be in doubt.

As endocrine research advanced, it became increasingly clear that a woman's reproductive system was regulated by a complex combination of hormones secreted by the ovarian interstitial cells, the Graafian follicles, the corpus luteum (a gland produced by the Graafian follicle following ovulation), and the placenta (if pregnancy should occur). At the time, researchers described general human endocrinology as a complex system of harmoniously self-regulating glands; the added complexity of the human female reproductive cycle made it an even more exemplary example of the endocrine system at work. In addition, the added complexity meant that women were more inclined to possible disorder, since there were more functions to correlate. Doctors described endocrine systems as being "delicately balanced": women depended on their particularly delicate balance to maintain periodic menstruation and reproductive health.[48] But the menstrual period itself was seen as upsetting to the human female endocrine system, and thus in need of expert supervision. Woman became the paradigmatic exemplar of human endocrinology: her system of internal secretions was eternally at risk of becoming unbalanced due to the natural forces of life and the unnatural stresses of modern civilization.[49]

Nelly Oudshoorn's essay "On the Making of Sex Hormones" examines the extent to which the early emphasis on the female reproductive endocrine system was at least partially the effect of women's and men's asymmetrical participation in clinical situations. At the time there was no male corollary to gynecology; Oudshoorn writes, "The medical specialty of andrology—the study of the physiology and pathology of the male reproductive system (and in this respect the counterpart of gynaecology)—emerged only in the 1960s. . . . Consequently, the development of knowledge about male reproduction was long delayed." [50] Without the ready supply of women to both provide research materials (urine) and be the recipients of the pharmaceutical products of the research, the history of endocrinology and its emphasis on female subjects might have been very different.

One result of the emphasis on women as the ideal subjects of endocrinology may have been the differing ratios of men to women seeking sex change: statistically, more men have, in the past, requested and achieved sex change. [51] There are a variety of reasons cited for the historical asymmetry in requests for sex change—among them, in Judith Shapiro's estimation, "the greater difficulty and cost of female to male sex change surgery, and its less satisfactory results; the greater propensity of men for the kind of experimentation, risk, and initiative involved in sex change surgery; the apparently greater propensity of males for sexual deviance in general; the dominant role of the mother in the rearing of children of both sexes; the relationship of transsexualism to other cultural institutions in which envious men are trying to appropriate the powers of women." [52] Yet in none of the critical or medical literature does anyone suggest that the discourses of "sex change" technologies (endocrinology and cosmetic surgery) have both constructed women as their ideal subjects. To become subject to the technologies in the context of sex change is to become a subject of the technologies—and vice versa. Thus, I would suggest that the historically higher numbers of men seeking sex change must somehow be correlated to the discourses within which both men and women who feel themselves to be "in the wrong body" construct themselves as entitled subjects of medical treatment. Transsexuals, as we shall see in chapter 5, evince a profound identification with (a fantasy of) their internal secretory processes; in the endocrine literature, this kind of identification between subjectivity and glands is highlighted for all subjects but emphasized particularly for women.

That sex hormone research emphasized the female reproductive system and generally supported nineteenth-century views that women were gonadal subjects in a more substantial manner than men does not mean that endocrine research was entirely circumscribed by the existing ideological paradigm. However, new discoveries about the "sex hormones" seem only to have challenged that paradigm in inconclusive ways. The discovery of sex hormones in the first half of the century produced a contradictory knowledge of the human body as a singularly sexed body: on the one hand, men and women were seen to differ from each other chemically; on the other hand, it was acknowledged (if grudgingly) that both males and females had the chemicals that construct the characteristics specific to the other sex, although in differing amounts. Nevertheless, most popular writers espoused the commonsense understanding that the sex hormones signified either masculinity or femininity.

Endocrinology was thus perceived as having established a chemical basis for sex differences in genitals, in secondary sex characteristics such as breasts and facial hair, *as well as* in behaviors. The "fact" of chemical sex difference supported numerous cultural stereotypes about men and women, from the aggressivity allegedly caused by (masculine) androgens to the periodic moodiness attributed to women. However, if endocrinology, like genetics, complicated the medical picture of sexual dimorphism by offering another possible site for sex differences (the hormones in addition to the gonads), it also provided the means by which the complications arising from "defective" or anomalous hormonal outputs could be rectified. In other words, endocrinology as science provided medicine with the tools to enforce sexual dimorphism—not only to examine and describe it.

Three theoretical elaborations appeared in both popular and scientific discourses concerning sex hormones, all of which were related intimately to the glandular thesis. First, sex differences were reduced to the chemicals that produce those differences. This is evident in the use of the terms "female" and "male" sex hormone. Second, there developed an idea of an index or continuum of sexual characteristics, with "masculine" on one extreme and "feminine" on the other. This appeared in relation to the notion of sex typing: so-and-so was called a "masculoid" woman or an "effeminate" man.[53] Third, physical and psychological sex characteristics were perceived to coincide, evidence of an assumption that the endocrine system regulated the continuity of "femininity" or "masculinity" across the psyche-soma boundary. Taken together, these theoretical variants suggested that the body was sexed in all of its characteristics, and that the sex of the body's "characters" determined the sexuality of the mind.

The idea that the body is sexed in all its characteristics was not a new one in the early twentieth century—especially concerning the bodies of women. In an influential essay concerning illustrations of the female skeleton in eighteenth-century anatomy, Londa Schiebinger claims that "[b]eginning in the 1750s, doctors in France and Germany called for a finer delineation of sex differences; discovering, describing, and defining sex differences in every bone, muscle, nerve, and vein of the human body became a research priority in anatomical science."[54] Thomas Laqueur understands this phenomenon to be connected to the emerging "two-sex" model of the human body, which superseded a "one-sex" model that understood the female body to be an inferior version of the male body.[55] Cynthia Eagle Russett, in *Sexual Science: The Victo-*

rian Construction of Womanhood, discusses how Victorian scientists and physicians perceived women's bodies to be "feminine" down to the last detail.[56] What endocrinology added was a physiological explanation for this extreme view of the sexed body—the sex hormones, coursing through the blood in minute amounts, made sure that the subject's sex touched all organs and affected all gestures and mannerisms. In this sense, we can see endocrinology as the culmination of a particular (and developing) medical vision of the sexed body.[57]

Among scientists of the pre–World War II period, there was a measure of ambivalence concerning the extent of the reduction of sex differences to specific hormones. Frank Lillie wrote, in *Sex and Internal Secretions*:

> There is no such biological entity as sex. What exists in nature is a dimorphism within species into male and female individuals, which differ with respect to contrasting characters, for each of which in any given species we recognize a male form and a female form, whether these characters be classed as of the biological, or psychological, or social orders. Sex is not a force that produces these contrasts; it is merely a name for our total impression of the differences. . . . In the strictly historical sense of the words, a male is to be defined as an individual that produces spermatozoa; a female one that produces ova; or individuals at least bearing the characters associated with these functions. But by extension, these terms have come to be applied also to the gametes themselves, to the determiners of male and female characteristics, and to the zygotes destined to produce a male or a female.[58]

What Lillie described was an example of semiotic transposition, whereby a sign becomes a signifier for something else. Thus "sex," the outcome or overall effect of specific physiological processes, was taken to motivate those processes to provide meaning for the smallest factors influencing the outcome. Lillie warned against this synecdochal reduction of sex, as a descriptor of species dimorphism, to the forces which produce this dimorphism. However, the tendency he opposed was as strong as his objection to it.[59]

Nelly Oudshoorn, in her article "Endocrinologists and the Conceptualization of Sex, 1920–1940," argues that the original, dualistic conception of sex hormones developed in the 1920s was "transformed into a less dualistic conception of sex" by 1940. She bases this argument primarily on the fact that during this period, endocrine researchers admitted that both "male" and "female" hormones could be found in either male or female bodies. She writes: "What label should be attached to substances isolated from male organisms possessing properties classified as being specific to female sex hormones? Scientists decided to name these substances female sex hormones, thus abandoning the criterion of exclusively sex-specific origin. Female sex hormones were no longer conceptualized as restricted to female organisms, and male sex hormones were no longer thought to be present only in males." [60] However, abandoning the "sex-specific origin" of so-called female and male sex hormones does not erase the fact that the labels "male" and "female" sex hormone characterize the substances that play a part in the construction of male and female forms as reduced examples of those forms. As in synecdoche, the "part" still stood for the "whole." The dualism therefore continued, although it became more complex. Indeed, even without the terms "male" and "female" sex hormone, researchers maintained the sexual dualism in the face of complex experimental results. [61]

Consider Bernhard Zondek's discussion of the fact that "follicular" hormone (an early name for the hormone secreted by the Graafian follicules of the ovary, that is, the "female" hormone later named estrogen) could be obtained from the urine of stallions:

> During the last two decades research work has succeeded in throwing light upon the nature of the female and subsequently of the male sex hormone. If the reverse order had been chosen, and if by means of a color reaction in urine and testes of the stallion large amounts of hormone had been found—before being discovered in the urine and ovary of the mare—this hormone found in the testis would certainly have been assumed to represent the male type. [62]

Folliculin/estrogen is no more "female" than testosterone is "male." As Lillie's argument suggests, these substances are chemicals that produce certain predictable physiological effects that, in turn, result in the application of the terms "male" and "female" to human and animal bodies. Both male and female bodies contain both "male" and "female" hormones, and would not be considered "normal" without the appropriate ratio of estrogenic and androgenic substances. It is not the hormones in and of themselves that produce these recognizable effects, but the overall hormonal ratio, the differential power of hormonal chemistry, and the ability of the bodily organs to metabolize each hormone differentially. [63] The term "male hormone" is thus a misnomer, a misapplied reduction of the concept of sex to the chemicals that produce sex effects. [64] The sign "sex" becomes a signifier for itself, as the "overall effects" of sexual dimorphism—male and female forms—become equivalent to the factors that produce them.

Zondek's discussion of what might have happened if researchers had looked in the urine of stallions for "male hormone" reveals that the researchers were already thinking of the so-called sex hormones as reduced versions of male and female forms. In addition, his comments suggest that had the researchers "mistaken" female hormone for male, endocrinology might have developed a different perspective on the relation of the sex hormones to sex itself. He believed that they would have been wrong in their designation; however, they might have realized a perspective on the activity of hormones in the "making" of men and women that would have refused the reduction of sex to the chemicals that produce it. Zondek's and others' insistence on the idea of male and female hormones was part of a growing blindness toward the available information concerning human sexuality and is an apt example of the medical appropriation of the body by the idea of sexual difference.[65] Instead of recognizing the increasingly unstable semiotic field of physiological sex—what we might now call the physiological "queerness" of sex, the seemingly innate capacity of sexual signifiers to be multiple and contradictory—these endocrinologists chose to insert the idea of sex hormones into the already established conception of stable sexual dimorphism.[66]

There was talk of a human sexual continuum, but this idea was largely undermined by the conception of strict sexual difference. For example, Louis Berman wrote that "when it becomes necessary to size the sex composition of a man or a woman, a measurement becomes establishable which may be spoken of as the sex index [or percentage]." Although he acknowledged that contemporary science lacked the ability to directly index the blood, he noted that "a scale of measurement of the secondary sex traits may be elaborated." This would demonstrate, for all those who suffer from "maladjusted sexuality, expressed and suppressed," that "we are all, more or less, partial hermaphrodites or intermediaries."[67] Nevertheless, when Berman wrote of "intermediary types," he did not invoke the notion of a universal, partial hermaphroditism, but of defective endocrine organs. Thus, in discussing femininity in women, he stated:

> A woman who has a delicate skin, lovely complexion, well-formed breasts and menstruates freely will be found to have a typical feminine outlook on life, aspirations and reactions to stimuli, which, in spite of the protests of our feminists, do constitute the biological feminine mind. *Large, vascular, balanced ovaries are the wellsprings of her life and personality.* On the other hand, the woman who menstruates poorly or not at all is coarse-featured, flat-breasted, heavily built, angular in her outlines, will also be often aggressive, dominating, even enterprising and pioneering, in short, masculoid. *She is what she is because she possesses small, shriveled, poorly functioning ovaries.*[68]

Here, the sex index represents a continuum from masculinity to femininity that is governed not by the natural intersexuality of the human species, but by an abnormality of specific organs of internal secretion. The "masculoid" woman and "effeminate" man were perceived to be the results of defective sex glands. The language suggests further that the hormonal secretions correspond in direct physical homology to the organs themselves.[69] Thus, while researchers accepted that men and women contain hormones that produced both "masculine" and "feminine" characteristics, they did not consider women who exhibited "masculine" characteristics to be normal (and vice versa). The sex index, it turns out, was a way to describe deviations from the ideal, not a normal spectrum of intersexuality within human sexual dimorphism.

Directly following the comments cited above, Berman wrote that "no better examples could be given offhand, of the *determining stamp of the internal secretions* upon mind, character and conduct."[70] This concept of a determining relation between the internal secretions and personality appears in much of the endocrine literature of the pre–World War II period. In *Endocrine Glands (In Health and Disease)*, a 1932 text, Chandra Chakraberty writes (preliminary to a discussion of the secretions of the ovaries): "From these observations it can be deduced that the internal secretion of the ovarian interstitial cells *determines* and develops the somatic and psychic feminine characteristics."[71] Louis Berman thought that the secretion of sex hormones correlated with male and female roles:

> Now if in the castrated male [rat] is transplanted an ovary, the positive characteristics of the female are evoked, such as enlarged mammary glands, and a tendency to secretion of milk. Experiments have also been reported in which an uterus was also placed in such an animal, with a means of entry [i.e., a vagina], and pregnancy follows. If in the castrated female a testicle is planted, the masculine traits become more marked and striking. *A direct exchange of the male and female roles can thus be achieved.*[72]

Here, Berman used the term "roles" to mean those postures associated with sexual activity. In the context of rat "culture," this primarily signifies mounting behavior. The following comment clarifies his intention to apply this term to human *social* roles as well:

> The womanly woman and the manly man, those ideals of the Victorians, which crumbled before the attack of the Ibsenites, Strindbergians, and Shavians in the nineties, but which must be recognized as quite valid biologically, are the masterpieces of these interstitial cells when in perfection.[73]

"Victorian" here signifies more than just a shift to human culture—it suggests the formal expectations of social sex role behavior characteristic of the Victorian period (a bourgeois ideal at that) and perceived as natural for all human subjects.

These three trends in theoretical and popular endocrinology—the reduction of sex differences to the chemicals that produce them, the notion of a sex continuum based on an ideal/defective dichotomy, and the belief in the determining influence of endocrine function on personality and social role—

contributed to the medical view of the body as being sexed at the level of its chemicals and its behaviors. Endocrinology offered physicians and others seemingly definitive proof of the pervasiveness of sex in the body and personality of human subjects. The essence of the person, but especially the woman, was perceived to reside first in her (sex) glands, and then later (with the advancement of endocrine technologies) in her (sex) hormones. This reification of the physical in the context of a normalizing medical specialty was, in the words of Margaret Mead, "consonant with other attitudes toward the body as a machine which should work; if it does not work it should be fixed." Indeed, many of the articles cited above abound in factory and other mechanical metaphors of the human body. Mead commented further that "people who fail to get [their body] fixed, to 'do something about it,' are given neither sympathy nor quarter by society."[74]

Since in the context of the glandular thesis and its specific applications to sex, to be normal was to embody the ideal and to represent the conventional social role for one's sex, it is not difficult to imagine that those who felt inappropriate or inadequate to the requisites of their social position would have sought to change their bodies rather than their minds. After all, the glandular thesis suggested that any perceived deviation from socially approved sex role behaviors could probably be traced to an endocrine deficiency or excess. The body and its behaviors became mere signs for the semiosis of the hormones at work (or on strike) within it.

Thus, endocrinological research into the differential effect of sex hormones on the psychology of the sexes was integral to the later-developing medical view of transsexualism. Endocrinologists were instrumental to the instantiation of transsexualism as a medical disorder and many believed sexual "deviance" would be explained in the future by an advanced technology able to discern chemical influences that at the time escaped medical practitioners.[75] This view implies that the endocrinologists' support for transsexual surgeries was contingent upon their belief that once the "real" (i.e., physiological) cause of the syndrome was found, medical science would be able to correct it so as to obviate the need for surgery. Thus, transsexuals' demands for surgical and hormonal interventions were perceived, at least partially, as an effect of a still developing medical technology that had yet to realize its full potential. This differentiates the medical practitioners from their transsexual subjects, for whom surgery was the final answer to their misery, a technological repair of "nature's mistake."

To connect this development with a concrete example, let us return to Michael Dillon's *Self: A Study in Ethics and Endocrinology*. As I suggested in the beginning of this chapter, Dillon's book exemplifies many of the tendencies in popularizations of the glandular thesis published during this period. In addition, in its direct advocacy of sex change for subjects who self-identify as the opposite sex, *Self* represents a prototype for the development of transsexual theory in the following decade. In examining *Self*, we can see concretely how the precepts of the glandular thesis served as discursive supports for the material practices of medical sex change.[76]

As noted earlier, Dillon opened his text with a reiteration of the glandular thesis:

> Here then is an attempt to put simply to the average reader the nature of certain parts of his body, the seven endocrine organs, parts which are somehow closely connected with his character, temperament and personality, so closely connected, in fact, that injuries to, or diseases of these glands may transform a man from a respectable citizen into a degenerate or criminal.[77]

In the chapter, "Mind: Masculine and Feminine," Dillon's allegiance to the glandular thesis becomes more evident. He identified the gonads as the origin of difference between men and women: "We know, too, as we have seen that the endocrine organs are the same in both, save in the one important instance of the cortex of the ovary and the interstitial cells of the testis, and that it is to this difference that we may, with some likelihood, attribute the psychological individuality of the male and the female."[78] In this chapter Dillon argued in addition that men were by nature more rational and that women were more emotional—characteristics built up by environmental influences over centuries but now part of the heredity of humanity[79]—a conviction that also fitted the investment of the glandular thesis in the idea of woman as the exemplary endocrinological subject. According to Dillon, her emotional nature connects her to the hormones, those chemical precursors of strong feeling, far more than does man's rational one. Man is not presented as having a similar dependence on the testosterone that regulates his sexual physiology. He transcends his endocrine nature, while woman is overwhelmed by hers.[80]

In the same chapter, Dillon presented the linchpin of the book's argument. After establishing that rationality is the inheritance of men and emotionality the inheritance of women, he stated:

> We may, perhaps justifiably, infer too that we cannot eradicate wholly the rational predominance in man, should anyone ever attempt such a task; hence, the personality of the other sex possessed by these people [cross-gendered persons], must inevitably be innate and not acquired as so many psychologists would have us believe. At least, this view must surely follow upon the acceptance of any distinction between the masculine and

feminine mind as being essentially different, and seeing that higher education does not seem to make a male personality out of a female, there seems little alternative to accepting it. . . . Within the limits of our present knowledge, therefore, and judging solely upon the probability, the balance would seem to tend toward the side of innate disposition and away from that of acquired habits.[81]

The conviction that personality structures were inherited and therefore innate, combined with the glandular thesis that located personality in the body (specifically in the glands), ultimately supported the argument that in cases of cross-sex personality it was the body and not the mind that should be changed. The whole of *Self* tends toward this assertion, ending with a final consideration of the subject's right to determine his or her fate—to decide, in other words, to change sex.

The "case" Dillon proved was largely his own—his decision to change sex through surgery and hormonal therapy. He used all available discourses and existing scientific terminology to make it; in addition, he focused his attention on syndromes or disorders that might explain his own particular situation— a "masculine" woman. Thus, in his discussion of the endocrine organs specific to women, Dillon concentrated on those irregularities (such as ovarian tumors) which "masculinize" women. In the introduction to the chapter concerning homosexuality, he wrote:

We have seen how injuries to, and diseases of, the endocrine organs can produce changes in the physical make-up and sometimes also in the mental make-up of the unfortunate individual affected. . . . How a tumour of the medulla of the ovary will make a pseudo-male out of a woman, while deficiency of the testis secretion will bring about a state of eunuchoidism in the male. And finally how the correct balance between the male and female hormones in each one of us is necessary for a normal character.[82]

He remarked, following the glandular thesis, that "there are not only two sexes but several grades."[83] This is a repetition of the connection between a continuum of intersexuality in human sexuality and the existence of endocrine abnormalities (i.e., ovarian tumors, undersized ovaries/testes). The idea of a gradation of human sexuality based on deviations from the norm or the normal ideal, however, problematizes the principle of a continuum of sex. This idea also contradicts Dillon's own reliance on the notion of inversion as a way to explain homosexuality and what we would now call transsexualism.

Like Havelock Ellis, Dillon understood true homosexuality to indicate a sexual attitude appropriate to the other sex, a flip-flopping into the opposite category.[84] Inversion, he believed, was due to abnormalities of the endocrine glands. Thus, the "natural invert," that is, the one "born that way," could look to physiology as the origin of his/her condition. Thus, while Dillon believed the psychologists would change the subject's mind to fit his/her body, the subject should be allowed to alter the body to fit his/her mind. In fact, Dillon asserted that "at all events it seems most likely that the cause is not to be sought in post-natal life at all but in foetal, since the child would seem to develop naturally enough *if only he belonged to the other sex.*" As further evidence, he suggested that to pass successfully as the other sex proved that there was a physiological origin to cross-sex personality.[85] This last point was contraindicated by Dillon's own experience, since previous to his mastectomy and testosterone treatments he was often questioned as to his sex.[86] Nevertheless, this conviction that the appearance of natural membership in the other sex category is indicative of the physical innateness of one's inversion underlies Dillon's entire argument. This conviction should be familiar by now, as it is based on a semiotics of sex that locates the origin and cause of appearance and behaviors (that is, socially recognizable signifiers of sex) in the chemical processes occurring within the body.

Discussing hermaphroditism, Dillon referred to scholars' assertions that most pseudohermaphrodites (those with two male or two female gonads but presenting indeterminate or cross-indicating genitalia) were acute male hypospadiacs (males with a congenital anomaly of the penis in which the urethra does not exit through the tip), a diagnosis which (potentially) confirmed his own case (just as the earlier discussion of masculinizing ovarian tumors did). He argued that a male assigned to the female sex might have realized the mistake at puberty when secondary sex characteristics developed (this assumes "normal" male hormonal function at puberty); alternatively, however, "the changes are not so evident so that the individual may live for some years under the delusion that he is a female unless his instincts gain the upper hand." Thus, pseudohermaphroditism might be indicated by the instincts alone, although a physical diagnosis was necessary to confirm this suspicion. To prove his point, Dillon argued that "normal" subjects would never have sought radical physical sex realignment, just as they would have wanted any excised parts (e.g., breasts) reconstructed following necessary surgery.[87]

Thus, the *desire* for "radical sex realignment" becomes, in his analysis, a sign of internal endocrine abnormality. Less than a decade later, this idea translated into the notion that the demand for technologically mediated sex change signified a physiological condition still outside the scope of medical knowledge but treatable with available medical practices. The belief that the articulation of this demand actually stood for some physiological disorder was so strong that physicians (notably endocrinologists Harry Benjamin and Christian Hamburger) argued that in the future medical science would find a physical cause behind the transsexual phenomenon even though they could not determine its specificity at the time.[88]

Dillon's text opens and closes with the phrase "Know thyself," which appears in both Greek and English on the page preceding the title page and again at the very end of the book, where he wrote:

Understanding is the keynote of Christianity, for what does understanding promulgate, save love, and what does love promulgate save understanding? But for understanding we must have knowledge and if we do not know ourselves, how shall we ever know anyone else? So much in ourselves is revealed to ourselves which, in another, is a closed book to us. Hence, what more fitting ending than the inscription over the temple of the Delphic Oracle:

ΓΝΩΘΙ ΣΕΑΥΤΟΝ
KNOW THYSELF[89]

In the context of the glandular thesis, to "know one's self" was to know one's glands. Endocrinology offered human subjects the fantasy of self-knowledge through chemical regulation and analysis. Transsexual discourses picked up this thread through the demand to change sex to match one's "true sex" or "true self." As will become evident, these discourses concerning self-knowledge and self-discovery mask other discourses about self-construction.

In conclusion, in the first half of this century, the glandular thesis created a semiotic economy within which physicians and others identified hormonal sex by external appearance and social mannerisms, even as the hormones were understood to be signifiers for these signs themselves. While endocrinological research complicated the idea that a singular physiological sex was the basis for human behaviors and personal appearance, researchers and clinicians continued to rely on the idea that the body would provide a unified sexual meaning. When it did not, they could produce one with the technologies at hand, all the while claiming to be facilitating the emergence of a "true" sexual identity latent in the body's tissue. The semiotic slippage from outside to inside escaped these physicians, however, as they were apparently unaware of the problematic implications of assuming that a physiological process follows from the observance of socially coded behaviors and compliance (or noncompliance) with socially approved and sexually marked standards of appearance.

As we shall see in chapter 2, where social conformity is concerned, endocrinology pales in comparison to plastic surgery. The latter medical specialty, particularly in the guise of cosmetic surgery, is less committed to describing the body than to changing it. Because of this, cosmetic surgery depends entirely upon people's desires to change themselves, whether it be to find the "true self" within or to create a new self from without. In the development of cosmetic plastic surgery as a reputable medical specialty and a reliable medical technology, we can reconstruct the necessary conditions for transsexuals' demands for "sex change surgery."

2

PLASTIC IDEOLOGIES AND

PLASTIC TRANSFORMATIONS

Plastic surgery as a technical practice is based on the transformative capacity of the human body and its organs. Many of the techniques of plastic operations, particularly classic rhinoplastic reconstructions, are centuries old. Medical advances in the nineteenth and early twentieth centuries, however, made many surgical operations routine. Specifically, these include the discovery of the importance of asepsis and antisepsis in operating room technique and surgical wound dressing, advances in anesthesiology, and the production and widespread prophylactic use of sulfa drugs and antibiotics. In addition, as war has been a significant factor in the development of medicine (especially surgical medicine), the twentieth century has provided two exemplary wars to impel the development of plastic surgical technique and to win its practitioners a permanent place in a recognized surgical specialty. As a result of developments in plastic surgery, people whose bodies have been deformed since birth or because of accident, injury, or illness, may become "whole" again, (re)gain for themselves a place beside the physically "normal" without fear of detection or ridicule.

Surgery is perhaps the most dramatic of medical specialties, primarily because the surgeon actively cuts and refigures human tissue. Unlike endocrinology, which as a research science as well as a clinical practice is at least nominally dedicated to describing human physiology (bringing the "real" code of the body into language), plastic surgery is mainly a technical craft. That is, while its practice is based on a descriptive discourse concerning tissue growth and behavior, the purpose of plastic surgery is not to describe the body but to reconfigure it. Consequently, plastic surgery does not depend as much as endocrinology on what Roland Barthes would call the terminological code that it produces as a basis for its treatment practices. Because of this, it is highly subject to ideological appropriation.[1]

This is evident in the development of the subspecialty of cosmetic surgery.

Cosmetic plastic surgery comprises procedures that have no functional justification but are undertaken because of the desire of the patient to look "better." These surgeries became increasingly prevalent in the 1930s, 1940s, and 1950s in the United States. They both depend on and produce standards of normal appearance. Their function is regulated by cultural expectations of beauty rather than medical determinations of physiological health. Cosmetic plastic surgeons of this period described their patients (potential and actual) as subject to psychological distress because of their (allegedly) anomalous appearance. The purpose of cosmetic plastic surgery is to make the external, visible body conform to the patient's idea of him/herself—an image of the psychological self externalized on the body's tissue.

Cosmetic plastic surgery is an activist medical specialty; that is, it attempts to bring patients into the operating room by consistently redefining the normal body and its reparable deviations. In this sense, it is similar to endocrinology in its approach toward menopausal women. Cosmetic surgeons must convince people that certain problems they experience in daily life can be attributed to deviations in physical appearance (such as aging) and that these problems can be alleviated by surgical intervention. Through its popularity and widespread acceptance, however, cosmetic surgery has contributed to the transformation of "normal appearance" that has taken place in the twentieth century. Thus, cosmetic surgeons have not only produced a discourse describing the human body's ability to be altered surgically (that is, the theoretical principles of physiological repair upon which plastic surgery is based), they have acted to change the kinds of bodies popularly considered in need of cosmetic transformation.

The advent and public acceptance of cosmetic surgery thus introduced specific circumstances into medical culture that were central to the emergence of transsexualism in the twentieth century. These developments include the technical procedures involved in genital conversion surgeries, surgeons' willingness to respond positively to demands for surgical treatment that had no physiological basis, and their practice of surgical therapy for psychological problems focused on the body. Most significant, however, was the growth of a medical specialty that enjoyed the prestige and security of membership in the American Medical Association, yet had only a loose and contingent relation to the established therapeutic discourses of medicine. As a technical craft, plastic surgery has transformed the face of modern medicine as well as the faces of millions of "disfigured" people. Insofar as it is subject to and a producer of the ideologies of modern culture, cosmetic plastic surgery has changed the expectations of external physical normality for everyone in the Western world.[2]

The American Board of Plastic Surgery first met on June 14, 1937. In an article about Vilray Papin Blair, one of the founding members of the new field of plastic surgery, Jerome Webster writes:

> At that time, the public generally considered plastic surgeons as "face lifters" and "nose whittlers." To be sure, a few surgeons throughout the country were known for their capabilities in special fields of plastic surgery. There were also those who were close to the border of being ethical, if not unethical, in their practice, and some definitely below that level.[3]

Eight months later, the Plastic Surgery Board had its first annual meeting, and established the standards for training. Plastic surgery had been a recognized hospital specialty only since the late 1920s, but those surgeons interested in professionalizing it lost no time. In 1927, the American Association of Oral Surgeons became the American Association of Oral and Plastic Surgeons, which in 1942 would become the American Association of Plastic Surgeons. This organization was select; new members had to be voted in by the standing membership. In 1931, the Society of Plastic and Reconstructive Surgery formed. This organization was larger than the association, and less select, as it followed a more open admissions policy. It became the American Society of Plastic and Reconstructive Surgery in 1941. In 1946, the society started a journal, *Plastic and Reconstructive Surgery*, which is the oldest English-language publication solely devoted to the topic.

In the early years when practitioners of plastic surgery tried to establish their work as a recognized medical specialty, there was conflict in the profession as a whole concerning the ethical dimension of aesthetic procedures. As in much of recent medical history, the conflict registered as one between "responsible" members of the profession and the "charlatans" and "quacks" who took advantage of the public's desire for cosmetic transformation. As Gustave Aufricht wrote in the first issue of *Plastic and Reconstructive Surgery*,

> Realizing the eagerness of the public to resort to surgery for the correction of deformities, irresponsible and poorly trained members of the profession exploited the situation. . . . In order to dissociate from this mercenary group, ethical representatives gave different names to the specialty, such as "reconstructive surgery," "reparative surgery," "facio-maxillary surgery," etc. Their position within the profession was not the easiest, as the importance of elective surgery was questioned and their work shifted from department to department in general hospitals.[4]

Maxwell Maltz, a plastic surgeon who wrote both a history of the specialty (*Evolution of Plastic Surgery*) and a popular text about the topic (*New Faces—New Futures: Rebuilding Character with Plastic Surgery*), remarked in the preface to the latter book, "Particularly is it hoped that the reader may come to realize that this branch of surgery is not an adjunct of the *beauty business* save when it is made a cloak for the operations of incompetent charlatans."[5] This characterization of the problem as a conflict between those entitled and those not entitled to perform plastic procedures, however, allowed the profession as a whole to displace the ethical issue at the heart of the matter — the issue of whether plastic surgeries for purely cosmetic reasons should be condoned and supported by the medical profession and performed by its licensed members. Instead, as more and more hospitals established plastic surgery services, many plastic surgeons became advocates of aesthetic surgeries and argued that these procedures resulted in significant psychological benefits for the patient.

For example, Harold Gillies, the prominent founder of British plastic surgery in this century, believed that surgeries that would improve the psychological functioning of the individual could legitimately be provided, even if there were no pressing physiological need. Gillies held that if a procedure enabled a patient to feel better about him- or herself, it was worthwhile to pursue it. This attitude supported his decision to offer reconstructive mammaplasty and breast reduction surgeries, as well as cosmetic reparations of the face, for those who desired such procedures. While he was upset about the way in which the cosmetic emphasis of early plastic surgery gave it a bad name in medical circles, he clearly set the stage for the legitimate practice of surgical reconstructions that had no other basis except for the demand of the patient and the physician's assessment that his or her physical anomaly could be made to look "better."[6]

This attitude toward plastic surgery was expressed in popular magazine articles of the period. A 1939 issue of *Reader's Digest* contained an article entitled "Cinderella Surgery," which read (in part),

> Today, thousands of men, women, and children disfigured by accident or from birth may find new hope in reconstructive surgery, which not only corrects visible deformities but, in doing so, banishes the feeling of inferiority that often accompanies them. *Psychiatrists are convinced that many cases of mental illness have been cured by the correction of a facial abnormality through plastic surgery.* . . .
>
> Of all plastic operations, the one still approached most cautiously by doctors is the surgical repair of women's breasts — pendulous or abnormally large. Many such requests are motivated by vanity, but most physicians and psychiatrists now admit that there are cases in which it is essential to a woman's mental and emotional well-being.[7]

A 1938 article in *Science Newsletter* stated that "plastic surgery has an esthetic as well as a reparative objective; it remedies the looks and appearances of indi-

viduals who enjoy good physical health but are weighed down by some deformity of appearance." Further, the article quoted a Dr. Henry Shireson of Philadelphia, who felt that "surgery for esthetic and psychological reasons will be
as commonplace in another five years as neatness and cleanliness are today." [8]
The next year, *Science Newsletter* published another short article on plastic surgery, "Skill of Plastic Surgeon Heals Personality Too." The author wrote that "a
physical deformity is a great handicap in keeping a job, winning a sweetheart,
making friends, finding happiness. *Warped personalities naturally result from twisted
bodies."* [9]

During World War II, most of the articles concerning plastic surgery dealt
with war wounds and the miracle cures of the plastic surgeons, but both before and after the war the "warped personalities" defense of plastic surgery was
a popular topic in magazine literature. In an issue of *Reader's Digest* from 1937,
one article asserted, "Popular psychology still accepts distorted features as a
sign of depravity and authorities know that they are reaching twisted minds by
rebuilding broken bodies and removing the stigmata of the criminal." [10] "The
Case of the Ugly Thief" was exemplary in this regard. This 1949 *Time* article
recounted the "psychological surgery" on an ugly man that cured him of his
criminality. The surgery, of course, was cosmetic. The article commented that
"psychiatrists are hopeful that John's new face has given him a new life." [11]
An earlier *Time* article discussed Chicago plastic surgeon John Pick's work at
the Illinois Stateville Penitentiary. "Pretty Does As Pretty Is?" introduced Pick's
eleven-year project "remolding faces and characters" of prisoners with the idea
that with less criminal "looks" they would leave their lives of crime. [12] And in an
issue of *Literary Digest* from 1936, an article concerning plastic surgery presented
a discussion of a young criminal with an ugly nose, a salesman with a protruding upper lip, and a woman with a receding chin: "In two years Helen became
popular, almost handsome; and she acquired a new and normal personality." [13]

Women's magazines concentrated, predictably, on the ways in which plastic
surgery might be beneficial to women and their children. "I'm Getting a New
Face," an anonymous article in a 1940 issue of *Good Housekeeping*, presented the
story of a woman who was self-described as "ugly" (she explained she had an
ugly nose and a "craggy" chin) and lived a lonely life. With a new face, she
believed she would get a new life. [14] Another 1940 *Good Housekeeping* article, "A
New Nose in a Week," asked (rhetorically), "Why should anyone suffer under
the handicap of a conspicuously ugly feature? *Why not let modern science give him a
normal face and an equal chance with other people?"* [15] This attitude was particularly significant with regard to surgeries on children. A 1952 article in *Better Homes and
Gardens* began with a discussion of "Henry," who became a young hoodlum as
a result of protruding ears. The judge in his case sentenced him to plastic surgery, after which a social worker reported: "He appears to have lost entirely

the old feeling of inferiority about his ears which drove him into seeking out acquaintances of dubious character, because he felt they were the only persons who would associate with him on an equal plane." The author went on to comment that "more and more, [Americans] have come to realize that many neuroses stem purely and simply from a malformed facial feature." The gist of the article was that parents should not risk their children's futures by allowing them to live with visible physical "deformities" that might give them inferiority complexes and lead them into lives of crime:

> Beauty may be only skin deep, as the philosophers insist, but as long as we live in a society where malformed or disfigured faces constitute a serious threat to an individual's health, happiness, and well-being, then a visit to the plastic surgeon may become a matter of sheer necessity, rather than of mere vanity.
>
> In the case of a child, no time should be lost in seeking expert advice. Early treatment may prevent his suffering personality damage.[16]

Along these same lines, in *New Faces—New Futures*, Maxwell Maltz told the story of "Miss Q," whose nose became disfigured in an accident: "Once pretty, she was now repulsive even in her own eyes. The realization that her family and friends pitied her added to her grief." Since she was about to enter college, Miss Q was particularly anxious to find out if she could have her nose rebuilt. Figure 7 demonstrates the "before" and "after" of her surgical intervention. Maltz wrote: "Four months later, when a freshman in college, she visited the office. The nose was completely healed. . . . She looked well and happy and said that she had regained her old personality." Figure 8 shows a girl with a "deformity" similar to Miss Q's, together with a warning about early treatment: "This deformity was corrected in childhood to prevent distortion of personality similar" to Miss Q's.[17]

Articles in *Cosmopolitan* more often concerned "mere vanity" than the "necessary" surgeries on children discussed above. A 1956 article by Elizabeth Honor had the matter-of-fact title "Cosmetic Surgery," but two years later the same author contributed a piece entitled "Beauty Can Be Bought." The first article maintained that the "patient should have wholesome, normal reasons for requesting cosmetic surgery" because "most surgeons simply do not have time for [luxury] cosmetic surgery when they can benefit the young person who wants a better start, the older person who wishes to extend his job expectancy, the girl who hopes to marry and live a normal life."[18] The second article contended, however, that "health and well-being are based increasingly on surgery that was once considered vanity or a 'luxury' item. Now we recognize it as a downright necessity."[19] The first article only recommended reduction mammaplasty, but the second suggested breast augmentation procedures, although

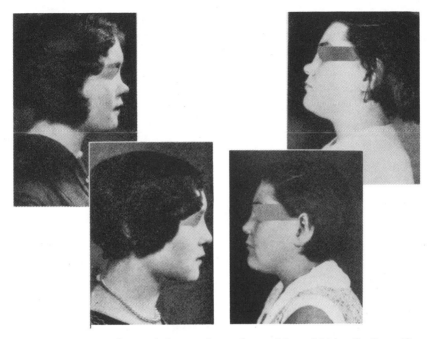

Figure 7. Correction of Miss Q's depressed nose. Source: Maxwell Maltz, *New Faces — New Futures: Rebuilding Character with Plastic Surgery* (New York: Richard R. Smith, 1936).

Figure 8. This deformity was corrected in childhood to prevent distortion of personality similar to that of Miss Q. This disfigurement and the crooked nose produced by accident can be corrected before the age of seventeen. Source: Maxwell Maltz, *New Faces — New Futures: Rebuilding Character with Plastic Surgery* (New York: Richard R. Smith, 1936).

Honor did mention that the current method (use of a plastic sponge) was still experimental and therefore possibly dangerous. "The operation is admittedly far from perfect," she wrote, "and its values are mostly psychological." The significance of psychology was not to be sniffed at, however:

> [T]he most exciting thing about cosmetic surgery is its dramatic results, in the form of better all-around health and social adjustment, evident in the youngster who is no longer afraid to go out and play, the business man who shucks off his shyness right along with his defect, the newly confident girl who may not look *that* much prettier but *feels* so much prettier that she has a better chance at marriage.

After all, the *real* tragedy of a "crooked or humped nose" was not that "it often creates difficulty breathing," but that it "often overwhelms an otherwise delicate young face."[20]

Many of the popular articles from the late thirties and early forties used

Maltz's New Faces—New Futures as a reference text. Maltz argued that because society could not be changed, and social attitudes required a certain standard of physical appearance, plastic surgery could offer "deformed" individuals a shot at physical normality. The benefit was far from solipsistic: "We cannot change society, but we can change the individual to make him conform more closely to man's ideal—both for his own benefit and that of society." Physically conforming to human ideals was, in Maltz's argument, a way of restoring psychological balance to the individual beset by ugliness. After a plastic operation to correct a deformity, "[t]he sense of inferiority disappears with the abnormality which produced it, and its place is taken by a new confidence, a fresh, healthy outlook on life." It is clear, however, that for Maltz, the "ideal" of the human body was also a measure of reality. Consider the following comments about the female breast:

> Normal mammary glands which reveal such positive esthetic ideals as symmetry, gradation, curvature and delicacy of contour, meet man's approval. Abnormal breasts do not. . . .
>
>   It is difficult accurately to describe the perfect mammary organ, but we can readily detect the normal one as portrayed by artists and sculptors. It is a hemispherical structure whose nipple projects from its center. According to Albrecht Dürer the nipple should be on the plane of an imaginary line drawn from the outer aspect of the shoulder to the umbilicus. The center of the breast should project from the chest in a position midway between the shoulder and elbow when the arm hangs at the side of the body.[21]

Dürer was an artist well-known for his detailed studies of human proportions. Nevertheless, to argue that an artist's representation of the human form demonstrates a "normal" anatomy rather than an ideal anatomy seems odd, especially when the norm is also defined as "reveal[ing] such positive esthetic ideals as symmetry, gradation, curvature, and delicacy of contour." Maltz collapses the distinction between the normal and the ideal, claiming to describe the normal but in fact delineating the latter. This is a strategy at the heart of the discourses of cosmetic surgery.

  The desire to embody the ideal in order to appear normal is an attitude that seems to have guided the actions of transsexual Roberta Cowell (possibly the "Male With Female Outlook" in Gillies's Principles and Art of Plastic Surgery). See figure 9. Cowell included in her autobiography this picture of herself looking at a Greek statue of a half-naked woman at the Louvre, with the caption: "Having reduced my figure to the correct proportions . . ."[22] The idea that the "correct proportions" might be indicated by a work of art mirrors Maltz's claims concerning Dürer's representation of the "normal breast" and demon-

Figure 9. In the Louvre, "Having reduced my figure to the correct proportions . . ."
Source: Roberta Cowell, *Roberta Cowell's Story* (New York: British Book Centre, 1954).

strates the problematic relation between the concepts of ideal and normal in the discourses of plastic and cosmetic surgery.

At the end of *New Faces—New Futures*, Maltz reiterated his claim that "[w]e cannot change society," adding that "[p]eople will always react in the same way to beauty and ugliness as long as the race exists." This staunch position about the intransigence of social attitudes regarded the actions of the plastic surgeon as neutral, without effect on social attitudes or expectation but merely in conformity with established and "normal" ideas concerning physical appearance. An emphasis on and reification of the "normal" surfaced consistently throughout Maltz's text, as in the following citations:

> Many anti-social individuals can be brought to *normality* and reclaimed for society by ferreting out the cause of their maladjustment, and in a number of cases it will be found that *abnormal* physical appearance has been the chief cause of faulty adjustment. . . .
>
> All of us want to be *normal*, for *normality* predicates a rational adjustment to the fundamentals of life which, in turn, bring happiness. . . .
>
> Of course, the psychotic or mentally diseased individual is not considered in this book. He [sic] cannot be helped by plastic surgery. We are concerned only with inherently *normal* people who become maladjusted because of disfigurement.[23]

That the desire to be "normal" is a "normal" (and therefore legitimate) desire is not as tautological as it may seem. The desire to be *physically* normal can only be seen as a normal *attitude* in a context where the (re)construction of physical normality exists as a technical possibility. Where that possibility does not exist, such a desire would be counterproductive and possibly antisocial—certainly not indicative of a "rational" or sensible approach to disfigurement.[24]

As we have seen, the development of plastic surgery techniques was accompanied by specific ideological developments that helped to establish (1) plastic surgery as a recognized and respected medical specialty, (2) elective cosmetic surgery as a viable option for both children and adults with congenital or acquired "deformities," and (3) a connection between personality (or behavior) and appearance. This last factor served as the justification for the surgeries, as their goal was baldly presented as psychological in nature. "Patient happiness," an elusive response, became the mark of the successful cosmetic procedure, since no functional goal could be sought. (Imagine open heart surgery, or even the removal of callouses, as having a primary goal of "patient happiness." Most functional surgeries aim to excise nonfunctional or anomalous tissue(s), to diminish pain associated with an injured area of the body, or to prevent the onset of disease by removing or repairing an organ or tissue.) And since the "aesthetic effect" is really only relative, the patient's happiness is based on the expectation of "improvement," which is never a fixed quantity. The new is always examined in relation to the old, and surgeons caution (and are cautioned) against taking patients who have so little relation to "reality" that they fantasize unrealizable surgical results. Such patients, we are told by both doctors and journalists, are rarely pleased with the actual surgical outcome.

Popular articles of the period in question even suggested that to make a "perfect" nose on a plain face was a mistake:

> [T]he results of plastic surgery must fit the patient's personality as well as his face. Sometimes a lesser correction is more suitable to his economic and social life, and, particularly if the patient is a man, to his other facial characteristics.[25]

The appropriate surgical intervention recognizes the social status of the patient as well as his/her sex, for too pretty a nose on a man would be a liability, as would too aristocratic a chin on a working-class "girl."

That "patient happiness" became the primary goal of cosmetic procedures demonstrates the extent to which cosmetic surgeries make use of psychological justifications. These surgeries are accepted as treatment for psychological problems that have as their central symptom an obsessive investment in a "flawed" or "defective" body part. But if a "beneficial" psychological result served as a guiding cause for early cosmetic surgeries (and it seems that as the profession has gained respectability the "Why shouldn't I?" approach has become increasingly acceptable),[26] there are indications that the surgery has its own, unpredictable, psychological effect(s). John and Marsha Goin, authors of *Changing the Body: Psychological Effects of Plastic Surgery*, write:

> The positive effects as well as the psychological dangers of most aesthetic operations are the result of altering the appearance of a body part and thereby producing changes in the body image. An understanding of the body image is the key to comprehension of the psychological aspects of most aesthetic procedures.[27]

Goin and Goin work as a team, one as plastic surgeon and the other as psychiatrist. In their book, the authors discuss the symbolic significance of different body parts, the possible impact of certain standard surgical procedures, and common patient profiles for specific surgeries. Their explicit goal is to alert plastic surgeons to the psychological dimensions of their craft. Nevertheless, they do not question the efficacy of cosmetic surgery or its goal of "patient happiness." For example, in discussing breast enlargement using prosthetic devices, they write:

Our view is that the augmentation mammaplasty is a psychologically superb operation which happens to have *serious technical drawbacks*, principally the present high incidence of capsular contracture and firmness. . . . There is reason to believe that the capsular contracture problem will eventually be controlled, but even if it is not, the operation, as judged by its *positive psychological effects* on patients, will continue to be justified.[28]

Recently, the "serious technical drawbacks" of augmentation mammaplasty with silicone gel implants have been exposed in the media, making it apparent that the companies that made these implants did not endeavor to study their possible side-effects with scientific rigor. In addition, doctors may have either ignored their possible danger to patients or concealed that information from their patients. Women report doctors who ignored the instructions for the implants that stated not to massage them once implanted. Possible side-effects include immunodeficiency disorders.[29]

Goin and Goin are primarily interested in avoiding malpractice—and, in more graphic terms, death. Their book opens with a story of the murder of a Madrid surgeon who was killed along with two nurses by an "unhappy" rhinoplasty patient. The chapter is aptly named, "The Ultimate Lesson." The authors explain that the surgeon should never have taken on this patient, given psychological contraindications.[30] In this context, understanding the psychological dimensions of plastic surgery means being aware of patient motivation and avoiding those patients who represent a hazard to the surgeon him/herself.

Yet much of their text demonstrates that cosmetic surgery patients do not register cosmetic procedures as real surgical events, with the potential of a "negative outcome," and, further, that these patients may experience their surgeries as fantasies. In their chapter on informed consent, the authors present studies demonstrating that a large proportion of cosmetic surgery patients do not recall having any discussion with the surgeon concerning the possible complications of their desired procedure. The authors use this information to support their suggestion that the surgeon's only recourse in this situation is to take extremely accurate notes of the conversations concerning informed consent, as evidence against malpractice. In the chapter about local anesthesia and intravenous injections, forms of anesthesia used in many surgical procedures and with which patients may remain drowsily awake during surgery, the authors document the fantasies of patients who overhear parts of nurses' and doctors' conversations and who invest their guilt or fears about surgery into their interpretations of those conversations. The condition of the patient— drowsy, restrained, drugged—may induce a paranoid response that affects surgical outcome (the "happy" result). Again, this information is conveyed as a warning to the surgeon to be aware of his or her operative dialogue, and not as an analysis of the problematical situation in which a medical intervention is carried out on the body for the purposes of psychological relief, an intervention which can have other unpredictable, and unfavorable, results in that very realm.[31]

One of the reasons that this situation can occur is that the body itself has an uncertain relation to psychology. Goin and Goin suggest that there are two existing views concerning the relation of neurosis (or obsessive investment in a "flawed" body part) to the body itself. The psychogenic point of view maintains that the symptom (hatred of one's nose, for example) is a psychological symptom that must be treated dynamically and in the context of psychotherapy. Revision of the hated feature will not remove the underlying cause of the neurotic fixation, and may cause the psychological situation to worsen once the offending object has been "fixed." The somatogenic position insists that surgery on the symptom can be quite effective in relieving the psychic trauma associated with the offending feature. Indeed, the authors argue that behaviorist psychology has demonstrated that the specificity of the cause of psychological distress is insignificant to the cure. This last view is the one adhered to by cosmetic surgery as a profession, for obvious reasons. Thus, while the authors agree with others that "the psychological relief which patients get from the correction of nasal defects is not measured by the size of the deformity but rather by the quantity of psychic energy devoted to it," they also maintain that surgery on the nose releases the psychic energy spent on the symptom, thereby rectifying the obsessive attitude.[32]

Ellen Berscheid, in "An Overview of the Psychological Effects of Physical Attractiveness," claims that from the 1930s to the 1960s there was a tendency to see neurosis as a causal factor in dissatisfaction with (disfigured) appearance. She suggests, however, that most of the early reports of neurosis ignored the true significance of physical attractiveness to psychological well-being. This was partially due to the history of psychological theories (such as phrenology) that "attempted to predict behavior from bodily characteristics." Because of their dismal failure to convince the public, "any attempt to associate behavior with physical characteristics of any kind smacked of charlatanism, and psychologists generally tended to shy away from any such research enterprise." For Berscheid, being "honest" about the social significance of beauty—which she believes most Americans are not—means condoning cosmetic surgery as a realistic response to social norms of appearance. After all, those norms exist and can be measured. They are "real."[33]

Norms of physical appearance, however, are not immune to cultural change. As Ronald Strauss suggests, plastic surgeons, through the practice of their specialty as cosmetic surgery, have shifted the boundaries of the categories "normal" and "abnormal" appearance such that the former has become smaller as the latter has grown.[34] Many of the physicians and social scientists who study plastic surgery approach the subject as if the "objective norms" that they study are immutable because they can be measured. Society, as Maxwell Maltz emphatically claimed, will not change. In this analysis individual and discrete surgical procedures do not register a measurable social effect. Ironically, this perspective deems the medical profession to have no sociocultural impact at all. Doctors and their advocates write themselves out of historical significance in the same breath with which they argue for the social utility of their therapeutic practices.

In "The Sociocultural Impact of Twentieth-Century Therapeutics," Edmund Pellegrino claims that "[e]ach new medical possibility forces a redefinition of the good life, the nature of man, and the purposes of his existence," and that "[i]n a pluralistic society, in which traditional values are eroded, what medicine *can* do easily becomes what medicine *should* do." Discussing the impact of modern medicine's ability to provide specific and successfully curative therapies for particular disease entities, Pellegrino argues that "medicine is emerging as a prime shaper of cultural values." His essay connects medical technologies (and the therapeutics which the technologies make possible) with specific sociocultural effects. Pellegrino's purpose is to identify the "dilemmas of modern therapeutics," which are, basically, defined by an ambivalence between the role of the physician as holistic healer versus that of a technician. At the end of the essay, he remarks, "The dilemmas of modern therapeutics are simply subsets of the wider problems which man's technological achievements will continue to create."[35] Throughout the essay, it is clear that one of the effects of "modern therapeutics" is a belief that with technology (either existent or in a more perfect future) medicine can cure all human maladies.

Medical technologies, however, work materially on the body and, as we have seen, often partake of somatogenic theories of human behavior that coincide with the behavioral emphasis of much of American psychology. Behavioral theories concentrate on symptom relief and often ignore the underlying causes of psychological distress. Certainly, modern medicine seeks to understand the underlying causes of physical disease. However, in the context of psychological disturbances, medicine has been happy to intervene at the site of the physiological symptom in order to effect a psychological benefit to the patient. This should be clear from the discussion of cosmetic plastic surgery above. Thus, one effect of modern therapeutics is a dependence upon technological intervention, even in cases of primarily *psychological* illness or distress.

Both plastic surgery and endocrinology are medical technologies that some have argued can (and should) be used to regulate human behavior through the production and maintenance of a physical "normality" that will lead to psychological "normality" and health. It is precisely the production and instantiation of this discursive network, the overlapping theories that claim the body as the basis for mental and emotional actions and attitudes, that sets the stage for the emergence of transsexualism in the 1950s. To advocate hormonal and surgical sex change as a therapeutic tool for those whose "gender identifications" are at odds with their anatomical sex, it is necessary to believe that physiological interventions have predictable psychological effects. In order to do this, evidence of the unpredictable psychological effects of plastic surgery must be marginalized, understood as aberrant (neurotic or psychotic) reactions, or controllable through patient selection—and certainly not the norm. It is necessary to believe, further, that patient "happiness" is a recognizable and realizable goal for surgeries that have no physiological indication. And, in addition, it is necessary to acknowledge a certain autonomy of the psychological realm such that the psyche is understood as the realm of stability and certainty, while the body is deemed mutable.

This last qualification was not entirely established by the ideologies of endocrinology and plastic surgery, although the development of their technologies made the body "plastic" and the target for medical interventions in significant ways. It was not until the intersex research in the 1950s that "psychological sex" —or gender, as it was named—gained prominence as a dependable category and the physiological sexes (in particular, secondary sex characteristics and genitalia) were understood as alterable in the face of the fixity of "gender." By that time, the technologies of plastic genital surgery had improved to the extent that they could serve as material support for the developing theories concerning the case management of intersexual subjects, which depended heavily on the concept of gender and its stability in the face of uncertain physiological sex.

The semiotic shift from sex to gender, from body to mind, relied on the use of plastic surgical technologies as putative treatments for impaired psychological functioning. The history of plastic surgery and the development of cosmetic surgery services in the early to mid-twentieth century demonstrates that plastic surgeons were actively involved in the delineation of the semiotic field in which they practiced. Unwilling to settle for the patients who would come to them due to accidents, car wrecks, or congenital deformities, cosmetic surgeons decisively rewrote the code of normal appearance to enhance their practices. Maxwell Maltz's comments (discussed above) concerning artists' renditions of the "normal" breast are a case in point.

More significant to this analysis, however, is the fact that cosmetic surgeons also produced surgical "treatments" for psychological disturbances, as well as a set of discourses defending and espousing the success of such "treatments." The practice of plastic surgery for the purpose of psychological health contributed to the elaboration of a semiotics of sex that upheld traditional values under the sign of cultural advancement. Advances in medical technology supported a seemingly progressive distinction between biological sex and cultural or psychological gender. However, one central tenet of plastic ideology held that cultural standards of appearance were irrefutable and immutable, just as a central component of the idea of "gender" (as we shall see in the next chapter) was its irrevocable establishment as a core aspect of identity by the age of two years. The body became the target of surgical interventions so that culture could be bracketed off (as "gender," "norms of appearance," etc.) and remain untouched by the semiotic changes effected through transformative medical technologies and physicians' activist appropriations of those technologies.

Women's bodies, of course, have been targeted for plastic transformation far more consistently than men's. In its initial stages, cosmetic plastic surgery, like endocrinology, constructed woman as its ideal subject. Most cosmetic procedures target women as their client base, although, as I will discuss below, men are increasingly singled out as entitled cosmetic surgery patients. In chapter 4 I will argue that the constitution of transsexual subjectivity around the demand for surgical sex change institutes a compulsion for surgical intervention that can help to explain the alleged "polysurgical attitude" evinced by many transsexual women. This is facilitated by their desire to become the ideal subjects of surgical technology, women whose bodies are the result of numerous plastic procedures: breast and cheek implants, rhinoplasties, Adam's apple reconfigurations, face-lifts, among other cosmetic operations. The position of woman as a subject ideally constructed through surgical engineering is central to the constitution of the transsexual demand for *surgical* sex change.

In an analysis of women's place in cosmetic surgical discourse and practice, it is difficult not to rest on interpretations that are not only obvious but ones which construe women as victims who are powerless in their relation to social norms of beauty, and thus, the cosmetic surgery establishment.[36] In traditional feminist analysis, women as a category are aligned with the bodily in a more intimate manner than men, thus, women invest in their bodies in more consistent ways than do men. Historically, the story goes, men have had greater access to political power and economic wealth than women have — their bodies mattered less in their ability to rise socially or maintain a socioeconomic position than did the bodies of their wives and mistresses. Much of plastic surgery is oriented toward delaying the material effects of aging, and women are denied "natural aging" in a culture that depends on them to eternally represent what one plastic surgeon called feminine "pulchritude."[37]

These are all valuable aspects of the scenario I have outlined. Nevertheless, I am dissatisfied with the simplicity of the argument that they suggest: cosmetic surgery is more of the same misogyny and sexism that are structures in the organization of our society. The rise of the cosmetic surgery industry and its focus on woman as the exemplary surgical candidate is also a result of the changing situation of medicine in the twentieth century. Doctors, with ever increasing ability to intervene in and on the human body, to enact what are construed as miracles of the flesh, play out fantasies of the normal and the ideal. The operative discursive opposition within which the cosmetic surgery "revolution" finds itself has more to do with the categories "normal" and "abnormal"—and the physicians' increasing authority to distinguish and shift those distinctions—than with an opposition between the categories "men" and "women."

Sexist, racist, classist, and other prejudicial biases make their way regularly through the discourses of plastic surgery. The juxtaposition of these structural prejudices with the categorical distinctions between normal and abnormal produces a situation within which differences are coded as deformities. In this interpretive context, women are perceived as less normal than men, who have enjoyed the normative position throughout Western history. Consequently, it is incumbent on women to produce themselves as more normal representatives of the nonnormative category. In order to do this, women attempt to represent the ideal—in other words, if they cannot be normal because of their sex, they might as well be perfect.[38]

In this context, Kathryn Morgan's provocative essay "Women and the Knife: Cosmetic Surgery and the Colonization of Women's Bodies" takes on an interesting spin. Morgan suggests that women might want to appropriate plastic surgery and use it to "deform" their bodies. She argues that by not actively engaging in a practice that uses cosmetic surgical technology to create "ugly" bodies, feminists may be demonstrating their continuing loyalty to the norms of patriarchal beauty. She suggests feminist women use the technology in a parodic and therefore subversive fashion. In suggesting that women use plastic surgical technology to remake themselves as "ugly," she is arguing for the parodic refashioning of women as extraeccentric to the category of the "normal." If women cannot be normal (that is, men) then they can be *really abnormal.* They can demonstrate their lack of filiation to the categories in play. Being surgically constructed ugly women is a way of upsetting the valorization of the normal that subjects women to the vagaries of cosmetic surgery in attempts to become perfect.[39]

One way to determine the impact of cosmetic surgeries on women is to look at books on cosmetic surgery targeted at a male audience.[40] Often, these will devote their introductions to defending cosmetic surgery for men, thereby providing the reader with insight into the current justifications for surgery and the ways in which men are interpellated into the discursive field. Men are brought into the field in much the same way as women, for example through claims to youthfulness and the alleged mismatch between an aged face and a young attitude. Physicians write that it is now acceptable for men to seek plastic alterations—implying that this is a step in the direction of liberation, a step toward personal fulfillment. Men, as potential candidates for cosmetic surgery, are constructed as equally subject to the vagaries of nature and aging as are women. As Ronald Strauss has suggested, the category of the "normal" is becoming more and more narrow. Men are losing their centrality, their normative status. Fantasies of ideality, and of immortality, are running rampant in the cultural imaginary. Through their influence and the increasing interventionary capacity and predilection of plastic surgeons, everyone becomes eccentric to the norm. That the difference between the numbers of men and women seeking sex change is narrowing only confirms this hypothesis.

In retrospect, this is clear from the presidential address delivered at the annual meeting of the American Society of Plastic and Reconstructive Surgery in 1954. President William Milton Adams stated that "comparatively few individuals who need plastic surgery find their way to our doors. To be convinced of this fact, one has only to walk a block down a busy city street; probably one of every five persons one meets will have some defect which could be improved or completely corrected by plastic surgery." His remedy for this obviously problematic situation was to "institute and vigorously pursue broad measures to enlighten the entire public—all those who live by the side of the road as well as the select few—regarding the type of services we provide in plastic and reconstructive surgery." He added that "it is [as] just and natural that any one with a structural defect should wish to have it corrected as it is that they should seek correction of an abnormally functioning gallbladder or other organ of the body. *The very fact that such a person seeks correction of a defect indicates a higher order of intelligence and a sane and realistic attitude toward his abnormal anatomy.*" [41] Cosmetic surgery has taken this basic perspective and exploited it to its extreme and logical conclusion: anyone can look better, and if one can, one should. Further, seeking cosmetic surgery becomes a way to prove one's psychological normality. [42]

The technological capacities of plastic surgery and endocrinology offered physicians the ability to construct physiological normality both discursively and materially. Yet the human body sets certain limits on the efficacy of the plastic ideologies. Sexual organs are not equal under the scalpel, and the differences between the sexes constrain the efforts of the plastic surgeons to construct female and (especially) male genitalia. This fact forces us to consider the materiality of sexual difference and the effects of technology on cultural ideologies.

The general principle of reconstructive plastic surgery is to transplant or transfer tissue from one site on the body to another and use the tissue to repair or reconstruct a damaged part of the body without the tissue dying in its new location or creating scars that would restrict both form and function of the repaired section. To move skin from one site to another, two general methods are used: flaps and grafts. A flap is a measure of skin where both skin and subcutaneous tissue are transplanted. Flaps are often "pedicled," which means that they are detached from their original site only after their attachment to the new site is safely established. Grafts are pieces of skin without subcutaneous tissue. They are called "split thickness" when they do not include the entire thickness of the skin and are often "free" grafts; that is, they are entirely separated from one site before transplantation onto another.

The development of the tubed pedicle flap is significant to the development of transsexual surgeries because it is one method of constructing an artificial penis. In 1916, a Russian doctor named Filatov raised the first human "tube pedicle flap," while independently, in 1917, Harold Gillies invented the same operation.[43] In "Operative Treatment of the Female Transsexual," John Hoopes wrote that "there is no literature [about the total reconstruction of the penis] prior to the 1920s, and that the currently accepted techniques are based on utilization of the Gillies-Filatov abdominal tube pedicle flap described in 1916."[44] One advantage of the tube pedicle flap over a conventional flap is that the tubed flap, wherever it is used, assures an adequate blood supply to tissue that is to be relocated, helping to deter infection and allowing for a longer flap of skin to be relocated. The tube itself is a skin flap that is raised and then sutured together to form a stalk, all the while remaining attached at both ends to the body. The skin underneath the pedicle is sutured. The pedicle can be walked or "wandered" across the body to the site of relocation, much like a regular skin flap, only with less risk of infection. Plastic surgeries with the tube pedicle technique are carried out in stages, like most flap procedures, allowing for the healing of one area before the skin is moved onto another. The invention of the tubed pedicle helped Gillies greatly in his reconstructions during World War I and in the immediate postwar period, as "this variety of flap is indicated in large skin replacements (especially facial) the blood supply of which and the resistance to infection being secured by the preliminary tubing of the flap."[45]

Liz Hodgkinson, Michael Dillon's biographer, writes that Harold Gillies made a tube pedicle penis for Dillon in the 1940s:

> By the 1940s, Gillies had perfected this technique as a means of reconstructing the penis. He did this by raising two abdominal tubes, one of which he inserted into the other, to produce a penile shaft and urethra. Into this he implanted a cartilage, to produce a semi-erectile condition.[46]

Gillies seems to have described this case in *The Principles and Art of Plastic Surgery*, although to do so he must have changed Dillon's biography to shield him. He claimed that the "new organ" was a success with the cartilage for stiffening and a working urethra.[47] As carried out today, this operation is still experimental, however, since there continue to be problems with the formation of fistulas that result from the grafting of hair-bearing tissue used for the constructed urethra.[48] Because the tube pedicle for the penis is first raised on the abdomen and then swung down, there tends to be extensive abdominal scarring. In addition, the "cosmetic results" of the penis itself are often poor.[49] Finally, a functional penis must be able to become erect and it must be able to urinate: these functions are specific and difficult to replicate. Dr. Stanley Biber, a surgeon who performs transsexual surgeries in Trinidad, Colorado, states that the most successful phalloplasties he has performed have been on Native American subjects whose abdominal skin is not hair-bearing and therefore does not create fistulas when formed into the internal tube of the urethra.[50] All attempts to construct a mechanical means of erection for (re)constructed penises have problems—for impotent men as well as for transsexuals—associated with the implantation of foreign materials in the human body. And the use of cartilage tissue for rigidity poses the problem of a constantly erect penis, certainly not a "natural" outcome.[51]

Vaginoplasty is physiologically an easier procedure than phalloplasty, although not without its own difficulties. The first successful attempts at vaginoplasty were performed in the early twentieth century.[52] One plastic surgeon describes six conventional techniques of vaginoplasty: free skin grafting (McIndoe's method); pedicle grafts (from the thighs or abdomen); use of the sigmoid colon (Schmid's method); rectal vaginoplasty (Schubert's method); use of the ileal loop of the intestine; and encouragement of secondary epithelialization of the granulating cavity (over a prosthesis that is worn continuously).[53] The last three methods are seldom used because they pose significant problems for the patient. The first is the most common method for cases of vaginal agenesis (absence of vagina) in genetic women, but the vagina thus made is "dry" and liable to contract and possibly undergo necrosis (that is, the tissue dies). Using the sigmoid colon to line the vagina is perhaps best for producing "normal" vaginal conditions—it is wet (though not as wet as the ileal loop) and, because it is already an internal organ, it does not tend to contract. However, the sigmoid colon procedure is not often engaged because it requires major abdominal surgery, and most gynecologists and plastic urologic surgeons are reluctant to do it.[54]

For male-to-female transsexuals, the most common procedure utilizes the skin of the penis for the lining of the new vagina and retains a portion of the erogenous tissue from the base of the penis for the clitoris. The scrotal tissue forms the labial folds. This technique is described by Gillies in The Principles and Art of Plastic Surgery and, if accomplished correctly, allows for vaginal feeling (even vaginal orgasm) because the penile skin used to line the vagina retains its nerve endings.[55] The procedure requires only one operation, although the recuperative period is somewhat lengthy and the new orifice must be maintained with a prosthesis to prevent closure. After the prosthesis is removed, the patient must dilate her vagina at least once every few days in order to maintain the vaginal form and prevent contracture; she may do this manually with a dildo or prosthetic device, by engaging in penile-vaginal intercourse, or by engaging in sexual relations that involve nonpenile vaginal penetration.[56]

Making a vagina is not merely the creation of a hole in the body, yet its construction is simpler than that of the penis, largely because it does not have to function in the manner of a penis—as an erectile tissue and as a urinary organ. Still, after it is constructed, a human-made vagina requires a lot of care and, as in other plastic procedures where tissue is taken from one place and put in another, the tissues are liable to become necrotic, infected, or to contract. Such a vagina has other limitations: it cannot take part in vaginal birth; it may need artificial lubrications; its size may be smaller than desired. Success is often measured by the ability to engage in penile-vaginal intercourse, a measure agreed on by many transsexual women and their doctors.[57] This is, of course, a decidedly phallocentric measure of success.

The differences between vagina and penis are not merely ideological. The difference between the sexes will never rest entirely on physiological distinctions between sex organs, but these distinctions are neither superfluous nor inconsequential. They constitute problems in the construction and reconstruction of matter that the plastic surgeon faces in his or her attempt to reorganize the physical signifiers of sex on the operating table. Any attempt to engage and decode the semiotics of sex in contemporary Western culture must acknowledge that these physiological signifiers have functions in the real that will escape, or exceed, their signifying function in the symbolic system. This is why ideological critiques of transsexualism should not ignore these material distinctions.

Marjorie Garber, in her article "Spare Parts: The Surgical Construction of Gender," discusses the relationship of surgical technologies to the incidence of female-to-male transsexualism, noting that because phalloplastic techniques are not well advanced, "sex reassignment surgery for female-to-males [is] less common" than for male-to-females. She remarks that "this [is] as much a political as a medical fact," arguing that in the context of sex reassignment surgery there remains "an implicit privileging of the phallus, a sense that a 'real one' can't be made, only born."[58] In effect, she subsumes any consideration of technology within an argument about ideology. The fact that techniques of phalloplasty lag behind those of vaginoplasty is not really presented as a medical *and* an ideological fact, but *only* an ideological one. As should be clear, making a penis that can both urinate and become erect is a vastly more difficult technical problem than constructing a working vagina, regardless of the ideological context within which the medical research takes place. In ignoring the specificity of the surgical techniques at issue, Garber demonstrates her investment in ideological analysis that refuses to acknowledge the resistances of the body to ideological captation.[59]

As I suggested in the introduction, it is not possible to understand how the gender system impacts the development of technologies unless we also examine how technical practices affect the gender system. As we shall see in the following chapter, the technical practices made available through developments in endocrinology and plastic surgery had a discernible impact on the discourses and clinical practices of psychiatric sexology and the medical management of intersexual subjects. Without the material means to regulate the hormonal sex of human subjects or to manipulate and (re)construct genital and secondary sexual organs, the current clinical protocols for the case management of intersexual patients would be meaningless. Indeed, they would have been unnecessary. In addition, and perhaps more important at the broader cultural level, the development of these technologies directly contributed to the production of the concept of gender. Plastic surgery, especially, invested itself in an ideological apparatus that depended on the idea of an identity prior to and within the body that theoretically should dictate the physical appearance of the subject.

Indeed, if endocrinology established a connection between external appearance and the internal circulation of hormones, presupposing a homology between culture and chemistry, cosmetic plastic surgery forged a relation between an internal sense of identity and how that self should appear to the public. We can see that this difference keeps endocrinology tied to the terminological system of medical description because its discourses must consistently return to the level of physiological description for support. Endocrinology, like any scientific discourse, is subject to ideological regulation, but that regulation is constrained by the relative significance of the terminological code for its treatment practices.

Cosmetic surgery, on the other hand, developed a discursive system that is more obviously motivated by cultural imperatives than that of endocrinology. This seems somewhat paradoxical, since plastic surgery is a more straightforward craft or technical practice than endocrinology. But it is precisely this loose hold on a descriptive system of the body that makes it ideal for ideological appropriation. Cosmetic surgery does not depend on a comprehensive description of physiological processes that would constrain its infiltration of the ideological field. Nevertheless, plastic surgery is constrained by the limits of physiological transformation. This fact keeps it at least partially connected to the materiality of the body and the body's relative autonomy, as plastic surgical practices must take account of sexual difference at the level of tissue function.

In its reliance on the idea of a self separate from physiology, however, plastic surgery participates in the transformation of sex into gender. In the case management of intersex subjects, the two practices of plastic surgery and endocrinology work together in the regulation of hermaphrodites into sexual difference. Technologically, the interventions are clear: the real code of the intersexual body is altered to fit a normative terminological system that mandates sexual difference between, and not within, subjects. Ideologically, however, these interventions depend upon the construction of a rhetorical system that posits a prior gendered self necessary to justify surgical intervention. Hormones work to figure the subject from the inside out; plastic surgery works to externalize the already existent internal self—or to produce that self through physical transformation of its somatic alibi.

3

MANAGING INTERSEXUALITY

AND PRODUCING GENDER

In 1990, Suzanne Kessler published an article in *Signs: Journal of Women in Culture and Society* on medical treatment protocols for intersexual patients. Entitled "The Medical Construction of Gender: Case Management of Intersexed Infants," the article is the end result of interviews conducted with "six medical experts (three women and three men) in the field of pediatric intersexuality," all of whom practiced in New York City. Kessler announces the focus of the article in its short preamble: "The process and guidelines by which decisions about gender (re)construction are made [in intersex case management] reveal the model for the social construction of gender generally. Moreover, in the face of apparently incontrovertible evidence—infants born with some combination of 'female' and 'male' reproductive and sexual features—physicians hold an incorrigible belief in and insistence upon female and male as the only 'natural' options. This paradox highlights and calls into question the idea that female and male are biological givens compelling a culture of two genders."[1]

Kessler examines the medical practices involved in the management of intersex infants both for their sexist biases and for the ways in which medicine upholds a two-gender system through masking the countersignification of bodies that transgress that system. She argues that "current attitudes toward the intersex condition are primarily influenced by three factors": advancements in surgery and endocrinology that make it possible to construct real-seeming genitalia and secondary sex characteristics, the influence of the feminist movement in "call[ing] into question the valuation of women according to strictly reproductive functions," and the development of the theory of "gender identity" which posits that "gender must be assigned as early as possible in order for gender identity to develop successfully."[2] This last factor, the gender identity paradigm, was inaugurated by John Money, Joan Hampson, and John Hampson in the mid-1950s, and developed further by Money, Anke Ehrhardt, and other intersexual researchers, as well as psychoanalyst Robert Stoller, in the 1960s and 1970s. The gender identity paradigm completely dominates the field of inter-sex case management, providing a philosophical basis for intersex treatment protocols, and was utilized by all the physicians consulted in Kessler's study.[3]

While she questions the data on which this hegemony is based, Kessler does not really examine the medical literature in which the claims for the gender identity paradigm are made. Rather, she is more interested in interrogating the ways in which the physicians' discourse and practice both construct two sexes and maintain that only two sexes really exist: "Case management involves per-petuating the notion that good medical decisions are based on interpretations of the infant's real 'sex' rather than on cultural understandings of gender."[4] She finds that in large part, the doctors perceive that decisions concerning assign-ment of sex need to be made quickly and are made, in fact, on the basis of phallic size: infants with male-like phallic structures are assigned to the male sex, while those with smaller phallic structures (micropenises or "normal" clitorises, depending on the physician's perception of the hormonal and/or chromosomal sex of the infant) will be assigned to the female sex.[5] Kessler concludes:

> If physicians recognized that implicit in their management of gender is the notion that finally, and always, people construct gender as well as the social systems that are grounded in gender-based concepts, the possibili-ties for real societal transformations would be unlimited. Unfortunately, neither in their representations to the families of the intersexed nor among themselves do the physicians interviewed for this study draw such far-reaching implications from their work. Their "understanding" that particular genders are medically (re)constructed in these cases does not lead them to see that gender is always constructed. Accepting genital ambiguity as a natural option would require that physicians also acknowl-edge that genital ambiguity is "corrected" not because it is threatening to the infant's life but because it is threatening to the infant's culture.[6]

Suzanne Kessler's essay is one that presents a fundamentally disturbing argu-ment about the perpetuation of ideas of "natural gender" in the face of their explicit simulation.

Nevertheless, Kessler misses a crucial opportunity to explore not the opera-tion of "gender" in contemporary culture, but the conditions of its production as a concept. In this chapter, I trace the introduction into medical discourses on intersexuality of the concept of gender as a separate experience of identity in sex, examining case studies of intersexual patients before Money's protocols were established in the 1950s and detailing the struggles of physicians to come up with a language about sex that would be appropriate to the new treatment practices available to them through advancements in endocrinology and plastic urologic surgery. From the perspective of this research, Kessler's claims about influences on the current attitudes about intersexual case management—technology, the women's movement, and the gender identity paradigm—are only partially correct: the first and third claims are accurate, but the second misrecognizes the physicians' ideological commitments. In this context of "making sex," the reproductive paradigm is not less important because feminists have convinced the medical establishment that women are not merely carriers of fertile ovaries, but because physicians are more concerned to maintain heterosexuality as the pattern of appropriate gender behavior than to recognize homosexuality as a potential sexual orientation for their subjects. This desire on the part of the "gender managers" overrides considerations of reproductive potential, as they argue that it is more important for their patients to be heterosexual than to be fertile but "perverted."[7]

Kessler's approach to the study of intersexuality is based on a perspective she developed with Wendy McKenna in their landmark study *Gender: An Ethnomethodological Approach*. Working from theories first developed by Harold Garfinkel, whose research on the intersexual/transsexual Agnes we looked at in the introduction, Kessler and McKenna claimed that perceptions of gender underlie all statements and observations about "sex": "We will use gender, rather than sex, even when referring to those aspects of being a woman (girl) or man (boy) that have traditionally been viewed as biological. This will serve to emphasize our position that the element of social construction is primary in all aspects of being female or male, particularly when the term we use seems awkward (e.g., gender chromosomes)."[8]

It seems to me, however, that this perspective fundamentally misconstrues the ways that physicians dealing with intersexuality and transsexualism utilize the terms "sex" and "gender" in their work. What I hope to show in the course of this chapter is that in examining the development of treatment protocols for the case management of intersexual patients, clinicians discursively and materially construct both sex *and* gender. To use "gender" to describe a physician's original assignment of an infant's sex or a surgeon's construction of a vagina for a male-to-female transsexual (as in "gender reassignment surgery") is to ignore or consider inconsequential the fact that these practitioners work with *material signifiers*. The significance of this distinction has to do with the way in which "gender" has been articulated in medical discourse as one component in a panoply of sexual signifiers, although different from the rest in that it is a psychosocial category rather than a physiological or anatomical one. The physicians treating intersexual conditions understand themselves to be working with "sex," in a context that accepts the nature/culture distinction between sex and gender.

Maintaining an analytic distinction between sex and gender does not relegate "sex" to the realm of scientific fact, but allows the critical thinker to make trouble in that very realm. Thus, I will not demonstrate that "gender" is always behind every claim made in the name of "sex"; rather, I aim to show that technology makes possible the distinctions between sex and gender that undergird the feminist conclusion that all sex is gender anyway. Indeed, my research suggests that prior to the introduction of "gender" into twentieth-century discourse as a signifier of "social sex," "sex" was a signifier encoding both biological and social categories. "Gender" was no less operative in social relations, but it went unmarked as a separate aspect of being a sex.[9] "Sex" came to refer solely to the biological realm when technology developed to the point that clinicians could routinely intervene at the level of (and therefore change) physical signifiers of sex.

Julia Epstein, in her important article "Either/Or—Neither/Both: Sexual Ambiguity and the Ideology of Gender," accounts for the significance of the technologies of sex change by arguing that "medicalization [of the intersexual condition] began in the sixteenth century and was nearly completed in the nineteenth, [but] its power did not alter the social condition of hermaphrodites until the availability of surgical and pharmacological interventions could control or create a public sexual identity for these individuals. In mandating binary sex differentiation for legal purposes, medical jurisprudence has, then, imposed a clearcut distinction even though in biomedical terms such a distinction has long been known not to exist."[10] The claim here is that the technologies of sex change have produced only the latest conditions in the increasing medicalization of hermaphrodites that now, because of the technology, can erase the signifiers of sexual ambiguity from the public realm. For Epstein, the instantiation of routine medical interventions to make intersexuals into males or females has had an ambivalent effect, given the historical treatment of hermaphrodites: "[T]he results of total medicalization [twentieth-century technological intervention] return us to the semiotics of teratology: individuals with gender disorders are permitted to live, but the disorders themselves are rendered invisible, are seen as social stigmata to be excised in the operating room."[11]

Thus, in Epstein's view, the more "fluid" medical perceptions of hermaphroditism that seemed to flourish between the seventeenth and the nineteenth centuries—perceptions that shifted hermaphroditism from the category of the monstrous to that of the natural anomaly within the taxonomies of natural science—were made moot by the establishment of technological intervention as the way to care for, as well as take care of, intersexuality. She concludes the essay with the following comments:

> The repression of the double-gendered in earlier centuries has now, far from being reversed by our liberal progression from "monstrosity" to "anomaly," been completed by the triumphant strategies of medical intervention in the service of civil taxonomizing: Suppression achieves its perfect form in "excision," and the Other's potential for subversive social arrangements is eradicated altogether. The varying approaches to gender ambiguity I have traced suggest that the assignment of a place in or the expulsion from legitimate social enmeshment represents an ideological project, a particular and paradigmatic instance of the cultural construction of gender, and one that reveals the powerful operations of homophobia in social practice. . . . Sexual ambiguity threatens the possibility of gender contrariety as the basis for social order and thereby threatens the hegemony of heterosexuality.[12]

While Epstein seeks to demarcate a shift in medical and legal perceptions of the "sexually ambiguous," she also looks for cultural patterns that recur—in this conclusion, she argues that medical technology has instantiated the "same old thing" with regard to society's desire to erase the possibility of gender confusion. This is a valuable analysis, but it nevertheless obscures the tremendous changes that twentieth-century technology offers to the ideological field. If this is the "same old thing," it is certainly the "same old thing" with a big twist.

Like Suzanne Kessler, Julia Epstein claims that everything is about "gender" rather than "sex." In "Either/Or—Neither/Both" this becomes quite a conceptual problem, as intersexual conditions are termed "congenital gender disorders" and the phrase "gender identity" is used consistently to describe individuals or circumstances in historical periods that predate its introduction into medical and popular discourse.[13] One of the reasons that this becomes a problem is that "gender disorders," a phrase Epstein uses to describe the case of Herculine Barbin (a nineteenth-century French hermaphrodite), is currently invoked to describe conditions such as transvestism and transsexualism: in current medical terminology, "gender" refers to the psychosocial realm, and not to the body.[14] However, even beyond that, this usage suggests, as Kessler's did, a misrecognition of the significance of physicians' *material* interventions into the realm of physiological and anatomical sex and the relation of those interventions to the social order understood as gender. In seeking to establish that ideological commitments construct two "natural" sexes, both Kessler and Epstein are unable to examine how ideological commitments vis-à-vis the perception of sex difference came to be understood precisely *as gender*.

My research suggests that physicians dealing with cases of intersexuality be-lieve in and subscribe to binary gender as a necessary social code. They accept, to a certain extent, the idea of "plural sex"; that is, the possibility of intersexu-ality as a naturally occurring form of physiological and anatomical sex. How-ever, they are willing to uphold binary gender by producing binary sex. It is technology and a certain attitude about technology that allows this capacity—both to perceive the multiplicity of sexual signifiers in one body and to make that body represent a singular sex identity—and thus it is technology that allows physicians to enforce binary gender through making males and females out of intersexuals.[15] In the following discussions of this chapter, I examine medical discourses on intersexuality in order to determine how physicians came to codify these beliefs in specific treatment protocols aimed at eradicat-ing intersexuality as a "natural" variation of the body's representation of sex.

From the first years of the twentieth century to its halfway mark, physicians confronted the problems of intersexuality with an increased capacity to inter-vene with both endocrine and surgical technologies. In addition, the growing fields of genetics and embryology contributed to the theoretical perspectives on intersexuality and, subsequently, to the practical applications of clinical treatment. In theories of human hermaphroditism prevalent in the nineteenth century and the first years of the twentieth, the body was thought to house a "true sex" evident in the histology of the gonads. But the advances of science in the early twentieth century dispelled this prior belief. The body was found to be unable to present unfailingly a unilateral or absolute sex.

The destabilization of the idea of an absolute sex is evident in the termi-nology used to describe subjects with ambiguous sexual signifiers. The terms "genuine" or "true hermaphrodite" are used to refer to individuals whose gonads are bisexual—that is, individuals with one ovary and one testis, at least one ovotestis, or both an ovary and a testis on at least one side. The "pseudo-hermaphrodite" is an individual with normal gonads of one sex or the other, but with ambiguously sexed genitalia and/or internal reproductive organs. A female pseudohermaphrodite is defined as having ovaries but masculinized ex-ternal genitalia; a male pseudohermaphrodite has testes but feminized exter-nal genitalia. Thus, the nineteenth-century belief in the true sex of the gonads continues in the terminology used to define hermaphroditic conditions and perpetuates in the perception that hermaphroditism is the result of the inter-mingling of the two sexes in one body, with one sex predominating.[16]

Michel Foucault suggests that in the eighteenth and nineteenth centuries the hermaphrodite's historical option to choose his/her sex at adulthood was undermined in favor of the notion of a true sex hidden within the appear-ance of two intermingled sexes, and that this belief in a true sex haunts us today, providing fuel for the current deployment of sexuality as the truth of the individual.[17] In the nineteenth century, surgery and microscopy made closer examination of gonadal tissues possible. It was within this context that Klebs classified true hermaphroditism as the existence of testicular and ovarian gonadal tissue, assuming that, in the words of Money and the Hampsons, "gonadal structure would determine sexual outlook and desires, even in those cases where gonadal structure and secondary sex characteristics at puberty were paradoxically contradictory." [18]

The distinctions between true and pseudohermaphroditism became unwieldy in the first half of the twentieth century because the terms no longer were able to describe in sufficient detail the conditions doctors met with in their hermaphroditic subjects. Advances in surgical anesthesia and sterile technique in the second half of the nineteenth century made the laparotomy (surgical examination of the peritoneum) a less risky procedure, allowing doctors to more routinely examine the contents of the abdominal cavity while the patient was still alive. This meant that pathological examination of the gonads through biopsy could contribute to diagnosis and treatment; previously, the histology of the gonads was generally available only after the death of the patient. Thus, the new technological capacity forced a reconceptualization of both the terminology describing hermaphroditism and the theories that attempted to explain its occurrence.

In chapter 1, in discussing the glandular thesis, I examined the idea of human intersexuality as a naturally occurring gradation of normal sexual variance that is nevertheless based on the idea of defective endocrine function. "Intersexuality" as a term was introduced into the diagnostic and descriptive lexicon in the 1920s by the German researcher Richard Goldschmidt, who suggested that all mammalian hermaphrodites were really "intersexes," having begun life as one sex or the other only to undergo a sex reversal as an embryo. The time of the sex reversal in the development of the organism was thought to determine the extent of the intersexuality. While Goldschmidt's specific theory of sex reversal has been refuted, his work remains significant, especially as the term intersexuality now coexists with the variants of hermaphroditism in the clinical literature.[19]

Theories of intersexuality, with the concomitant notion of a continuum of physiological and anatomical sex differences, challenged the idea of a "true sex" hidden within the body's tissues. In the twentieth century, with the development of technologies such as sex chromatin testing and the classification of different kinds of intersexuality (that is, internal distinctions between the broader categories of male and female pseudohermaphroditism that recognized specific and very different physiological causes and consequences), the notion of a "true sex" broke down. After all, there can be no true sex if no single "kind of sex" (chromosomal, gonadal, hormonal, among others) can be invoked infallibly as the final indicator of sex identity, as gonadal sex had been in the previous century. Thus, although the terminology of true and pseudo-hermaphroditism is still in use, intersexuality is more likely to be invoked as the larger category within which types of hermaphroditism are classified.

This is where the work of Money and the Hampsons is most significant. Their work demonstrates the gradual shift in interest away from the "true sex" as that which will ultimately determine the subject's gender destiny, toward the idea of the "best sex," that sex which would be most appropriate or advantageous, given the individual's genital morphology and psychological makeup. They could only pursue this course because medical technologies of "sex change" had, by the 1950s, become routine enough for physicians to offer them in the service of maintaining intersexual subjects as verisimilar representatives of one sex. It is in this context that binary gender could be enforced through the material production of sex (as opposed to other means).

The central question for physicians dealing with cases of hermaphroditism in the second quarter of the twentieth century was what to do now that they could actually intervene effectively to maintain a patient as a viable representative of a given sex. The recognition that there were numerous developmental reasons why physiological and anatomical sex might produce conflicting signifiers made a biological rationale for treatment less and less convincing. In addition, physicians were increasingly concerned with the psychological adjustment of their patients. Nevertheless, the nineteenth-century absolutism of anatomical sex identity ("a woman is a woman because of her ovaries") died hard, and the increasing scientificity of medicine made any dependence on the "soft data" of psychology difficult to accommodate. Fortunately, the rise of psychological tests of masculinity and femininity eventually offered physicians a "scientific" method of measuring sex role and therefore a way to use psychosocial sex identity as a factor in their treatment practices.[20] Even without this dependence on psychological profiles, however, in the 1920s through the 1940s physicians began to express hesitation—and anxiety—about deciding the sex assignment of intersex individuals.

The anxiety of making a decision concerning an intersexual patient with lateral hermaphroditism (ovary on one side, testis on the other) is apparent in a case reported by the urologic surgeon Hugh Young in 1924. Young wrote that an eighteen-year-old male came to him presenting hypospadias with severe chordee, an undescended left testicle, and a painful mass in the left inguinal canal.[21] Upon operation, Young discovered that the "mass" was in fact an ovary attached to an embryonic uterus and fallopian tubes. He described his dilemma in the following manner:

At this moment the problem seemed to me to be as follows: a normal-looking young man with masculine instincts [athletic, heterosexual] was found to have a normal tube and a functioning ovary in the left groin. What was the character of the scrotal sac on the right side? If these were also undoubtedly female, should they be allowed to remain outside in the scrotum? If a male, should the patient be allowed to continue life with a functioning ovary and tube in the abdomen on the left side? If the organs of either side should be extirpated, which should they be? It seemed imperative, therefore, to make an incision in the right groin to determine the nature of its contents.[22]

Fortunately for this physician, the right gland was a testis, although without signs of spermatogenesis. Young excised the ovary and tubes. His dilemma proved inconsequential because this patient was a "true hermaphrodite." The surgical intervention could follow the sex of assignment and rearing because there was at least one testicular gonad.

In a similar case many years later, Young was more secure in making a decision concerning the course of surgical intervention:

The question arose whether the gonad [in the hernial sac] was an ovary or a testicle. It was impossible to say definitely what the structure was, but it was small and apparently functionless, and *as the patient was distinctly masculine in figure, habits, and desires* it was decided to remove the uterus, the tube, and the gonad.[23]

Young's original desire for a biological or physiological basis for his decision gave way to an acceptance of a decision based primarily on psychosocial grounds.

A series of cases reported by a French doctor, G. Cotte, demonstrates a similar ambivalence that eventually led to an acceptance of a psychological justification. Cotte reported on three cases in "Plastic Operations for Sexual Ambiguity," of which the first and third are most significant here. Case one was a sixteen-year-old "boy" who was found to have female internal structures, although the vagina opened onto the urethra. Cotte wrote: "The result [of the plastic surgery] was excellent. Morphologically, I succeeded in changing the external genital organs from their masculine type into the feminine. Then I succeeded in constituting a vulva."[24] While the operation was ostensibly carried out on wholly physiological grounds—because the patient presented a demonstrably female physiology with some external masculinization—Cotte added:

I have to add that the patient, who up to then had been educated as a boy but whose tastes and character adjusted itself badly with her comrades at school without knowing why, is very happy that her sexual ambiguity has disappeared. . . .

From that moment on, the patient, whose latent femininity could not express itself, has been living as a woman.[25]

As in Young's first case, the decision based on biology was found to corroborate a psychosocial orientation. However, in Cotte's third case, the situation was precisely the opposite.

A twenty-two-year-old "woman" who had had a hernial operation at age eighteen was not menstruating and wanted to get married. Two testicles had been removed during a previous operation. Cotte diagnosed her as a "cryptorchid subject . . . with absence of scrotum and a vulvaform hypospadias."[26] The following citation from his article demonstrates the factors contributing to the decision to intervene:

> Operative intervention opened many grave problems. Here we were dealing with a masculine subject, neutral at present because of the resection of the atrophied testicles but in regard to civilian status the subject had already been considered as a girl. She was engaged in feminine work and how could she accept all of a sudden the status of a boy; more so because she had met a boy of whom she was very fond and to whom she revealed her malformation and who was willing to wait until she was operated upon and then marry her.
>
> In regard to the sex, the subject has feminine behavior and . . . one cannot impose the male sex on a subject who is not menstruating, who has no penis and who is incapable of having sexual intercourse as a male. It was therefore thought advisable to create a neo-vagina. *The subject being declared as a girl or female, there was no objection to her marriage because marriage consists only of uniting two individuals of different sexes.* The question may be asked whether a surgeon performing a plastic operation does not aid in deceit by hiding a deformity which involves sterility and which may later be the cause for divorce. The patient, on the other hand, declared that if she was not operated upon she would commit suicide. From the moral point of view her friend knew that she had no vagina, no uterus and that she would never have children but he accepted these conditions. It was therefore decided to intervene.
>
> . . . *The foregoing observations seem to me significant enough to be described because they show how surgeons are capable of modifying malformations and thereby ease their effect on the psyche.*[27]

The justifications presented are interesting for a number of reasons. First, and perhaps most significantly, "sex" in this passage clearly denotes a status or classification: it is a state that "ought not be imposed" as well as a category of declaration. It was not, in Cotte's argument, the subject's "sex" that was a problem, but her deviance from the morphology and physiology of those commonly included in her "sex." The problem was resolvable largely because the subject in question was engaged to be married. The fact of her heterosexuality, then, alleviated the dilemma associated with a change of sex status because it demonstrated her feminine attitude. Thus, Cotte banished the specter of homosexuality—what might have happened if she had been reassigned to the male sex as a result of the status of her reproductive organs and genitalia.

Cotte mentioned that he was worried about engaging in a deceitful act by "hiding a deformity which involves sterility and which may later be the cause for divorce." As the patient had threatened suicide, the operation to establish morphological femininity seemed the better course of action. However, it was the fiancé's acceptance of the patient even though he knew of her anatomical state that, at least rhetorically, immediately preceded the decision to intervene. It is as if Cotte needed the approbation of another male to admit this masculine subject into the female sex, or as if the fact of the fiancé's approbation made it clear that surgery was a better course than the probable suicide. The patient would, at least for a time, become a *married* woman; that is, the surgical intervention would insure her heterosexuality.

In the first case reported by Cotte, the decision to intervene based on biological physiology turned out to have facilitated a latent psychosocial orientation toward femininity. In the other case, the decision to intervene was based almost entirely on psychosocial orientation. Cotte argued for the ethics or morality of each decision, even though they had distinctly different legal implications. In the first case, the subject was reregistered as a girl, in keeping with the surgical "reassignment," while in the other case the original registration of sex was used as an argument for the subject's marriage despite the existence of testes, which indicated gonadal maleness: "The subject being declared as a girl or female, there was no objection to her marriage."

In article after article, especially from the late 1930s through the 1940s but appearing even before, physicians argued that the treatment of hermaphrodites needed to be correlated with what Money and the Hampsons would later call the sex of assignment and rearing.[28] In these articles, most (if not all) of which are case studies, we can read the consolidation of the concept of psychosocial sex identity, a term designating a complex of ideas that needed a simpler unifying principle or name. For instance, in a 1947 article in *Surgical Clinics of North America*, Francis Ingersoll and Jacob Finesinger wrote that a fifteen-year-old "girl" with gonads similar to prepubertal testes identifies with the mother and shows no need for competing with males. The female qualities of neatness, orderliness and compliance are seen as desirable and leading to success. She wishes to be a woman and accepts the feminine role. The conclusions drawn from the [psychological] test battery reinforce the clinical opinion that the patient has socialized in a feminine pattern of behavior with which she identifies. She rejects striving and masculine attitudes. There is agreement among the various tests in that the patient's personality is definitely feminine.[29]

The authors concluded the article by stating that the "evidence indicates that situational and cultural factors played the significant role in the patient's emotional development. Psychiatric and psychological study can define the sexual and social orientation of the patient. Once this is established, the surgeon can transform the external genitalia to fit the psychosexual behavior of the patient."[30] A 1949 article by Louis Fazen made a similar point:

> It becomes apparent that the plan of management of intersexuality depends primarily on the psychologic and emotional factors involved in each case, and the anatomic structure of the gonads should be the least determining factor. The course which promises the greatest improvement and causes the least disturbance should be followed.[31]

Nevertheless, in the case described by Fazen, the decision concerning medical intervention was made, at least partially, on the basis of technological capacity. The patient was six years old and presented cryptorchid testicles and a blind vaginal pouch. Fazen wrote that the testicles were excised, among other reasons, "because it is impossible to create functioning male genitalia out of normal-appearing female genitalia; and because this child should make a satisfactory adjustment as a female."[32]

In a 1945 study, Albert Ellis reviewed the literature concerning hermaphroditism in order to ascertain whether psychosexual behavior is physiologically determined or learned. By psychosexual behavior, Ellis meant sexual drive or orientation. He concluded that physiology had little if any influence on it. He noted that none of the hermaphrodites raised as males were willing to give up that status and assume a feminine social position, although those raised as females were not as fixed in their sex role. This fact he attributed to the social organization of European and American societies as male-dominated social and cultural formations. In conclusion, he wrote that "it may be inferred from this study that while the *power* of the human sex drive may possibly be largely dependent on physiological factors—such as the quantity and/or quality of sex hormone secretions—the *direction* of this drive does not seem to be directly dependent on constitutional elements."[33]

Many others agreed with Ellis and argued that in treating intersexuality environmental influences were, by and large, the most important factors in determining a subject's psychological identity and sex role orientation. F. Guternatsch summed up the prevalent line of thought in his review article "True Hermaphroditism: Concerning the 37 Cases Reported":

> While the older anatomists and pathologists as a rule presented merely descriptive reports of their cases, it is gratifying to learn from the reports of the last decade that it was possible, in some cases at least, through either surgery or hormone treatments, or with a combination of both measures, to bring medical aid to these individuals by shifting their anatomical, physiological and psychological imbalance from the state of bisexuality to a somewhat more determined state of male or female sexuality. The social significance of such corrective measures cannot be overestimated.[34]

The "social," however, enters into the diagnosis and treatment of intersexuality in another significant way, as suggested by some of the cases above, specifically through the consideration of cultural factors in the determination of the "best sex" for the intersexual patient. One way to assess the extent of the physicians' investments in producing appropriately sexed *social* subjects is to analyze their use of photographs to corroborate the claims of their clinical experiences. Authors use photographs and graphical illustrations to demonstrate and support specific treatments for physiological and anatomical sex variations, yet the medical illustrations demonstrate as well importance of the visual presentation of their patients in the cultural interpretation of sex.

For example, in the 1947 case by Ingersoll and Finesinger discussed above, the intersexual subject was raised as a girl. As an adolescent, she experienced phallic growth—that is, what was originally thought to be her clitoris grew so that it was considered abnormally large—and the deepening of her voice. There was no breast development at puberty. A gonadal biopsy demonstrated one cryptorchid testis and one underdeveloped or streak gonad that was thought to contain testicular tissue. There was no spermatogenesis present. Psychiatric studies suggested an orientation toward the "female role," in both sexual and social aspects. The subject's parents were against changing her assigned sex. The authors wrote that through psychiatric evaluation "the true nature of this patient's sex could be determined." The eventual treatment included synthetic estrogens and the excision of the enlarged clitoris.[35]

Figure 10 shows the "before" shots. In the photograph on the left, the bandages appear because the picture was taken after the gonadal biopsy surgery. According to the caption below, the purpose of this photograph is to document the "maleness" of the patient before treatment. Two things stand out, however: the striped socks and the overpowering accompanying photograph

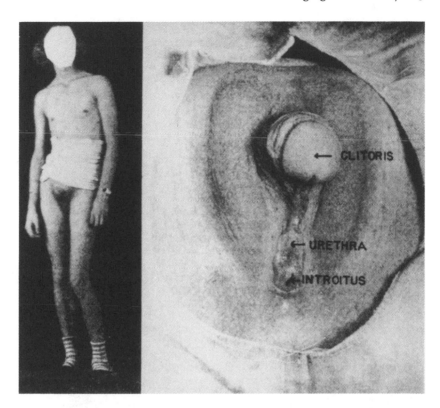

Figure 10. *Left:* Patient in November 1943. Note male physique and lack of breast development before treatment. *Right:* Patient in April 1946, showing perineum, enlarged clitoris, female urethra, intact hymen, and introitus. Source: Francis M. Ingersoll and Jacob E. Finesinger, "A Case of Male Pseudohermaphroditism," *Surgical Clinics of North America* 27 (October 1947): 1219. Reprinted with the permission of W. B. Saunders Company.

of the patient's genitalia. There, the penis-like "clitoris" commands substantial attention. The label "clitoris" is clearly meant to designate the "true identity" of the organ. The socks, in this period, signify "girl." [36] In addition, the body of the patient is posed as if to suggest a typical *feminine* stature with knees together and pelvis swayed forward.

The "after" pictures also appear in tandem (see figure 11). Here, we are asked to judge the patient's success as an "acceptable" female subject. The photograph on the left shows the patient naked, except for what appear to be bedroom slippers. Note that she is not wearing socks; her posture is straight, almost military in its bearing. We are asked to pay attention to her "enlarged breasts and darkened areolae after stilbestrol therapy." In the right photograph the patient is dressed in a woman's suit. The authors consider her "acceptable" with re-

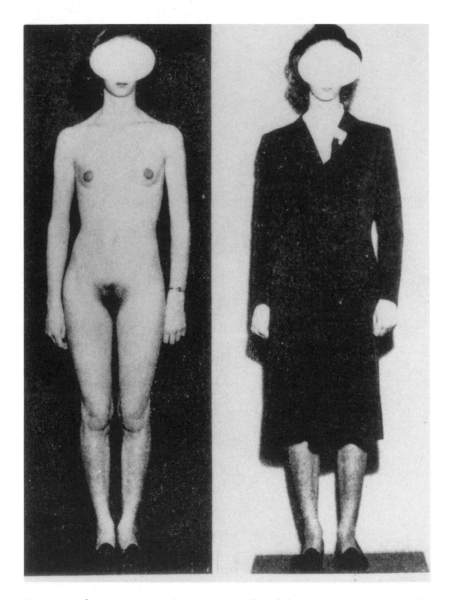

Figure 11. *Left*: Patient in April 1947. Note enlarged breasts and darkened areolae after stilbestrol therapy. *Right*: Note acceptable female appearance after therapy. Source: Francis M. Ingersoll and Jacob E. Finesinger, "A Case of Male Pseudohermaphroditism," *Surgical Clinics of North America* 27 (October 1947): 1223. Reprinted with the permission of W. B. Saunders Company.

gard to her appearance as a female. Here, it is not the body itself that is asked to verify the patient's femininity, but the patient clothed as a cultural subject.

Although the "before" pictures were supposed to convince us of the patient's male physique, there are messages that this subject is really a woman after all— her stature in the first photograph, her girlish socks, and the genital tubercle that is labeled a "clitoris" (as opposed to "micropenis" or "phallus"). This patient, the "before" pictures tell us, should be a woman because she already signifies as one. The "after" pictures suggest that the patient makes a very good woman after all, reassuring the reader that a correct diagnosis has been made.

In an article entitled "Pseudo-Hermaphroditism" by Leona M. Bayer, also published in 1947, the patient, "Helen," is described as a "masculinized girl." She had underdeveloped female internal reproductive organs—atrophic ovaries, tubes, and a uterine ridge. Her external genitalia included only a short urogenital sinus and a hypertrophied (that is, large) clitoris. She had to shave in order to "control" her facial hair. She had a consistently high output of 17-ketosteroids—this indicates a substantial presence of androgens in her system. She underwent clitoral amputation, estrogen therapy, and removal of her adrenal glands, the last of which had no appreciable effect on her hirsutism (excessive hairiness). The text is accompanied by a series of photographs of Helen at various ages, mostly to assess her growth rate (see figure 12). In addition, the author includes a chart to interpret the photographic illustrations.[37]

What is exemplary about this chart (illustrated in figure 13), "Androgynic Patterns of Body Form: Rating Profile," is that it represents a precise, semiotic guide for interpreting the photographs of Helen's (or any other intersexual's) body. The purpose of the chart is to interpret the physical signifiers of the whole body form for the reader. And, according to this chart, Helen receives between asexual and masculine as her "androgyny score": her "characteristic description" is "bisexual." The other exemplary aspect of the chart is the interpretation of the anatomical signs of sex. For example, the "hyper-feminine" trunk contour is "frail, softly fat," while the "hyper-masculine" trunk contour is "massive." Feminine legs have little or no muscular development, while masculine legs "bulge" with muscle. And, finally, a very large penis indicates hypermasculinity, while large breasts indicate hyperfemininity. This chart demonstrates in bold relief the kind of implicit semiotic apparatus or interpretive schema many clinicians of the period engaged as they treated intersexual patients. What might rightly be considered comical stereotypes of masculine and feminine body shapes were considered indicators of the body's "true" identity in sex.

In an article entitled "Social and Psychological Readjustment of a Pseudo-hermaphrodite under Endocrine Therapy," Rita S. Finkler provides the following information and analysis: The intersexual patient was raised as a girl, but

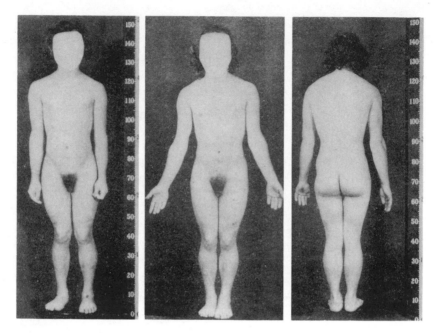

Figure 12. *Left:* Age 11 years, 6 months. *Center and right:* Age 15 years, 9 months. Source: Leona M. Bayer, "Pseudo-Hermaphroditism: A Psychosomatic Case Study," *Psychosomatic Medicine* 9 (1947): 246. Reprinted with the permission of Williams and Wilkins.

during puberty, her clitoris began to grow and she "developed an emotional interest in a girl and began to feel the urge to assume a masculine role in this relationship." She resisted attempts at feminization. Her labia were "somewhat shrunken," the vaginal opening measured eight centimeters, her voice was deep, there was no male hair pattern, no evidence of a prostate, and no evidence of (female) pelvic organs. Hormone treatments and a laparotomy demonstrated the existence of infantile testes, with no ovarian tissue present. The patient was placed on testosterone therapy and the patient was legally changed from female to male, and assumed male attire.[38]

Figure 14 shows the patient before testosterone therapy, while figure 15 ostensibly demonstrates the effect of the testosterone therapy on the patient's biceps. The placement of the subject's arms is meant to demonstrate precisely this muscular development. It would seem, however, that this stereotypical posture of masculinity makes its point in another sense. Indeed, in all three of these cases, the photographs or illustrations accompanying the text make their points in "another sense," that other sense being the presentation of appropriate cultural signifiers of masculinity or femininity. In other words, the pictorial or graphical accompaniments to the diagnostic/textual presentation had as their

Bayley-Bayer Standards*
17–18 Year Norms

| Name Helen | Sex M/F | Date Nov. 11, 1944 Age 18-4 | Skeletal Age Adult | Case Number |

ITEM ("A" through "H" from rear-view photographs)	Hyper-masculine 1	Masculine 2	Intermediate, A-sexual, or Bi-sexual 3, 3a, 3b	Feminine 4	Hyper-feminine 5
I. A. Surface modeling	Exaggerated hardness of relief.	Strong muscle molding. Bone, vein and tendon prominences.	b. Muscular and fat. / a. Little muscle or fat.	Smooth and soft, with little muscle.	Very soft, fat, no muscle.
II. Trunk Contours B. Shoulder girdle	Massive.	Appears wide, heavy and muscular.	b. Muscular and fat. / a. Narrow, "bony."	Slight, soft and narrow.	Frail, softly fat.
C. Waist line	Marked torso narrowing to low waist; may have minimal indentation.	Slight indentation due to narrowing of torso.	b. Broad hip and shoulder; little indentation. / a. Slight symmetrical high concavity.	Definite line accentuated by hip widening.	Marked indentation.
D. Hip flare	No widening.	Slight widening of hips from waist.	Intermediate.	Flares into wide hips laterally and posteriorly.	Marked flare.
E. Buttocks	Very flat.	Flat and angular.	Intermediate.	Rounded and full.	Very broad and rounded.
III. Leg Patterns F. Thigh Form	Cylinder and/or bulging muscles.	Approaches cylinder. Lateral outline convex.	Intermediate.	Funnel, fat and rounded. Lateral outline concave.	Fat, wide-top funnel.
G. Interspace (whole leg)	Very open.	Open center above and below knees.	Intermediate.	Closed center except small space below knees.	Thighs and knees together, etc.
H. Muscle bulge (lower leg)	Strong bulge, no fat.	Prominent inner bulge of gastrocnemius.	b. Moderate muscle bulge. / a. No muscle bulge; spindly.	Slight inner bulge; shapely, smooth, outer curve.	Very little muscle, but smoothly rounded and outer curve.
J. Penis size	1 Very / 1.5 Large	2 Average	2.5 Small / 3 Very		
K. Breast size			3 Very / 3.5 Small	4 Average	4.5 Large / 5 Very
L. Body hair density	1 Heavy on thighs, etc.	Easily discernible	2.5 Sparse (3)	4 Absent	
M. Pubic pattern	Disperse / Acuminate.	Sagittal	(Horizontal)		
N. Bieristal/Biacromial Index	–68 69	73 74	76 77	82 83	
P. Strength (Kg) Grip (R+L)+Thrust +Pull; Grip (R+L)	+244 243 / +126 125	186 185 / 95 94	148 147 / 80 79	110 109 / 59 58	
Androgyny Score (Sum of "A"–"H")	8	12 13	19 20 / 25 26	34 35	40
Characteristic Description (Circle one)	Hypermasculine	Masculine	Intermediate (Bisexual) Asexual Disharmonious	Feminine	Hyperfeminine

Figure 13. Androgynic patterns of body form: Rating profile. Source: Leona M. Bayer, "Pseudo-Hermaphroditism: A Psychosomatic Case Study," *Psychosomatic Medicine* 9 (1947): 249. Reprinted with the permission of Williams and Wilkins.

purpose the demonstration of the intersexuals' "proper" sexual performance, according to conventional standards of masculine or feminine deportment and/or measurement. It is this developing perspective that led to the work of Money and the Hampsons, whose coining of the term "gender role" crystallized the trend of the preceding decades of clinical treatment of intersexuality.

The medical record is not without contradictions, however, and before moving on to a discussion of the work of Money and the Hampsons, I would

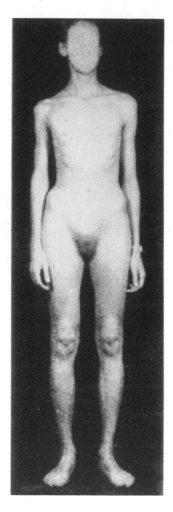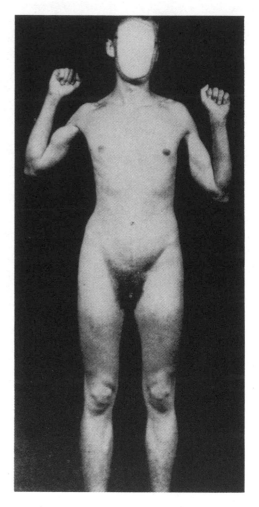

Figure 14. Patient W. D. Age 21. Before therapy. Height 71 inches. Weight 120½ pounds. Source: Rita S. Finkler, "Social and Psychological Readjustment of a Pseudohermaphrodite under Endocrine Therapy," *Journal of Clinical Endocrinology* 8 (1948): 89. Reprinted with the permission of the Endocrine Society.

Figure 15. Patient W. D. After testosterone therapy. Height 71 inches. Weight 151½ pounds. Source: Rita S. Finkler, "Social and Psychological Readjustment of a Pseudohermaphrodite under Endocrine Therapy," *Journal of Clinical Endocrinology* 8 (1948): 93. Reprinted with the permission of the Endocrine Society.

like to discuss some of these cases. It is important to understand how contested the treatment of intersexual patients was, and how tenacious the ideas of the physicians were concerning the constitutive aspects of a proper female or a proper male. For while doctors were coming to a sort of consensus concerning the direction of treatment for intersexuals, there was a lot of "messing around" in the body that, in retrospect, demonstrates the contingent quality of the identification of tissue as "male" or "female," as well as the power of medical practices to transform lives.

A case in point was described by Hugh Young in his landmark text, *Genital Abnormalities, Hermaphroditism, and Related Adrenal Diseases.* Young, whose work we have already examined in part, was a urologist at the Johns Hopkins Hospital. *Genital Abnormalities* is a compendium of information on both "true" and pseudohermaphroditism, and provides a wealth of case material for any avid researcher in this field. In keeping with his specialty, Young was particularly interested in the surgical repair of genital abnormalities, and the text is replete with detailed drawings of the various stages of plastic urologic surgery.[39]

Young's fifth case of male pseudohermaphroditism is of interest here. In 1925 a seven-year-old child was brought into the hospital because of undescended testes and a hypospadiac penis. The child had been brought up as a boy in a male orphanage. During an exploratory laparotomy, the doctors discovered some internal female organs (a uterus, a fallopian tube, and what they believed to be an ovary), and did not find any testicular tissue at all on the right side. The child was "put into girl's clothing [and] transferred to [a] female orphanage." There, the child "developed [a] marked habit of masturbation"; apparently, the "clitoral appendage" was also "annoying to the child, so that she has to wear a suit of underclothes all the time, in order to keep other children from seeing her."[40]

The child was brought into the hospital again to check on the possibility of removing the "clitoral appendage." Despite the fact that the appendage was "about the size of a ten-year-old boy['s penis]," the doctors recommended amputation: "Owing to the continued masturbation, the very frequent erection of the clitoris, the fear of exposure and as the previous laparotomy showed the patient to be 'definitely female,' it was decided to amputate the penis-like 'clitoris.' " The doctors report that "the convalescence was uneventful."[41]

At age sixteen, this same child "was admitted to the hospital complaining of a mass in the left inguinal region of about 5 years' duration." Interestingly, the patient made it clear to the doctors that "she" intended to "assume male attire" as soon as "she" was out of the orphanage. The physicians examining "her" found a testicle on "the left side, with a definite vas; also a Fallopian tube leading to an undeveloped uterus behind the bladder; and a Fallopian tube also on the right side, but no gonad." Young reports, "After a long discussion, it was decided that, as the penis had been excised 6 years before, it would be best to excise the testicle with as much as possible of its mesentery containing the supposed vas deferens, and also a large part of the Fallopian tube."[42] This decision was made despite—or in spite of—the patient's articulated desire to assume the social position of a man upon reaching the age of majority.

Young's final comments are perhaps his most interesting:

> During the past year (1935) the patient has become more masculine in character and interests. His mental outlook has been completely trans-formed and he is apparently happy although living as a male without penis or testicles and with the vagina still present. If *implantation of ovaries ever becomes successful in the human should this be done?*[43]

For these physicians, it was inconceivable (or practically inconceivable) that a human subject could be happy and masculine without penis and/or testicles. Thus, despite the patient's stated intention to follow a masculine line of work ("mechanical trades") and to "assume the attire of a man," because they had already excised the "penis-like clitoris" the physicians proceeded to remove what they knew was viable testicular tissue (although seemingly incapable of spermatogenesis).[44] And while the subject persisted in a "masculine" life, Young still wondered about the possibility of implanting *ovaries* into "his" body.

In other cases, the physicians seem to have responded more favorably to the demands of the patient to remain in a given sex despite physiological or ana-tomical evidence to the contrary. However, with respect to one of these cases, Young makes a comment similar to that quoted above: "Patient now apparently living happily as a woman, although neither uterus nor ovaries present."[45] In both cases, he finds it questionable that a subject can really be a sex with-out the matching gonads or reproductive/genital organs. In the 1950s, Money and the Hampsons would have claimed that both these patients were "being a sex" through appropriate performance of and identification in their gender role, and they would have argued that in the case of the "boy" raised in the orphanage, everything possible should have been done to maintain "him" in that sex category since by the time "he" was taken to the hospital "he" had already established that identification. Whether or not this case verifies their later theories, however, seems less important than noting Young's reluctance to believe that performance and satisfaction as a sex could really occur in a body without the right sexual apparatus(es).

Another "case" discussed by Young seems to refute Money and the Hamp-sons' later theories concerning the necessity of establishing an identity as one sex or the other. This was a subject whose "sex" was undetermined—meaning that he/she did not submit to a laparotomy to determine the histology of his/her gonadal tissue. He/she was what Young called a "practicing hermaphro-

dite," meaning that he/she lived with knowledge of his/her anomalous condition and, in fact, exploited it somehow (in this case, he/she used both sets of
genital organs for sexual pleasure). The subject was married as a woman to a
man and participated in sexual relations with "girl friends" using his/her "enlarged clitoris."

After describing the patient's life story, as well as the findings of an external
exam, Young records the following conversation:

> The patient was asked if she were satisfied with her present life.
>
> "No," she said, "I feel, sometimes, as if I should like to be a man. I have
> wondered why my passions always have been directed towards women.
> I have derived great pleasure from many sexual affairs with women, and
> never with my two husbands."
>
> "Would you like to be made into a man?" "Could you do that?"
>
> When assured that this would be quite easy, that it would only be nec-
> essary to remove the vagina, and do a few plastics to carry the urethra
> to the end of the penis the patient said, "Would you have to remove that
> vagina? I don't know about that because that's my meal ticket. If you did
> that I would have to quit my husband and go to work, so I think I'll keep
> it and stay as I am. My husband supports me well, and even though I don't
> have any sexual pleasure with him, I do have lots with my girl friends." [46]

This exchange demonstrates that it is perhaps possible for a human subject
to produce an identity that takes into account what Julia Epstein would call a
"sexually ambiguous" anatomy. Because this patient was an adult, the physicians could not enforce any specific form of treatment for his/her anomalous
condition—and on this point it is clear that Young and his associates could
make decisions for the orphaned child precisely because that child was a ward
of the state and had neither his/her own parents nor his/her own say in the
matter. [47]

Further, and perhaps most significantly, this last case demonstrates the extent to which the intersexed subject him/herself understood his/her desire
for women to be indicative of his/her "masculinity," but could at the same time
refuse to give up "female organs" that were of value to him/her. Anne Fausto-
Sterling writes that "Emma's [the patient's] reply strikes a heroic blow for self-
interest," highlighting what we might call (after Freud) Emma's "instinct for
self-preservation." [48] However, I would argue that what is most interesting here
is the way in which his/her experience of sexuality, identity in a sex category,
and performance in a sex role were embedded in a complex social, economic,
and ideological context that he/she refused to make more "coherent" through
the excision of some tissue and the building up of some other tissue.

This is precisely the potentially subversive power of intersexuality that Julia

Epstein suggests at the end of her article, when she states that "[g]ender ambiguity does more than merely turn the world upside down, a gesture that, after
all, fundamentally maintains the notion of hierarchy even when it reverses it.
Sexual ambiguity threatens the possibility of gender contrariety as the basis for
social order and thereby threatens the hegemony of heterosexuality." Epstein
adds, as the final line in her essay, that the history of sexual ambiguity "demonstrates that this threat has been met with the heaviest artillery available to the
professional discourses of medicine and jurisprudence that establish human
definitions and boundaries."[49] Fausto-Sterling would agree, as she writes in
"The Five Sexes":

> The treatment of intersexuality in this century provides a clear example
> of what the French historian Michel Foucault has called biopower. The
> knowledge developed in biochemistry, embryology, endocrinology, psy-
> chology and surgery has enabled physicians to control the very sex of the
> human body. The multiple contradictions of that kind of power call for
> some scrutiny. On the one hand, the medical "management" of intersexu-
> ality certainly developed as part of an attempt to free people from per-
> ceived psychological pain. . . . And if one accepts the assumption that in
> a sex-divided culture people can realize their greatest potential for happi-
> ness and productivity only if they are sure they belong to one of only two
> acknowledged sexes, modern medicine has been extremely successful.
>
> On the other hand, the same medical accomplishments can be read not
> as progress but as a mode of discipline. *Hermaphrodites have unruly bodies.* They
> do not fall naturally into a binary classification; only a surgical shoehorn
> can put them there. . . . Inasmuch as hermaphrodites literally embody
> both sexes, they challenge traditional beliefs about sexual difference: they
> possess the irritating ability to live sometimes as one sex and sometimes
> the other, and they raise the specter of homosexuality.[50]

The protocols for the medical management of intersexuality that Fausto-
Sterling refers to were first introduced in a series of essays published in the
1950s by John Money, Joan Hampson, and John Hampson.[51] All four articles
concerned what the authors called "human hermaphroditism," and in each
the authors made a pitch for the significance of the "sex of rearing" as the
most important determinant of what they called "gender role": "By the term
'gender role' we mean all those things that a person says or does to disclose
himself or herself as having the status of boy or man, girl or woman, respectively. It includes, but is not restricted to, sexuality in the sense of eroticism.
A gender role is not established at birth, but is built up cumulatively through
experiences encountered and transacted. . . . In brief, a gender role is established in much the same way as is a native language."[52] In effect, these articles

codified the prevalent trend in the medical management of intersexuality by arguing that neither hormonal, chromosomal (genetic), or gonadal sex, nor internal reproductive structures, nor even external genital morphology, were as important in determining an individual's "gender role and orientation" as the assigned sex and sex of rearing of that individual.[53] Based on their determination that gender role and orientation become fixed somewhere between the ages of eighteen months and two years, Money and the Hampsons advocated parental decision making concerning sex of rearing before that time, taking into account the feasibility of constructing natural-looking genitalia and the ease of "fitting in" (visually) as a member of the assigned sex. After the acquisition of gender role, they advised surgical and hormonal interventions to accommodate the subject's body to the established role.

In the introduction to this book, I drew attention to differences between the entries for "gender" in the two editions of the Oxford English Dictionary, differences that imply a shift in twentieth-century usage of the term, specifically with regard to "sex." Previously, the OED informs us, "gender" was used as a direct substitute for the word "sex," while since 1962 (the date of its first example under the new definitional entry) it has also been used "to emphasize the social and cultural, as opposed to the biological, distinctions between the sexes."[54] An interview with John Money, published in Omni magazine in 1986, clarifies how this came about:

In working with hermaphrodites, Money confronted a new problem: how to talk about not only copulatory roles but also mind-sets of people whose social or legal sex is discordant with their chromosomal, gonadal, or body status. "People may be absolute about male and female," he said. "Nature is not." To spring himself from this semantic trap, Money borrowed the word gender from philology, the study of languages. Gender signified a person's personal, social, and legal status as male or female without reference to the sex organs. From this, he coined the term gender role. The phrase caught on, and today just about everybody uses it without always knowing precisely what they're talking about. For Money, gender role means the things a person says or does to reveal him- or herself as having the status of boy or man, girl or woman. He soon found it necessary to combine the term into gender identity/role. Gender identity became the private experience of gender; gender role, one's public presentation as male or female.

As he explores new territory, Money makes up new concepts along the way.[55]

From this quote, we can see that Money did not want to use the term "sex role," which was already in circulation and which would seem to describe the same phenomenon as "gender role," precisely because he did not want to suggest that this role acquisition had anything to do with aspects of biological sex.[56] In a 1991 article, Money relates essentially the same story to account for his coining of the term "gender role" to relay the "totality of masculinity or femininity."[57]

Money and the Hampsons presented their overall argument through the four articles in a piecemeal fashion, first offering their recommendations, then their evidentiary support. In "Hermaphroditism: Recommendations Concerning Assignment of Sex, Change of Sex, and Psychologic Management," they recommended that for infants and neonates, sex should be assigned primarily on the basis of the presentation of their external genitalia, giving due regard to the effects of possible hormonal and surgical interventions. For older children and adults, they believed that the first consideration must be given to the extent of the establishment of gender role and orientation. A change of sex should be avoided unless the subject exhibited behaviors considered appropriate to the other sex. They postulated that after the transition from infancy to childhood—which in this essay they marked at between three and one-half and four and one-half years of age—"it is too late to impose a change of sex."[58] Indeed, they claimed that gender awareness usually becomes established at around eighteen months, although "as in all matters pertaining to development and maturation, it is not the same age for all infants."[59] Throughout the article, Money and the Hampsons emphasized that assignment of sex should be made as soon as possible after birth, because "the most complex problems of psychologic management arise in those hermaphroditic children who are exposed to equivocating indecision and doubt on the part of parents and physicians and whose sex is debated or ridiculed by their contemporaries, so that they do not establish their gender with unambiguous certainty."[60]

"An Examination of Some Basic Sexual Concepts: The Evidence of Human Hermaphroditism" reported on a study in which Money and the Hampsons compared the sex of assignment and rearing of intersex subjects to other contradictory sex indicators such as sex chromatin, gonadal sex, internal reproductive organs, and external genital morphology. In this article, they argued that the sex of assignment and rearing was the best indicator of gender role and orientation. Indeed, they claim that "from the sum total of hermaphroditic evidence, the conclusion that emerges is that sexual behavior and orientation as male or female does not have an innate, instinctive basis."[61] However, the authors are quick to argue that this does not mean that just because gender role is established during postnatal development and does not have an innate or instinctual basis that it is "easily modifiable. Quite the contrary! The evidence from examples of change or reassignment of sex in hermaphroditism . . . indicates that gender role becomes not only established, but also indelibly imprinted."[62]

In "An Examination of Some Basic Sexual Concepts" Money and the Hampsons also present an addendum to their definition of gender role, concerning their methods of measuring its acquisition and its direction: "Gender role is appraised in relation to the following: general mannerisms, deportment and demeanor; play preferences and recreational interests; spontaneous topics of talk in unprompted conversation and casual comment; content of dreams, daydreams and fantasies; replies to oblique inquiries and projective tests; evidence of erotic practices and, finally, the person's own replies to direct inquiry."[63] These criteria reveal quite specifically the nature of Money and the Hampsons' conceptions of "gender role," and the extent to which clinicians' assessments of the patients' proper gender role involved making judgments about the appropriate sexual fantasies and desires of male and female subjects.

This aspect of gender role assessment is made very clear in the next article in the series. "Sexual Incongruities and Psychopathology: The Evidence of Human Hermaphroditism" presented evidence that the "reassignment of sex of rearing during early months of life was extremely conducive to subsequent psychologic healthiness," and that a "healthy" rating was more likely with those intersex subjects whose genitals were more "normal looking."[64] However, in the "mildly nonhealthy" group (as opposed to "moderately nonhealthy" or "severely nonhealthy"), Money and the Hampsons included "three patients, living as women, who had homosexual desires and inclinations. One of these, an introverted and shy person, had not been a partner in homosexual practices; the other two, whose erotic practices had been bisexual, were not introverted and shy in day-to-day routines and affairs."[65] Thus, nonheterosexual sexual practices were perceived by these authors to be indicators not only of improper gender role but of psychologic unhealthiness—although it is to their credit that the researchers did not put these individuals into the two "unhealthiest" categories of their taxonomy.

The last article in this series, "Imprinting and the Establishment of Gender Role," argued that gender role was neither purely hereditary nor purely environmental (socially constructed). Instead, the authors asserted that gender role acquisition was something of a semiotic learning process, similar to that of language acquisition or the imprinting of patterned behaviors. They used the example of Konrad Lorenz imitating a female mallard duck, "discovering that wild mallard ducklings, immediately upon being hatched, could be induced to react to him as if he were their mother." The authors also reiterated the idea that "once a person's gender role begins to get well established, an attempt at its reversal is an extreme psychologic hazard."[66]

While Money and the Hampsons can be seen as having asserted a constructionist rather than an essentialist position concerning the relationship between physiological sex and the development of "psychological sex" or gender role, they established a new essentialism that fixed gender role and orientation within an exclusively heterosexual framework.[67] For example, in their first article of the series, they wrote that a "chief objection" against their recommendation was that it

> flagrantly disregards the possibility of depriving the group of nonsterile hermaphrodites of fertility in adult life. The answer to this objection is that actual child bearing as distinguished from potential biological fertility is not determined by chromosomal, hormonal, and gonadal sex alone. It is also determined by the social encounters and cultural transactions of mating and marrying, which are inextricably bound up with gender role and erotic orientation.[68]

Safeguarding fertility might, as a corollary effect, produce homosexual adults: "Thus a boy, changed to wear dresses once ovaries were discovered, may continue to think, act and dream as the boy he was brought up to be, eventually falling in love as a boy, only to be considered homosexual and maladjusted by society." The authors mentioned another possibility—that the child may not make the gender role switch completely and thus may be subject to psychologic disorder "sufficiently disabling to prevent marriage." Thus, managing intersex subjects with specific regard to genital morphology and the establishment of gender role and orientation had as one explicit object the maintenance of heterosexuality among intersexual subjects.[69] Their ambiguous physiological presentation, threatening to the cultural imperative of a binary opposition between the sexes, was contained within the heterosexual imperative with the aid of surgical and hormonal technologies.[70]

Money and the Hampsons were not the first clinicians concerned with intersexuality to be alarmed at the potential perversity of their patients. In a 1938 article, James McCahey wrote:

> Erections of the phallus in genetic females is pathological, even though some of these individuals have well marked somatic and psychical traits of masculinity. The erections may be so strong that male-like potency becomes established. Should such individuals contemplate matrimony as males, in justice to the intended wife, the true state of affairs should be made known and correctional procedures advised. Genetic females with no abnormal sex urges, who have become economically adjusted as males, may be left undisturbed.[71]

This passage is remarkable for its (paranoiac) lack of specificity. Are these "correctional procedures" disciplinary or surgical? If the latter, which direction would they go? And what if the "intended wife" knew of the intersexuality of her intended and thought it was fine? McCahey's desire to avoid pathological sexuality—that is, the "perverse" orientation of homosexuality—was not uncommon among physicians dealing with intersexuality at the time, and in other situations led to some startling rhetorical justifications for medical intervention.

Another case report from the same period discussed "Eloise," an intersexual African-American subject brought up as a girl. Eloise, who later took the name Louis, underwent surgical treatment to excise a hernial sac and to determine his/her appropriate sex. The doctors chose (allegedly with their patient's consent) to establish Eloise/Louis as a male, a decision apparently motivated by the fact that the patient lived with a woman in a sexual relationship and had a relatively well-developed penis, since the gonad that was found was an ovotestis. The authors wrote that they "must consider the possibility of this individual being psychologically a homosexual female; but *by making the patient male, the perversion socially ceases to exist.* This, of course, is desirable from the standpoint of the community." At the end of the article they added that "since our patient has been wearing men's clothing he has exhibited no overt desire to return to the female method of dress. This would be evidence against the belief that he may be psychologically a homosexual female." [72]

Why this would be evidence against female homosexuality is not clear, since female transvestism has been an alleged sign of female homosexuality for centuries. Wearing female dress, in their eyes, must have been a sign of psychological femininity. The logic continues that since Eloise/Louis was happy to be dressed as a man, he/she must have felt him/herself to be a man. Therefore, his/her relations with the "opposite sex" were understood as heterosexual, and having nothing to do with his/her prior status as a female.

The circumstances under which Eloise/Louis came to the attention of the physicians were not insignificant to the outcome of his/her case. The authors describe these circumstances as follows:

Eloise H., a 27 year-old negro . . . came to the attention of the civil authorities in January, 1935. At that time he [sic] was living with a woman who had deserted her husband and her 3 children. His mistress was pregnant but claimed that her husband was the father of the coming child. However, the husband denied the paternity of the child and the patient was accused of being the father. In April, 1935, this woman was delivered of a male infant.

In view of the part the patient had played in disrupting the marital union, in addition to the suggestion of his hermaphroditic nature and possible paternity of the newborn child, he was brought before the Municipal Court on a bench warrant. Two court physicians examined him, made a diagnosis of "pseudo-hermaphroditism and inguino-scrotal hernia." . . .

On January 15, 1936, he was committed to the Philadelphia General
Hospital, Psychopathic Ward, for observation. On admission, the patient
was fully attired in female clothes from hat to chemise but was placed in
the men's division because of what seemed to be a predominantly male
type of psuedo-hermaphroditism.[73]

As stated above, upon surgical inspection, Eloise/Louis was found to be a "true
hermaphrodite," with at least one ovotestis. While the authors claim that Eloise/
Louis concurred with them in their decision to become a male—they write,
"He always thought of himself sexually as a male"[74]—since it does not seem
that he/she had much say in the issue of treatment, their assertions are suspect.
Indeed, his/her experience with the medical institution is reminiscent of the
young orphan whose "clitoris" was extirpated due to excessive masturbation.[75]

If Money and the Hampsons' protocols for the case management of intersexual subjects can be said to continue this kind of treatment, codifying into
medical practice the physicians' preference for heterosexuality even at the cost
of fertility (although, in the case of Eloise/Louis, as in the case of all "true hermaphrodites," fertility was probably not a possibility as either sex), their own
language belies a tendency to continue to think of and represent sex organs as
primarily reproductive. Significantly, the points at which this tendency exerts itself
occur in relation to the information that should be given to intersexual children about their sexual organs. For example, Money and the Hampsons write:

> An hermaphroditic child needs only eyes and ears to know that the focus
> of medical attention is on his or her genitals, even if the hermaphro-
> ditism is concealed. . . . [I]t is actually a lifting of the burdens of secret
> worries and doubts for the doctor to talk frankly with children. . . . One
> cannot, of course, say very much about the reproductive system without
> explaining the facts of reproduction. These items of information can be
> given quite intelligibly to young children, as they become ready to as-
> similate them, in terms of a *baby nest* or *pouch*, a *baby tunnel* or *chute*, an egg
> without a shell, and sperms that swim from the penis and up the baby
> tunnel in a race to see which one can win.[76]

In a related comment, they write: "Not only should children be informed of
the prospective surgical plan, but also they should invariably be given a simple
explanation of what to expect of an operation. . . . Girls should also know,
incidentally, that whereas boys have a penis, girls have a vagina—*in juvenile vocabulary, a baby tunnel*—as double insurance against childish theories of surgical
mutilation and maiming."[77]

It is interesting to note that the euphemisms for sexual organs—"baby tunnel" for vagina, "baby pouch" for uterus—all designate *female reproductive or sexual organs*; there is no "juvenile vocabulary" for penis. Indeed, the sperm have a race, while the eggs are simply "without shells." However, more significant to our interests here is the fact that the euphemisms are reproductive in nature— the female sexual organs are represented as baby-related organs or structures. This seems astounding in the context of an article that argues *against* a fertility-oriented rationale for treatment. In other words, in the context of a theory that eschews fertility as the guiding criteria for treatment of intersexual subjects, Money and the Hampsons advocate "speaking plainly" to children about their sexual ambiguity completely within the terms of reproductive sexuality. They never consider the paradox of this position, that in talking about "baby tunnels" and the like to gonadally masculine "girls," they may be setting up expectations for future reproductive experiences that can never be met. In another perspective, however, it is clear that this strategy makes a lot of sense, because it is partially through expectations of future reproductive experiences—one's special role in those experiences as a male or female—that "gender role," as Money and the Hampsons define it, becomes established.[78]

Another problematic element of Money and the Hampsons' treatment protocols concerns their understanding of "gender role" as an irrevocably imprinted orientation of the subject. They claimed that gender role was both socially constructed and imprinted. By imprinting, they meant behaviors acquired through nonconflictual learning processes that are fixed—like instincts —in the subject. To suggest that socially constructed behaviors are *imprinted*, that is, established irrevocably and without flexibility, is, however, to lend tacit support to culturally hegemonic rules and expectations. The concept of imprinted behavior suggests the idea that while there is one correct pattern (heterosexuality with its concomitant masculine or feminine gender role expression), this pattern can be wrongly imprinted. Because the notion of imprinting suggests irrevocably established behaviors, the only way to affect (or "cure") the anomalous imprint—so that the subject can engage in cultural activities as a "normal" person—is to alter some other aspect of the subject. In the context of intersexuality, after gender role has been imprinted, the subject's genital morphology and hormonal makeup become targets for medical intervention. The same holds true for transsexualism and it is in this connection to intersex research that transsexualism appropriated one of its strongest arguments for surgical and hormonal sex change, as transsexuals are understood to be subjects who for some reason develop the "wrong" gender identity for their anatomical sex.

In a later elaboration of his ideas about gender role—one that substantially shifts the emphasis of these ideas as well—John Money and Anke Ehrhardt write that "[t]here is room for argument as to whether it is correct to apply the term, imprinting, to human beings as well as to birds. However, it is the concept, not the term, that is important, and there seems to be every good reason to distinguish the acquisition of language and core gender identity from other, more transient learning, such as memorizing the summer bus schedules. The distinction makes sense in view of the fact that errors of core gender identity are notoriously resistant to change."[79] It does seem, however, as if the authors' counterexample to "imprinting" gender identity — "memorizing summer bus schedules" — is somewhat disingenuous, at least insofar as it does not in any way represent an analogous experience, as would understanding oneself as a citizen of a particular nation or ethnic group. In addition, the authors' reliance on an argument that dismisses the significance of a "word" in deference to the concept that it represents seems odd in the face of John Money's extensive coinage of new terms for sexological research, the most significant of which — "gender role" — we are investigating here.[80] Finally, one might assume that those objecting to the use of the term "imprinting" are doing so because it is the *concept* (not just the word) that they believe to be misapplied.

In spite of these conceptual difficulties, Money and the Hampsons' work came to define the field of the medical management of intersexuality. In addition, their work was instrumental in the development of gender theories applicable to the transsexual experience, insofar as they used the category of psychological sex to distinguish it from its biological counterparts and acknowledged contradictions between different aspects of "sexual identity." But it was not until psychoanalyst Robert Stoller added the concept of "gender identity" to the panoply of sexes (that is, chromosomal, gonadal, hormonal, and so on) that transsexuals were able to make claims about the incongruity of their gender identity with their expected gender role as males or females.[81] In the words of Jan Wålinder, Robert Stoller "formulated the concept of 'core gender identity' for the feeling of 'I am a male' or 'I am a female' as distinguished from 'gender role' for a masculine or feminine way of behaving" in 1964.[82] Stoller wrote that "the advantage of the phrase 'gender identity' lies in the fact that it clearly refers to one's self-image as regards belonging to a specific sex." [83]

The later addition of the concept of gender identity as an aspect of psychological sex distinguished from gender role behaviors was not commented on in *Man and Woman, Boy and Girl*, Money and Ehrhardt's 1972 popular account of sex and gender development. In this text, gender identity appeared as a complement to and substitute for gender role: "Gender identity . . . is the private experience of gender role; and gender role is the public manifestation of gender identity. . . . '[G]ender identity' can be read to mean 'gender identity/role,' unless the context signifies otherwise." [84] Thus, the concept of gender identity was integrated into the established lexicon of diagnostic categories for sex. The fact that it partially subsumed the earlier term "gender role" testifies to its significance within the increasingly specified application of these categories in the management of intersexual and transsexual cases.

It makes sense that Stoller would reorient the terminology from that of "role" to that of "identity"—he was a practicing psychoanalyst whose primary interest was defining the etiology of transsexualism from the evidence of early childhood relationships. In fact, in the essay in which he introduced gender identity, Stoller contrasted it to sexual identity, not gender role:

> This term "gender identity" will be used in this paper rather than various other terms which have been employed in this regard, such as the term "sexual identity." "Sexual identity" is ambiguous, since it may refer to one's sexual activities or fantasies, etc. . . . Thus, of a patient who says "I am not a very masculine man," it is possible to say that his gender identity is male although he recognizes his lack of so-called masculinity.[85]

Stoller considered gender to be a category untainted by the problems of sexual activity and fantasy, and gender identity to be a term that consolidated the best aspects of its predecessors—sexual identity and gender role—by suggesting an internal, felt sense of belonging to a social category.

In describing gender identity, however, Stoller used Money and the Hampsons' terminology for gender role. He maintained that gender identity was produced by the "anatomy and physiology of the external genital organs," "the attitudinal influences of parents, siblings, and peers," and a "biological force."[86] In his later work *Sex and Gender* (1968), Stoller discussed the differences between gender identity and gender role, writing that "Money and the Hampsons have expressed the view with which I agree: Gender identity is more or less fixed by primordial experiences, especially in the first eighteen months of life," citing the 1956 article discussed above.[87] In that article, however, Money and the Hampsons talked about gender *role*, not gender *identity*.

Earlier in the book, Stoller had defined the "adult male transsexual" as a man "who has been very feminine all his life" and "feels he is truly a woman (a *role* and an *identity*) and a female (a *biological state*), and wishes his body to be 'corrected' so that it anatomically approximates a female's."[88] In retrospect, Stoller's taxonomy was internally inconsistent: one cannot really feel oneself to *be* a role. Stoller redefined gender role as the performative expression of gender identity (the true category of "being"). However, gender identity absorbed its predecessor gender role as "role" became a term increasingly applied to external activities and performances, and not associated with an internal sense of authenticity. In this context, a theory of gender "identity" was necessary to

make the protocols for the case management of intersexual subjects and transsexuals coherent, as they were dependent upon a terminology borrowed from
social psychology that subsequently turned in a different direction.[89]

In *Sex and Gender*, Stoller further distinguished gender identity, a general category, from "core gender identity," or "the person's unquestioned certainty that
he belongs to one of only two sexes."[90] He writes, "This essentially unalterable
core of gender identity [I am a male] is to be distinguished from the related
but different belief, *I am manly* (or masculine). The latter attitude is a more subtle
and complicated development. It emerges only after the child has learned how
his parents expect him to express masculinity."[91] One's sense of one's masculinity becomes, in this theory, a part of overall gender identity, which develops
throughout the person's childhood and adolescence. This sense of general gender identity is most closely related to Money and the Hampsons' articulation of
gender role, as it involves social expectations and regulations about behavior,
as well as parental attitudes about appropriate compliance with those social
codes. The idea of "core gender identity" that Stoller elaborates in his studies of
intersexual patients and transsexuals concerns the (imprinted) establishment
of the subject's identity as a sex that occurs before the age of two years.

In his initial statements about the term "gender identity" in the preface to
Sex and Gender, Stoller comments that "I am using the word *identity* to mean one's
awareness (whether one is conscious of it or not) of one's existence and purpose in the world or, put a bit differently, the organization of those psychic
components that are to preserve one's awareness of existing."[92] As for "gender," he presents the now classic distinction between "sex" (as biological) and
"gender" (as cultural): "Dictionaries stress that the major connotation of *sex* is
a biological one, as, for example, in the phrases *sexual relations* or *the male sex*. . . .
It is for some of these psychological phenomena [behavior, feelings, thoughts,
fantasies] that the term *gender* will be used: one can speak of the male sex or
the female sex, but one can also talk about masculinity and femininity and not
necessarily be implying anything about anatomy or physiology."[93] "Core gender identity" comes to signify, however, less of an awareness of oneself as a
sex than a *conviction* of that fact—it is a profound feeling that arises even in the
face of seemingly incontestable contrary evidence, as some of Stoller's cases
demonstrate.

As Stoller develops his theory of the etiology of male transsexualism—based
at least partially on the infant boy's physical closeness to the mother's body—
he depends upon a notion of aberrant core gender identity as transsexualism's
incontrovertible sign. Thus, it is not just that the transsexual feels uncomfortable with the gender role expectations commensurate with his (or her, although
Stoller doesn't really know what to do with female transsexuals) sex, but that

he feels himself to truly be a member of that other sex. Stoller's introduction of the idea of gender identity and his later elaboration of the idea of core gender identity thus transformed the originally quite simplistic scenario of identity in "gender role" introduced and elaborated by Money and the Hampsons. This transformation conferred on the theory of gender an enhanced discursive power, as it suggested both the depth of individuals' investments in gender and the variability (within any given individual) of those investments. More categories in gender suggested the possibility of more subject positions—including, as I will argue at the end of this chapter, the opening up of the possibility of transsexualism as a disorder of gender identity.

There is another, more subtle reason why the term "gender identity" came to identify the paradigm of intersexual and transsexual treatment protocols: in Money and Ehrhardt's revision of Money and the Hampsons' work, there is a decided emphasis—absent in the earlier research—on the possibility of hormonal influence in the prenatal environment having an effect on the eventual gender orientation of the subject. This turn toward a biological explanation of gendered behaviors—although tempered with Money and Ehrhardt's reiterations that any biological influence can be overridden by postnatal environmental factors—is reflected in the use of biologistic language to discuss gender identity. For example, Money and Ehrhardt open the book with the following paragraph:

> In developmental psychosexual theory, it is no longer satisfactory to utilize only the concept of psychosexual *development*. Psychosexual (or gender-identity) *differentiation* is the preferential concept, for the psychodevelopment of sex is the continuation of the embryodevelopment of sex. Alone among the divers functional systems of embryonic development, the reproductive system is sexually dimorphic. So also in subsequent behavioral and psychic development, there is sexual dimorphism.[94]

Later in the text, they write,

> Gender identity, nonetheless, differentiates generally so as to be rather remarkably fixed in adulthood. Typically, it differentiates as primarily or exclusively masculine in boys, and feminine in girls. Possibly, however, differentiation may be unfinished as either completely masculine or completely feminine, but ambiguous instead. It is probably impossible for gender identity to be totally undifferentiated. The same is all but true for the embryonic anlagen of the reproductive anatomy, for in the case of anatomy, arrested development of the male is synonymous with development as a female: arrestment of female development results in no genitalia at all.[95]

Their attempt to describe psychological development of gender identity along the lines of embryological sex development—that is, as *differentiation* rather than development—represents a desire to establish a "symmetry" between somatic sexual dimorphism and psychological sex. However, Money and Ehrhardt's statement that the symmetry between psychic and embryologic sexual development is "all but true" hardly accounts for the asymmetry evident in their last statement: "arrestment of female development results in no genitalia at all." Apparently, symmetrical male/female differentiation is disrupted by a third term: no genitalia at all. In other words, the use of the word "differentiation" to denote sex dimorphism into male and female forms is perhaps a misnomer even in the realm of biology.[96]

Money and Ehrhardt use differentiation to suggest development as one of two options (in this case either male or female, masculine or feminine) that counterbalance one another. Gender identity, not gender role, defines something that can "differentiate" because it is perceived to be a "thing" inside the subject that develops rather than an external structure or system of behaviors to which the subject adheres. This is how the term "gender identity" becomes not only useful but necessary to Money's theory of gender acquisition as that theory becomes more dependent on a biologic paradigm.

Ruth Bleier and Anne Fausto-Sterling have published scathing critiques of the Money and Ehrhardt hypothesis, especially concerning the researchers' suspect data on fetally androgenized females. However, as both Bleier and Fausto-Sterling suggest, Money and Ehrhardt's work together, as well as their subsequent collaborations with other researchers, relies on what are now considered to be the established "facts" concerning the relationship between social behaviors and the fetal hormonal environment. Fausto-Sterling comments:

Despite . . . recent tempering of their analysis and conclusions, a disingenuous flavor remains. Money, Ehrhardt, and other coworkers have published paper after paper, given symposium talk after symposium talk, describing studies aimed at factoring out which components of human behavior are biological and which result from socialization. They have been attacked on the one side by biological determinists and on the other by environmental determinists. They call themselves "interactionists," believing that the interplay between biology and environment creates personality. And yet their work seems most often to weigh down the biology side of the seesaw, and their attempts to explain their results in any other fashion remain feeble. It is not surprising, then, that others use Money's, Ehrhardt's, and Baker's [a later collaborator with Ehrhardt] work over and over again to argue that prenatal hormones cause sex differences in behavior. Given such use it becomes especially important to spell out in detail the fundamental problems from which the studies on AGS [adrenogenital syndrome; chromosomally female infants subject to fetal androgenization] and progestin-exposed children suffer. Not to put too fine a point on it, the controls are insufficient and inappropriate, the method of data collection is inadequate, and the authors do not properly explore alternative explanations of their results.[97]

In a later paper, Fausto-Sterling also includes a critique of some of the data used by Money and the Hampsons in the initial four articles that inaugurated the management protocols for intersexual patients.[98] Other critics have questioned whether Money and coworkers' assertion that an "integrated theory involving biology and culture" is really being presented.[99]

This lack of legitimate scientific support, although significant, does not really address the issues at stake in my analysis, primarily because I am examining the importance of the development of the "gender identity paradigm" insofar as its introduction into medical discourse and practice came to have far-reaching effects on cultural notions of the relation between the sexed body and its behaviors. In this context, the fact that Money, the Hampsons, Ehrhardt, and others may have been scientifically deficient in collecting data, and therefore wrong in their conclusions, is not as significant as the fact that they were able to produce a discourse about the body and human identity in sex that became powerful both as a justification for medical practices and as a generalized discourse available to the culture at large for identifying, describing, and regulating social behaviors. In their attempt to present consistent criteria for reliable treatment protocols in the case management of intersexuality, Money and the Hampsons, in effect, established (or crystallized an already established trend toward) a new conceptual realm of "sex": gender. What they argued, in a sense, was that those subjects unable to represent a sex "authentically" could simulate one through adequate performances of gender that would fix one's identity irrevocably in a sex category. In other words, if you aren't born into a sex, you can always become one through being a gender.[100]

Although it was not acknowledged by those theorists introducing the terminology, the shift from gender role to gender identity in the literature on intersexuality and transsexualism was instrumental to the historical emergence of the transsexual subject. While the shift occurred after Christine Jorgensen's surgery in 1952 and the demands that followed its publicity, the widespread use of the term "gender identity" after its inauguration in 1964 attests to its significance in the field as a theoretical concept and diagnostic tool. The theories of gender produced through studies of intersexuality offered sexologists a way to discuss the cross-sex identification experienced by transsexual subjects. Transsexual core gender identity was described as being at odds with anatomical sex *and* expected gender role. Transsexuals' inability to conform to expected gender role behavior and the ineffectiveness of therapeutic interventions to effect such a change led medical sexologists to the conclusion that anatomical sex should be altered to alleviate patient suffering. Thus, the incongruity between gender identity (on the one hand) and the physical genitalia, sex of rearing, and expectation of performance in a gender role (on the other hand) was ameliorated by the reassignment of sex through hormonal and surgical interventions to reconfigure the genitals and secondary sex characteristics.

This analysis differs from that offered by Dwight Billings and Thomas Urban in their important 1982 article in *Social Problems*, "The Socio-Medical Construction of Gender." There, they argue that the significance of intersex case management protocols for the development of transsexualism was not in the development of the categories of gender role and gender identity, but in the occasional practice of surgical sex reassignment for adult hermaphrodites. Thus, they claim that the acknowledgment on the part of intersex researchers that "sex reassignment could be made in later years if hermaphrodites themselves felt some error had been made in their assigned sex [was] a concession that proved important for the treatment of transsexuals."[101] However, it is clear in the history of the case management of intersexual subjects that it was the establishment of the concepts of gender role and identity that made sex reassignment on the basis of psychological or social factors the criteria for management protocols. This, and the differentiation between gender role and identity, allowed physicians to diagnose certain subjects as transsexuals; that is, subjects with a disturbance of core gender identity that leads them to feel more comfortable in the clothing, social role, and genital morphology of the other sex. That there were some sex reassignment surgeries of adult hermaphrodites because of Money and the Hampsons' management protocols perhaps had an impact on the history of transsexualism, but in the context of the treatment of intersexuality, a physiological rationale is always available to support specific practices. Transsexualism needed a rationale that would work in the absence of a physiological justification for surgical and hormonal sex change.

Gender offered precisely this rationale. As a psychologized signifier for sex and sexual difference, gender shifted the semiotics of sex out of the confused geography of the physiological body and into the putatively stable realm of psychology and the social. Nevertheless, given its history as a concept produced in order to direct the treatment of intersexual subjects, gender maintained a relation to physiology through medical intervention, becoming an indexical sign directing clinicians to the appropriate sex for a given individual. It is through this relation, as I argue at greater length in chapter 6, that gender comes to provide a conceptual basis for the idea of sexual dimorphism. The idea of gender, specifically a gender based in a "core gender identity" that can override the power of physiological signifiers (like genitals, gonads, or chromosomes) to indicate sex, disrupts the conventional relation between body and sex on which the entire sense of "sexual difference"—as a binary distinction of the body—had hitherto historically depended.

The "intersex managers" felt they had to make treatment decisions based on the psychological health of their patients. Psychological health, they believed, correlated not to physical sex but to the sense of rightful belonging in a sex category. Psychic health, in other words, was more closely regulated by the constraints of culture than the mandates of biology. What the researchers and clinicians did not account for was their active role in producing discourse and therefore enabling new subject positions. In effect, they codified a whole new way to be a sex, enabling their intersex patients to be legitimate and entitled members of one sex or the other.

There was no way to exclude other subjects from capitalizing on this discursive development. But because only those with recognizable physiological intersexuality were immediately accorded access to sex reassignment technologies through the discourses of gender identity, others had to demand that access as entitled subjects. This is how the constitution of transsexual subjectivity in the demand for sex change was initiated. The logic of gender identity was available only if they could insert themselves into it in a convincing way. Once gender identity disrupted the idea of sexual difference based entirely on physiology, transsexuals could not be denied access to technological sex change, because they could demonstrate their aberrant gender identity through a phenomenology of gender role behaviors.

4

DEMANDING SUBJECTIVITY

By demanding technological intervention to "change sex," transsexuals demonstrate that their relationship to technology is a dependent one. Ostensibly, the demand for sex change represents the desperation of the transsexual condition: after all, who but a suffering individual would voluntarily request such severe physical transformation? Yet it is through this demand that the subject presents him/herself to the doctor as a transsexual subject; the demand for sex change is an enunciation that designates a desired action *and* identifies the speaker as the appropriate subject of that action. Demanding sex change is therefore part of what constructs the subject as a transsexual: it is the mechanism through which transsexuals come to identify themselves under the sign of transsexualism and construct themselves as its subjects. Because of this, we can trace transsexuals' agency through their doctors' discourses, as the demand for sex change was instantiated as the primary symptom (and sign) of the transsexual.

It is important to underscore the agency of transsexual subjects insofar as they forced the medical profession to respond to their demands. Transsexuals needed the services of professional physicians to achieve their goals, and their ability to work with physicians to create a discourse describing their condition and advocating surgical and hormonal interventions was central to realizing those goals. Transsexual agency is not unproblematic, but to acknowledge its significance to the emerging diagnostic categories in psychiatric sexology is to recognize that transsexuals were (and are) not the passive recipients of medical intervention. This dialectical process between transsexuals and physicians resulted in the codification of transsexualism as a "gender identity disorder" in the *Diagnostic and Statistical Manual of Mental Disorders* in 1980.[1]

Many of the documents I discuss in this chapter were written before the terms "gender role" and "gender identity" became common in medical discourse concerning cross-dressing and the desire to change sex—even before "transsexualism" became an accepted term to designate those who wish to change sex. My discussion concerns how the demand for sex change became the most significant symptom of transsexualism, its irrefutable sign. The demand for sex change was not produced as the central symptom of the transsexual syndrome by physicians wanting to legitimate their treatment of transsexual subjects, as some critics have suggested, but was evident in the earliest phases of the emergence of transsexualism.[2] By demanding sex change, transsexuals distinguished themselves from transvestite and homosexual subjects—the other designations available in the sexological discourses of the period to identify cross-sex proclivities—and thus engaged actively in producing themselves as subjects.

Since the nineteenth century, Western sexologists have occupied themselves with teasing out the fine distinctions between "sexual aberrations" that have come to be called homosexuality, transvestism, and transsexuality. The ways these three broad groups of behaviors were understood by doctors and by transsexuals is significant with regard to the development of clinical treatment protocols for transsexualism, especially as the discourse of gender identity gained precedence as the paradigm within which perceived cross-sex behaviors came to be defined. The way transsexuals understood themselves from the 1950s through the 1960s shifted as the diagnostic discourses concerning transvestism and homosexuality and their relation to transsexualism changed, and it is through finely articulated differences in behavior, sensibility, and etiology that transsexuals were able, in dialogue with clinicians, to demand separate consideration in the form of different treatment protocols, practices, and therapeutic goals.

The late nineteenth- and early twentieth-century sexological discourses concerning the relation between cross-dressing and homosexuality are interesting in this regard, as they demonstrate the extent to which language concerning "deviant" sexual behaviors changed from the end of the nineteenth century to the middle of the twentieth and how sexologists refined their categories of sexual aberration. To preface my discussion of "demanding subjectivity," I explore how cross-sex behaviors were theorized by Richard von Krafft-Ebing, Havelock Ellis, and Magnus Hirschfeld. These prominent sexologists set the terms within which clinicians in the mid-1950s maneuvered their discourses concerning the demand for sex change and its meanings. It is in the context of the history of sexological taxonomy that transsexualism was separated out from transvestic and homosexual behaviors, and it is in this context that we can examine the significant difference that technology makes in the construction of the modern transsexual subject.[3]

Psychiatric sexology is a clearinghouse of taxonomical classifications of sex. In the twentieth century, the nineteenth-century category of "antipathic sexual feeling" became three categories that have been codified by Western psychiatric and sexologic practice as homosexuality, transvestism, and transsexualism, each understood as a distinct pattern of behavior with specific etiological causes and possible treatments. The creation of three related but distinct categories within the sexological taxonomy of sexual aberration enabled more subjects to recognize themselves within the specific definition of each category and to consolidate identities under their signs. Thus, changes in sexological classifications might be characterized as "progress" to the extent that sexological discourses now can more clearly distinguish periodic cross-dressing (classic fetishistic transvestism) from homosexuality from transsexualism. It is important to recognize, however, that this "progression" has also brought with it an increasing tendency to hierarchize sexual behaviors, as well as classify them.

Sexologists in the late nineteenth and early twentieth centuries were largely concerned with the legal ramifications of "sexual deviance." Krafft-Ebing strove to enlighten the public with knowledge of sexual disease—a knowledge that located the origin of that disease in the mind or the body of the offender—in order to determine what the individual must be responsible for, before the law. His purpose was to take sexual "deviates" out of the court system and place them in what he considered their rightful place—the doctor's office. We can see in *Psychopathia Sexualis* (1886), Krafft-Ebing's monument to the taxonomic classification of sexual behaviors, sexology's classic move in modern Western society: the decriminalization and subsequent medicalization of sex and sexual behaviors. After Krafft-Ebing, in the work of Magnus Hirschfeld, Havelock Ellis, and even Sigmund Freud, there was a corollary move to depathologize sexual behaviors—that is, to define "deviance" as a statistical variation within a given population ("the norm"), and not as a term signifying a moral code. Alfred Kinsey is perhaps the twentieth-century sexologist who best represents this last position.

For Richard von Krafft-Ebing, "sexual instinct" was part of what constituted "sex determination," a category inclusive of nonbiological components.[4] He wrote that "[t]he form of the sexual glands [as ovaries or testes] is therefore not the qualifying element of sex determination, but we must look rather to sexual sensations and the sexual instinct."[5] In this sense, one's "sex" was not merely that biological category to which one was assigned at birth, but a complex of factors including sexual orientation, sexual behaviors, and other psychosexual indicators. Krafft-Ebing used the term "sex of the individual" to designate strictly biological sex; this is closer to the definition of "sex" that would prevail in sexological discourses in the twentieth century, signifying the sexual anatomy and physiology of the subject. "Sexual instinct" identified what we would now call sexual orientation or preference. Krafft-Ebing believed that there was an "instinct" characteristic to each sex, and to exhibit the instinct characteristic of the other sex was to have "antipathic" or contrary sexuality.[6]

For Krafft-Ebing, it was important to determine whether the antipathic sexual behavior was acquired or congenital: the former type were thought to be due to unfortunate circumstances (no members of the other sex available) or temporary difficulties (such as depression, excessive masturbation, or disappointment in love, among others). Those who committed perverse acts because of a congenital sexual anomaly were the victims of a degenerative pathology that was generally perceived to be neurological in origin but could also result from masturbatory practices. Two of the four types of "abnormal congenital manifestation" of antipathic sexual instinct that Krafft-Ebing delineated can be considered precursors to the modern sense of transsexualism. These types were (1) persons whose "entire mental existence is altered to correspond with the abnormal sexual instinct (effemination and viraginity)" and (2) those for whom the form of the body began to approach "that which corresponds to the abnormal sexual instinct."[7] Identification with the other sex was considered in conjunction with, or as an aspect of, homosexuality: it was an analogous perversion of sexual instinct, a turning away from what was characteristic of one's sex. Thus, "contrary" or "antipathic sexual feeling" defined a large, amorphous, and diverse group of behaviors and subjects: part of its taxonomic appeal was an ability to synthesize diverse sexual "aberrations" under a singular banner. This ability was directly connected to the inclusiveness of the idea of sex utilized by Krafft-Ebing. Subsequent to his work, "sex" became a category designating the biological components of sex identity and the category of "antipathic sexual feeling" divided into discrete categories. Both Magnus Hirschfeld and Havelock Ellis were directly responsible for the elaborate taxonomies of sexology that resulted.

In the introduction to *Sexual Anomalies*, a posthumously published text, Magnus Hirschfeld's students wrote that like many of his sexological precursors, Hirschfeld held to a belief in "psychophysical parallelism," the belief that "the abnormal manifestations of the sexual impulse [are] constitutional phenomena arising from the individual's physical and psychic make-up" and that "constitution and character were manifestations of the same vital principle, as though nature were expressing the same idea by two different media." However, unlike his precursors, Hirschfeld brought these ideas in line with the discovery of the "chemistry of sex"—endocrinology—thus giving the theory of psychophysical parallelism a "firmer basis" as well as "greater precision."[8]

The discovery of endocrines and the system of "ductless glands" is crucial to understanding Hirschfeld's influence on sexology. Before the twentieth century, there was no concept of the hormonal regulation of the body's biochemistry. Thus, while not an endocrinologist himself, Hirschfeld was convinced of the relevance of "glandular science" to the field of sexology.[9] He believed that both homosexuality and transvestism could be explained by variations in sex hormones. These variations were explained by the theory of the intersexes that delineated the degree and kind of "mixture" that determined hermaphroditism, androgyny, transvestism, and homosexuality.[10]

In a direct refutation of Krafft-Ebing's (and others') classification of transvestism as "but a variant of homosexuality," Hirschfeld believed transvestism to be an independent phenomenon. He also posited heterosexual, homosexual, and bisexual transvestites, an idea that is only beginning to resurface in clinical theories of transvestism today.[11] At the time, Hirschfeld was arguing against a sexological establishment that believed all transvestites to be homosexual. Thus, Hirschfeld analytically separated transvestism from homosexuality, defining the latter as the true "contrary" (or antipathic) form of sexual activity, while the former represented an intersexual variant that could encompass a range of sexual activities. Both were "natural variants" of the norm, heterosexuality.[12]

Havelock Ellis came up with the theoretical categories utilized most heavily by those developing theories of transsexualism in the 1950s. Ellis's volume concerning "Sexual Inversion" was one of the first published as part of the *Studies in the Psychology of Sex* in the late nineteenth century. His specific work on transvestism, or "eonism" as he called it, was published later, and in it he criticized Hirschfeld's term ("transvestism") because he claimed that it reduced a complex phenomenon to only one of its components—dress.

"Sexo-aesthetic inversion," Ellis's descriptive term for eonism, was not considered an inversion in the same sense as sexual inversion, although Ellis thought that both had an "organic basis." Sexual inversion meant a "sexual impulse [that] is organically and innately turned toward individuals of the same sex." [13] (Terminologically, for Ellis "homosexuality" was "used more comprehensively of the general phenomenon of sexual attraction between persons of the same sex, even if only of a slight and temporary character.") [14] Specifically, Ellis wrote:

> We have further to distinguish sexual inversion and all other forms of homosexuality from another kind of inversion which usually remains, so far as the sexual impulse itself is concerned, heterosexual, that is to say, normal. Inversion of this kind leads a person to feel like a person of the opposite sex, and to adopt, as far as possible, the tasks, habits, and dress of the opposite sex, while the direction of the sexual impulse remains normal. This condition I term sexo-aesthetic inversion, or Eonism.[15]

Ellis suggested that both homosexuals and transvestites were "intermediate sexual anomalies" that could be explained by the theory of "organic bisexuality." Physical hermaphroditism and gynandromorphism or eunuchoidism (men with female characteristics or vice versa) could be understood similarly. Ellis also stated, in keeping with Hirschfeld, that "it is probable that we may ultimately find a more fundamental source of these various phenomena in the stimulating and inhibiting play of the internal secretions" (that is, hormones).[16]

In "Eonism and Other Supplementary Studies," in the Studies in the Psychology of Sex, Ellis argued against the psychoanalytic interpretation of transvestism as fetishistic behavior. He used the term "Eonism" because of its reference to the Chevalier d'Eon, who, in the eighteenth century, "adopted feminine dress on his own initiative, and became commonly regarded as a woman."[17] The chevalier was instrumental to the French diplomatic corps, and appeared as a woman both officially and in the privacy of his home. The choice of the Chevalier d'Eon as the eponym of the term for "sexo-aesthetic inversion" is significant, given that Ellis noted that the chevalier "had a constitutional predisposition for the life he adopted, aided by an almost asexual disposition," and he added that "in people with this psychic anomaly physical sexual vigor seems often subnormal."[18] According to Ellis, the chevalier did not periodically cross-dress; rather, he chose to live his life as a woman.[19] The asexuality ascribed to him is now considered part of the transsexual syndrome. Ellis's description of Eonism locates the tension between the two types of cross-sex behavior that will, in the mid-1950s, be split into the two distinct categories, transvestism and transsexualism: cross-dressing for its own pleasures and cross-dressing as one expression of a profound identification with the other sex.[20]

Eonism, for Ellis, was a phenomenon

> of erotic empathy, of a usually heterosexual inner imitation, which frequently tends to manifest itself in the assumption of the habits and garments of the desired sex; for the important point is that this impulse springs out of admirations and affection for the opposite sex.[21]

He also described its cause as an oversympathy to the aesthetic and emotional situation of the loved one, a desire to be in the place of the loved one, "an emotional identification with the beautiful object."[22] Ellis's scenario depended on representations of the other sex (implicitly female), whose situation (as defined by dress, mannerisms, activities) was idealized and desired. The identification with the feminine other was realized through one's representation of an idealized version of her.

Carroll Smith-Rosenberg writes that the "sexologists struggled to reverse [the Church's] vision of sexual perversion as moral license. Arguing for an organic model, they insisted that sexual perversity, especially homosexuality, was a physiological abnormality."[23] Ellis's and Hirschfeld's incorporation of the discoveries of endocrinology into their own work presaged the later collaboration between endocrinologists and sexologists in the sphere of transsexualism. As endocrinology developed, it presented sexology with a seemingly meaningful way to analyze cross-sex behaviors as effects of cross-sex hormonal influences. As we have seen, however, this is only possible when hormones are taken to represent the physical and psychological sexual characteristics that they are thought to produce.[24] In the context of the glandular thesis, endocrinology offered both a theory of cross-sex behavior and a technology for its rectification.[25] One result of this was the elaboration of hormonal "treatments" for cross-sex behaviors, once popular for homosexuality and transvestism, and now generally accepted only in cases of transsexualism.

The classification of aberrant behaviors is central to differential diagnosis, the diagnostic technique with which psychiatrists define and categorize mental illnesses. Differential diagnosis is at the heart of the *Diagnostic and Statistical Manual of Mental Disorders*, the official compendium of the American Psychiatric Association.[26] Richard Docter's book *Transvestites and Transsexuals: Toward a Theory of Cross-Gender Behavior* represents one of the most recent examples of sexology's intense classificatory impulse to define and regulate the distinctions between cross-sex proclivities in human subjects. Docter laboriously works through the distinctions between different kinds of transvestic and transsexual behaviors, noting "five heterosexual behavior patterns involving cross dressing"— fetishism, fetishistic transvestism, marginal transvestism, transgenderism, and secondary transsexualism (transvestic type)—and "four homosexual behavior patterns involving cross dressing"—primary transsexualism, secondary transsexualism, "so-called drag queens," and female impersonators.[27] Each pattern has a distinct symptomatic history and, Docter presumes, a different etiology.

This kind of classificatory zeal presupposes that the categories described are largely static and are therefore "discovered" by researchers. However, it is important to question whether the Victorian subject who told Krafft-Ebing that he felt like a woman in a man's body is articulating the same sensation as the mid-twentieth-century subject who asks his doctor for a sex change because he feels like a woman in a man's body. The idea of "being a woman trapped (or enclosed) in a man's body" was first used by Karl Heinrich Ulrichs, a nineteenth-century German homosexual writer and theorist, as a description of *homosexuality*.[28] Is the same statement being made when, for the latter subject, the possibility of a "change of sex" exists (at least superficially)? Can the term "transsexual" be used to designate those subjects who expressed a desire to be (or the feeling of already being) the other sex before the advent of surgical and hormonal sex reassignment?

The horizon of technical possibility changes the nature of these statements about "being a woman in a man's body," and "transsexual" is not a term that can accurately be used to describe subjects exhibiting cross-sex behaviors prior to the technical capacity for sex reassignment. After all, representing oneself as the other sex, expressing a desire to be the other sex, or even stating a belief that one is the other sex, are not the same as demanding to be *made into* the other sex. As Catherine Millot puts it, "Today, transsexuality combines an inner conviction and a demand vis-à-vis the other. The latter element is new, for it assumes there is an offer to satisfy it—that of science. There is not transsexuality without the surgeon and the endocrinologist; in this sense, it is an essentially modern phenomenon. But there is also the inner conviction, which antedates science." [29] In their recent book, Vern and Bonnie Bullough write: "The appearance of the new diagnostic category [transsexualism] was not the result of a theoretical breakthrough. Rather, it appeared on the scene as the result of the development of a surgical treatment for the extreme form of transvestism." [30] In these conceptualizations of transsexuality, science/technology create the element crucial to its construction: the possibility of a material response to the conviction of being the other sex. [31] ·

However, it is not just the technology alone that makes transsexualism possible: the technology enables the development of a set of discourses within which the idea of the transsexual becomes conceptually possible. As we saw in the preceding chapter, the development of sex change technologies facilitated the creation of the conceptual apparatus of "gender" in the terms of the gender identity paradigm. Once gender identity was established as the basic criteria for intersex treatment protocols, transsexuals could request treatment of their condition with the same discursive machinery. Because they did not exhibit the physical signs of intersexuality, however, transsexuals had to demand entitlement to the same procedures routinely practiced on intersexes. In the documents discussed below, we will see how before the official establishment of the gender identity paradigm, transsexuals and physicians negotiated the discursive terrain around the technologies of sex change, and transformed that discursive terrain so that gender identity could become a clinical sign indicating the propriety of medical intervention to change sex.

That transsexuals are aware of and utilize changes in sexological discourse is acknowledged by many researchers and clinicians. This becomes clear in a comment by Richard Docter concerning the veracity of transsexuals' statements about their "condition":

Confounding the problem of assessing gender dysphoria is the fact that transsexual applicants are typically very much aware of the gender dysphoria thesis and seize upon this as a causal attribution to explain their own behavior. Their proclamations, if accepted at face value without external validation, may constitute key misleading statements in the gender history. It is obvious that the clinician as well as the researcher must be sensitive to this potential distortion.[32]

Other researchers—notably Anne Bolin—have remarked on this problem.[33] Transsexuals keep up with the burgeoning sexological literature on cross-sex identification and identify themselves under its categories.[34] In many ways, the narrowing of diagnostic categories made their task easier, insofar as the range of symptomatic behaviors became increasingly specific for transvestism, transsexualism, and even homosexuality. The increasingly narrow taxonomic classifications of "aberrant" gender behaviors helped some transsexuals to improve their chances of obtaining surgery because these taxonomies specify the exact behaviors and histories necessary to obtain the appropriate diagnosis. In other words, the proliferation of sexological categories worked, to a certain extent, in the interest of transsexuals who sought surgical and hormonal sex change and who, in order to achieve that goal, had to be recognized by clinicians as deserving of it.[35]

The agency of transsexual subjects—in defining the categories that came to designate their "problem" and identify its solution—will become clearer as I trace the history of the demand for sex change in the twentieth century. This discussion of transsexual agency does not suggest that transsexuals are all-powerful in the context of the medical establishment, nor that this agency is unproblematic. Transsexuals' personal narratives are studded with comments concerning unsympathetic physicians and mental health care providers.[36] However, any critical analysis of the emergence of transsexualism in the twentieth century must confront the fact that the psychiatric diagnosis of transsexualism takes as its central symptom the subject's demand for sex change. This fact in and of itself suggests transsexuals' dialectical involvement in that diagnostic protocol; in other words, doctors did not act alone in creating these sexological categories. As Richard Docter writes:

> Transsexualism has been said to be the only major surgical procedure carried out in response to the unremitting demands of the patient. While this may not be entirely correct, it is true that the currently accepted definition of transsexualism rests, quite insecurely, upon the reported subjective feelings, beliefs, and self-perceptions of the person involved.[37]

Robert Stoller comments that with gender dysphoria "we are not dealing with a syndrome—that is, a complex of signs and symptoms—but rather with a desire (wish, demand) that is embedded in all sorts of different people who suffer all sorts of signs and symptoms."[38]

In the late 1940s and early 1950s, transsexual subjects as we understand them today appeared on the medical and social landscape of the West. The term "transsexual," although introduced into the sexological literature in David O. Cauldwell's 1949 article "Psychopathia Transexualis," did not take hold in the discipline until after the early 1950s, when transsexualism as a medical syndrome was clinically differentiated from transvestism.[39] This differentiation occurred in the context of papers written by Christian Hamburger (and colleagues) after the celebrated surgery on George/Christine Jorgensen in 1952 and by Harry Benjamin, the so-called father of "Benjaminian transsexualism." Both Hamburger and Benjamin were endocrinologists. Their medical backgrounds encouraged them to believe in somatogenic theories of human behavior, as well as to look toward medicine's future when perfected technologies would offer the truth of the transsexual enigma. They distrusted psychiatric—especially psychoanalytic—approaches to the transsexuals' dilemma. Most significantly, they helped to establish the demand for sex change as the central signifier of the syndrome.[40]

In "Psychopathia Transexualis," Cauldwell argued that the term "psychopathic transsexual" could be applied to those individuals who are "unfavorably affected psychologically" who decide "to live and appear as a member of the sex to which he or she does not belong." The term "means, simply, that one is mentally unhealthy and because of this the person desires to live as a member of the opposite sex." For Cauldwell, mental ill-health was considered both precursor and cause of the pathological disorder. Thus he represented a twentieth-century version of the nineteenth-century sexologist who looked for pathology in sexually anomalous behavior, connected that behavior to other socially degenerate activities, and represented the sick subject's degenerate tendencies as a group of symptoms suggesting an inborn deficiency. When Cauldwell was beset by the demands of "Earl" for surgical sex change (female to male), he responded that while surgery was possible for those entitled to it for biological reasons, "what she desired was impossible." The crux of the matter, for Cauldwell, was that although mastectomy, female castration, and the construction of an artificial penis were possible, the latter would be of "no material use on a female" and would have no sexual feeling. "Material use" referred to reproductive potential, sexual activity, and possibly also to urinary capacity. The first would be an impossible outcome of medical intervention, the next two unlikely ones. Cauldwell argued, in addition, that it would be criminal for a surgeon to proceed in an operation to remove healthy breast and ovarian tissue.[41]

In his introduction to the 1956 anthology *Transvestism . . . Men in Female Dress*, D. O. Cauldwell stated categorically, "*Trans-sexualists* (those who wish to change their sex) are always transvestites. Were this not so, they would not desire to be transformed into members of the sex to which they do not belong. In this

connection, it is appropriate to state that change of sex is impossible."[42] Cauldwell's response to the demands of transsexual subjects was quite different from
the responses of certain other physicians who were similarly subject to the demand for surgical and hormonal sex change. Cauldwell is an example of a perspective that has always existed in the medical community and may represent
a majority of American physicians.[43] What was necessary to produce a situation favorable to the emergence of transsexual subjectivity was not a whole-
sale positive assessment by the majority of the medical profession, however,
but acceptance by a significant group of well-placed doctors who had at their
disposal resources to make sex-change surgery and cross-sex hormone treatments possible. These doctors, who responded favorably to the demand and
theorized the helpful nature of surgical and hormonal interventions in specific cases, helped to consolidate transsexual subjectivity around the demand
for surgery. Their encouraging response worked to heighten the expectations
of self-diagnosed transsexuals, who then sought medical sex change.[44]

In late 1952, the world learned that a former GI named George Jorgensen
had been transformed into Christine earlier that year, through hormonal treatments and plastic genital surgery (which did not include vaginoplasty).[45] Her
doctors, the foremost of whom was Christian Hamburger, published an account of the case in the *Journal of the American Medical Association*. The authors pur-
ported to "outline the characteristic features of eonism (or 'genuine transvestism')" as distinct from the run-of-the-mill fetishistic male transvestism that
currently fascinated sexological researchers. They stated that "transvestism, in
the widest sense of the term, must be regarded as a symptom that may appear
in a number of conditions, and only by thorough clinical analysis is it possible
to distinguish between these states." Hamburger and his coauthors were interested only in the small group of "transvestic men in whom the desire is so
dominant as to justify the designation 'genuine transvestism' or 'psychic hermaphroditism.' "[46]

Jorgensen's doctors took Havelock Ellis's term "Eonism" and used it to designate those transvestites who felt that they were "victims of a cruel mistake —
a consequence of the female personality in a male body." This was a narrower
category than that designated by Ellis himself.[47] The authors preferred the term
"genuine transvestism" to "Eonism," however, although for unstated reasons.
They may have wanted to link Jorgensen's condition with the accepted sexological category of transvestism. Their use of the modifer "genuine" suggests
that they saw Jorgensen as one position on a continuum of cross-sex behaviors — "genuine" signifying a most extreme position on that continuum. The
authors stated that their subject "yielded to his pronounced transvestic tendencies. He acquired a complete set of women's clothes and secretly put them on.
This relieved the psychic pressure he invariably felt when in men's clothes."[48]

Thus, the term "transvestism" continued to designate those subjects who requested a change of sex for a few years after the term "transsexual" was introduced by Cauldwell. This caused discursive problems for Christine Jorgensen, who in her autobiography vehemently denied ever having been a transvestite, even though in the authorized story of her life published soon after her sex change she wrote: "My own case has been classified as one of transvestism. Medical science has not yet succeeded in revealing the cause, or the causes, of this disease. A variety of factors may play a part, when a person has an irresistible feeling of really belonging to the opposite sex."[49]

The genuine transvestite, in the eyes of Hamburger, Stürup, and Dahl-Iversen, was "disgusted by relationship with homosexual men" and was not a fetishist. Homosexuality and transvestic fetishism represented the two other diagnostic options within medical sexology at the time. The "dominant feature" of the genuine transvestite's situation was "the urge toward attaining the 'ideal of perfection.'" They remarked that "the eonist's feeling of being a woman is so deeply rooted and irresistible that it is tempting to seek deeper somatic causes of the disease"; however, while they presented a hypothesis of intersexuality for pronounced transvestites, they were unable to substantiate it and looked to the future for further corroboration of this idea.[50]

Noting that there was no known psychotherapeutic procedure to cure these subjects of their affliction, Hamburger and his colleagues stated that "the object of the medical profession, therefore, is to bring about—as extensively as possible—conditions that may contribute toward the patient's mental balance and a certain sense of 'purpose in life.'" They strengthened this claim by stating that "it is understood in medical ethics that if a disease cannot be cured an attempt should be made to improve the stress and inconvenience of the patient in order to make his life as tolerable as possible." In the end, Hamburger and his co-authors remarked that due to the numerous letters they received following the publicity surrounding the Jorgensen case, "it has been an exceedingly depressing experience to learn the degree to which these persons feel they have been let down by the medical profession and by their fellow men." Given that "the possibilities of treatment are considerably limited by the legislation governing castration in each country," the authors argued that castration would have to be legally sanctioned so that it would be possible "to remove in transvestites those organs the presence of which seriously impair their mental health."[51] They did not, however, recommend vaginoplasty—the surgical construction of a vagina.

In 1953 Hamburger also published an article in Acta Endocrinologica entitled "The Desire for Change of Sex as Shown by Personal Letters from 465 Men and Women." After the publicity of Christine Jorgensen's transformation, Hamburger (the physician named in the newspaper articles) was besieged by letters from "unfortunates." In this article he stated that "the desire for change of sex is most apparent in patients suffering from transvestism, and is the predominant symptom in genuine cases of this condition." [52] This was the beginning of the determination of the "primary symptom" of transsexualism: the demand for surgery.

The major portion of the article detailed the statistical data from the letters and discussed its significance. In conclusion, Hamburger restated some of the sentiments expressed in his earlier article:

> These many personal letters from almost 500 deeply unhappy persons leave an overwhelming impression. One tragic existence is unfolded after another; they cry for help and understanding. It is depressing to realize how little can be done to come to their aid. One feels it a duty to appeal to the medical profession and to the responsible legislature: do your utmost to ease the existence of these fellow-men who are deprived of the possibilities of a harmonious and happy life—through no fault of their own. [53]

Hamburger represented the physician as one who was bound by duty, as well as sympathy, to respond to these victims who have no one to blame for their misery. It was the charge of the physician to bear the burden of rectifying this disorder without a known cause. For Hamburger, an endocrinologist, discovering the true cause was again projected into the future when endocrinology could detect with greater accuracy the existence of intersexuality or hormonal imbalance. For the present, the least that the medical practitioner could offer was some therapeutic token that would make life easier for those afflicted with the desire for change of sex: surgical and hormonal transformation.

Hamburger mentioned Harry Benjamin, an American endocrinologist, in the *Acta Endocrinologica* article, and cited a 1953 essay by Benjamin. In this essay, entitled "Transvestism and Transsexualism," Benjamin (who was to become a significant advocate of transsexuals and sex change surgery) suggested the term "transsexualism" as the name for the disorder. He wrote that "transvestism . . . can be powerful and overwhelming, even to the point of wanting to belong to the other sex and correct nature's 'anatomical error.' For such cases the term Transsexualism seems appropriate." Much of the article argued against psychoanalytic, psychiatric, and other psychotherapeutic "treatments" for transvestism and transsexualism. Benjamin believed that the body was implicated in these disorders far more than practitioners in these fields would readily admit: "[T]he soma, that is to say the genetic and/or endocrine constitution (often a psychosexual infantilism), has to provide a 'fertile soil' on which the 'basic conflict' must grow in order to become the respective neurosis." In addition, he went on to suggest (in agreement with Hamburger and his colleagues) that "more perfected future methods of endocrine or constitutional diagnoses may reveal more organic contributions to neurotic disorders, suggesting also more effective treatment."[54]

For "milder cases of transvestism," Benjamin suggested psychotherapy, along with "supplementary endocrine treatment" with "maturation and masculinization as its objective" (that is, to try to masculinize "effeminate" male transvestites, their ostensible problem being too many "female" hormones). For "transsexualists," the "most disturbed group of male transvestites," he believed that psychotherapy was useless. Benjamin stated that these types "harbor a female 'soul' . . . in their male body."[55] He added that "they demand a 'conversion operation,'" but stated that "a radical operation of this nature is rarely indicated." Benjamin believed that because genetic sex cannot be altered, only the "secondary sex characteristics" could be changed; nevertheless, surgical as well as hormonal interventions might be indicated "in suitable cases." He wrote: "A patient like that has every right to be accepted as a woman and lead a woman's life. Blind prejudice alone would deny her this right to which her own nature, science and humanity entitle her." In addition, while "the sexual life of the feminized male may be lively," it was "largely non-genital. His (or rather her) libido is 'cerebral.' It could be aroused and gratified by the fact of 'being a woman.'"[56]

Benjamin added that the patient would not need an artificial vagina for herself, except indirectly, insofar as it would serve her male sex partner. Thus, as he noted in an addendum to the essay, his conclusions concerning vaginoplasty for transsexuals were the same as those of Hamburger, Stürup, and Dahl-Iversen. The construction of an artificial vagina was not necessary because it was not part of the demand of the patient.[57] In terms of the larger issue of medicine's responsibility to transsexuals, Benjamin clearly stated that medical practitioners must act in the service of scientific truths that would banish the power of cultural prejudice: "Where such behavior does not intrude on the rights of others, it should be viewed in the light of science and common sense and not, as it is now done, in the twilight of prejudices and misconceptions."[58]

In an article published the following year, Benjamin further delineated the distinctions between transvestites and transsexuals: "[T]he transsexualist always seeks medical aid while the transvestite as a rule merely asks to be left alone. To put it differently: In transvestism the sex organs are sources of pleasure; in transsexualism they are sources of disgust."[59] In his comments about treatment, he reiterated his belief that "psychotherapy for the purpose of curing the condition [transsexualism] is a waste of time." Instead, Benjamin suggested that the only possible role for the psychiatrist of a transsexual is to "relax tension, to develop and reinforce realistic thinking, and to supply guidance." However, Benjamin was not entirely sanguine about the therapeutic benefits of sex change surgery. The operation, consisting in "castration, the amputation of the penis (peotomy) and the possible plastic formation of an artificial vagina," might not "always solve [the transsexual's] problem. *His feminization cravings may never end.* The later realization that a complete change of sex including the ability of child-bearing is impossible and that only a change of secondary sex characteristics has been and can be accomplished, may leave some patients still frustrated after a more or less extended period of relief." He went on to comment that a patient "on the verge of a reactive psychosis" or one who is "in danger of suicide or self-mutilation" should not be turned away "unequivocal[ly]." Nevertheless, Benjamin cautioned that "the physician's sympathy should not tempt him to give in too easily to the patient's persuasive arguments"; the final word should be that of the psychiatrist.[60] This position is particularly interesting given Benjamin's antitherapy bias, and suggests the ambivalent relation between psychiatry and clinical endocrinology in the treatment of transsexualism. Benjamin wanted psychiatry to enable clinicians to determine those most worthy of surgery and those most liable to benefit from it; he did not see psychiatry as being able itself to treat transsexualism, and therefore, to have any real authority over its diagnosis.

Published with Benjamin's article, as part of the symposium on transsexualism and transvestism, was an article by Emil A. Gutheil, "The Psychologic Background of Transsexualism and Transvestism." Gutheil's approach was largely psychoanalytic, as indicated in the following comment: "We must show [transvestites] how, while fantasying a future physical metamorphosis, they are, in reality, harking back to their neurotic past, to their infantile fears and pleasures, and point out to them how futile it is to try solving one's sexual problems — in effigy." He also discussed the "poor therapeutic results" of psychotherapy for transsexual subjects. In disagreement with transsexual surgery advocates, Gutheil believed that these poor results "do not necessarily prove that the etiologic concept is wrong. If our therapy does not succeed, we must investigate the causes of our failure, learn from our mistakes and improve our approach. In most of the unsuccessful cases the patients' uncooperative attitude may be considered as the main source of failure."[61] Gutheil's position — that psychotherapy is the correct mode of treatment for transsexualism, since the syndrome is based on unresolved neurotic conflicts of childhood — directly opposed that of Benjamin. The conflict between the two, largely a conflict concerning the efficacy of psychotherapeutic treatment and whether a lack of therapeutic effectiveness demonstrates a failed theoretical apparatus, is at the center of debates concerning transsexualism to this day. Transsexuals, predictably, continue to advocate and proselytize Benjamin's position as established fact.

Harry Benjamin consolidated his theoretical contribution to the study of transsexualism in a book, *The Transsexual Phenomenon*, in which his sexological classifications were presented in tabular form. Three types of transsexual appear: nonsurgical, true (moderate intensity), and true (high intensity). The "true" transsexuals (of both categories) request surgery, the high-intensity transsexual with urgency. The nonsurgical candidate might be attracted to sex change, but does not admit the attraction or request surgery. The "classic Benjaminian transsexual" is the high-intensity, true transsexual, the one most likely to attract the attention of physicians because he is "a candidate for self-mutilation, suicide, or its attempt." [62] In other words, the demand of this subject is all the more convincing because it is made in conjunction with threats of self-destructive actions.

A few other aspects of Benjamin's book merit commentary. First, in the text Benjamin changed his perspective regarding vaginoplasty. Whereas in earlier articles he denied its necessity, in The Transsexual Phenomenon he treated it as a routine aspect of sex conversion surgery. More significant, however, are Benjamin's comments concerning the relation between "sex" and "gender" as conceptual tools in the clinical diagnosis of transsexualism. He wrote: "It will become apparent in the following pages that 'sex' is more applicable where there is the implication of sexuality, of libido, and of sexual activity. 'Gender' is the nonsexual side of sex. As someone once expressed it: gender is located above, and sex below the belt." [63] It is in the context of this discursive logic that Benjamin wrote, "The transvestite has a social problem. The transsexual has a gender problem. The homosexual has a sex problem." [64]

These distinctions between "sex" and "gender" helped identify transsexualism as a "gender problem," a confusion of psychological sex or of masculinity/femininity. While Benjamin continued in The Transsexual Phenomenon to rely on the idea of a "fertile" somatic ground for transsexual development—even without any data to support this hypothesis—he prepared the way for the elaborations of gender identity theory in the 1960s by articulating sharp theoretical distinctions between what was "below" or "above" the belt.[65] But Benjamin advocated surgical "treatment" for transsexualism—that is, treatment "below the belt"—for what he believed manifestly to be "above" it: "Since it is evident, therefore, that the mind of a transsexual cannot be adjusted to the body, it is logical and justifiable to attempt the opposite, to adjust the body to the mind." [66] Therefore, although in his own words the transsexual had a *gender* problem, treatment for transsexualism, in Benjamin's view, should target precisely what was *not* the problem—the transsexual's nonabnormal genitalia and endocrine system.

The other significant accomplishment of The Transsexual Phenomenon was to establish the term "transsexual" as the appropriate signifier for those subjects requesting sex change. Benjamin made the term "transsexual" stick, and he effectively linked it to the idea of gender disorders. Even after other terms were introduced (see below) "transsexualism" still defines the phenomenon of subjects requesting sex change.[67]

Benjamin's distinctions between "gender" and "sex" problems were made possible by the work of Money and the Hampsons in the 1950s. As we saw in chapter 3, the treatment protocols they established for the case management of intersexuality inaugurated the semantic split between (biological) sex and (psychosocial) gender that undergird Benjamin's designations "below" and "above the belt." At the same time that Benjamin was doing his work, Robert Stoller was developing increasingly specific etiological criteria for the diagnosis of transsexualism, as well as his theory of gender identity.[68] Stoller's work led to the conceptualization of transsexualism as a "gender identity disorder," a designation signifying that the individual had developed the wrong gender identity for his or her sex.

In the 1970s, the term "gender dysphoria" began to be substituted for transsexualism. As a diagnostic label, gender dysphoria "is much broader than transsexual[ism]. This term is the only one available to refer to the whole gamut of individuals who, at one time or another, experience sufficient discomfort with their biological sex to form a *wish for sex reassignment*."[69] Diagnoses of Benjaminian transsexualism and gender dysphoria therefore relied upon the articulation of a *request or wish for surgery* as a sign of the disorder. The intensity of the demand, as observed by the physician or therapist, indicated the severity of the disorder and thus, eventually, the possibility of surgical and hormonal interventions for the subject. In 1980, the category "gender identity disorders" appeared in the *Diagnostic and Statistical Manual of Mental Disorders* (DSM-III). Among these disorders, transsexualism could be identified by the "persistent wish to be rid of one's genitals and to live as a member of the other sex." In addition, "[t]hese individuals often find their genitals repugnant, which may lead to persistent requests for sex reassignment by surgical or hormonal means."[70]

"Gender dysphoria" and "gender identity disorders" are not entirely the same: the first term designates a more general category within which the second is understood to fall. In the context of the DSM-III, transsexualism is a gender identity disorder. Gender dysphoria is not part of the DSM-III definition of gender identity disorders or transsexualism; it describes an underlying cause or sensibility made manifest in those disorders.[71] Its introduction into the diagnostic lexicon allowed clinicians to perceive themselves as treating a widespread phenomenon with a variety of clinical manifestations. Some who supported the idea of a "gender dysphoria syndrome" were opposed to the idea that differential diagnosis was central to the determination of treatment for those demanding sex change. Indeed, while "gender identity disorder" suggested Stoller's strict etiology concerning the development of male transsexualism in very young boys, "gender dysphoria syndrome" opened up the possibility of sex reassignment for those unable to produce a personal history consonant with Stoller's scenario.

Dwight Billings and Thomas Urban argue that with the terminological shift from transsexualism to gender dysphoria, "physicians de-emphasized the technicalities of diagnostic differentiation [differential diagnosis] and stressed behavioral criteria instead."[72] Norman Fisk, one of the first proponents of the term "gender dysphoria syndrome," wrote:

> As originally intended, the term *transsexual* was to specifically identify a person who was not to be confused with a homosexual or a transvestite. . . . I feel rather strongly (given the experience of the Stanford University gender dysphoria program) that the differential diagnosis aimed at clearly identifying a subgroup of patients termed transsexuals is in many instances a rather non-productive effort. Beyond this, differential diagnosis does not significantly bear upon the success or failure of ensuing treatment.[73]

While the request or demand for sex change surgery continued to identify patients to the program at Stanford, "the overtly present common denominator was the high level of dysphoria concerning the individual's gender of assignment and rearing."[74] Fisk outlined the components of gender dysphoria in the following manner:

> The dictionary definition of gender as applied to its non-grammatical meaning, merely states *sex*. It is well known to students of biology and behavioral science that gender is a complex and convoluted compilation of a number of biological, psychological and psychosocial factors. Chromosomal make-up, sex of assignment and rearing, external and internal genital morphology, pre-natal and post-natal endocrinologic factors, as well as behavior, are all seemingly interrelated within the concept of the gender. A dictionary definition of dysphoria includes dissatisfaction, anxiety, restlessness and discomfort.[75]

The "phenomenological" approach suggested by the term "gender dysphoria"—a clinical emphasis on behavioral criteria rather than a strict adherence to the specific etiological and symptomatological picture necessary to insure the differential diagnosis of transsexualism[76]—allowed physicians to regroup the categories "transvestism," "transsexualism," and "homosexuality" into a continuum of gender-aberrant behavior. (The consolidation of these discrete categories within an umbrella term repeats the categorization "antipathic sexual feeling" of the nineteenth-century sexologists—although the emphasis on "gender" reflects the shift in medical thinking from a sex paradigm to a gender one.) Within the context of "gender dysphoria," subjects seeking sex change could present distinctly different patient histories; those who were best at proving their "stability" in the cross-sex gender role were perceived to be viable candidates for surgery. In Fisk's words:

> Dr. Donald Laub, who heads the surgical team that performs the re-constructive operations, feels very strongly that the flexible, yet at once somewhat rigid, behavioristic requirements for acceptability into our program represent a very unique and distinctive form of behavioristic psychotherapy. Many patients who are initially denied surgical sex conversion are placed on a "hold" status to be re-evaluated later. Implicit in this delay is the message that they should improve the overall stability of their life-style. For many patients this involves a waiting period of two to four years, and during this period pronounced changes in at least superficial behavior are observed. If one adheres to a doctrine of thought that believes a person eventually becomes what he or she seems to be, then Dr. Laub's supposition would indeed seem to be correct.[77]

Note that it is the *plastic surgeon* who made these comments concerning the *psychological* development of the candidates for sex change.

The introduction of "gender dysphoria" also facilitated the surgical sex change of many subjects who did not fit the picture of the "classic Benjaminian transsexual." Billings and Urban argue that "diagnosis in the post-Benjaminian era remains a subtle negotiation process between patients and physicians, in which the patient's troubles are defined, legitimated, and regulated as illness. . . . We found that admission to surgery depended less on formal, rational, or fixed criteria than on the commonsense of clinicians." They continue, with reference to Norman Fisk:

> Despite physicians' belief that the semantic shift to "gender dysphoria syndrome" was effective in "allowing and encouraging our patients to be honest, open, and candid, with the result that our overall evaluations quickly became truly meaningful," patient screening and interviewing still function as patient socialization.[78]

According to this argument, the ultimate effect of the introduction of gender dysphoria as a diagnostic label was to encourage more subjects to identify as transsexuals and to seek surgical sex reassignment. Billings and Urban write that "transsexual therapy, legitimated by the terminology of disease, pushes patients toward an alluring world of artificial vaginas and penises rather than toward self-understanding and sexual politics. Sexual fulfillment and gender-role comfort are portrayed as commodities, available through medicine." The result of "the legitimation, rationalization, and commodification of sex-change operations" is the production of "an identity category—trans-sexual—for a diverse group of sexual deviants and victims of severe gender role distress."[79]

Billings and Urban's arguments are cogent and persuasive, especially insofar as they attempt to assess the political implications of transsexualism as a medically regulated form of social identity. Much of their argument hinges on the claim that physicians who responded favorably to the transsexuals' demand for surgery and hormonal treatments constructed that demand as a central symptom of the disorder in order to counter the allegations by other doctors who were opposed to conversion surgery and hormone therapies. These latter, many of whom were psychoanalysts, accused the transsexual advocates of collaborating with their patients' psychotic demands.[80] This argument suggests that the physicians involved with the development of transsexualism as a medical syndrome treatable through surgical and hormonal therapies elevated the demand to the level of symptom solely in order to make their endeavor seem legitimate.

It is evident, however, that physicians were already responding to a demand for surgical and hormonal sex change as early as 1949, which would suggest that subjects requesting sex change presented the demand for medical intervention as integral to their case histories before the question of medical legitimacy became significant for the profession as a whole. The essays by Cauldwell and Hamburger verify this claim. That the demand for sex change became the key signifier for transsexualism demonstrates the centrality of technology to the consolidation of transsexual subjectivity—asking for technologically mediated sex change is in one and the same gesture to name oneself as transsexual and to request recognition as a transsexual from the medical institution. In addition, by making their desired treatment absolutely clear, transsexuals encouraged a therapeutic response on the part of clinicians. In this way, transsexuals were actively engaged in defining their position within medical discourses.

Billings and Urban are correct to note that many doctors have claimed merely to be responding to their patients' requests and have not recognized their involvement in the construction of a transsexual subjectivity that is founded (at least in part) in a symptomatology produced through the doctor-patient relationship. However, they neglect the historical significance of the relation between the demand for sex change and the development of those specific medical technologies that make transsexualism possible. The well-publicized, positive response of certain physicians encouraged the development of the demand as central to transsexual identity—that Hamburger was deluged with letters following the publicity surrounding Christine Jorgensen's transformation demonstrates this process. The demand was linked to the availability of surgical and hormonal technologies, which were then further refined with use. These refined techniques became the object of the demands of a new generation of transsexual subjects who knew of their existence and their potential uses. By underestimating the significance of technology in the emergence and development of transsexualism in the twentieth century, Billings and Urban deny a crucial aspect of the phenomenon.[81]

Hamburger and his colleagues clearly demonstrated that transsexual subjects sought to distinguish themselves from homosexuals and transvestites, which in the 1950s medical context were the diagnostic labels that represented the other subject positions available for those exhibiting cross-sex behaviors.[82] Transsexuals worked to reconfigure the psychiatric categories detailing what were originally known as sexual deviations. They challenged the prevalent discourses and practices concerning sexual deviance with other discourses and practices gaining relevance in other sectors of medicine. Physicians and transsexuals together eventually succeeded in displacing the diagnosis of sexual deviance by redirecting the discourses of the intersex researchers (Money, for example) to define their condition in terms of gender.

The development of the idea of gender dysphoria as an underlying condition for manifestations of transsexualism can be understood as part of this activity, since it opened up the clinical situation to phenomenological criteria of which the patients were more in control. As Billings and Urban write:

> Diagnosis is linked to routine everyday gender typifications. More than anything else, physical appearance enables patients to control screening interviews; successful cross-dressing often truncates the screening process. When patients appear at a clinic convincingly cross-dressed, verbal slips or doubtful acounts are set right by covering accounts—or are simply glossed over because physical appearance confirms the gender claimed.[83]

Theoretically, the introduction of gender dysphoria (and the related "gender identity disorders") to refer to the condition underlying a continuum of cross-sex behaviors undermined the centrality of the demand for sex change as the primary symptom of transsexualism. To quote Steiner, Blanchard, and Zucker again, "The diagnostic label *gender dysphoric* . . . refer[s] to the whole gamut of individuals who, at one time or another, experience sufficient discomfort with their biological sex to form the wish for sex reassignment."[84] The continued appearance in gender clinics of subjects who demanded sex change yet did not "fit" the previous sexological categories placed a consistent pressure on clinicians to develop new diagnostic distinctions. (The broadening of diagnostic criteria may also have encouraged the development of "transgenderism" as an optional position for those subjects experiencing "gender dysphoria.")[85]

The pressure to expand the diagnostic taxonomy is documented in changes in the psychiatric classifications of transvestism and transsexualism between the early 1950s and the late 1980s. In the first *Diagnostic and Statistical Manual for*

Mental Disorders, published in 1952, "sexual deviations" were described under the larger heading of "Personality Disorders." The sexual deviations included homosexuality, transvestism, pedophilia, fetishism, and sexual sadism. In the second edition (1968), the sexual deviations constituted their own category and, in addition to those delineated in the first edition, included exhibitionism, voyeurism, masochism, and "other sexual deviations." The third edition (1980) introduced the gender identity disorders under the heading "Psychosexual Disorders." The other three psychosexual disorders were defined as the paraphilias ("characterized by arousal in response to sexual objects or situations that are not part of normative arousal-activity patterns and that in varying degrees may interfere with the capacity for reciprocal affectionate sexual activity"), the psychosexual dysfunctions, and the "other" psychosexual disorders. Significantly, while transvestism remained a paraphilia in 1980, homosexuality did not. Finally, in the revised third edition (1987), gender identity disorders were classified as "disorders usually first evident in infancy, childhood, or adolescence." They appeared after eating disorders and before tic disorders, and while differentiated from transvestic fetishism, are not included in the same classification.[86] Of interest here is the way in which transsexualism moved from consideration as a sexual deviation to a gender identity disorder located near other *compulsive behavior* disorders. This corresponds to the increasing theorization of gender in psychiatric sexology, and the development of the idea of core gender identity as central to the stability of personhood. Transsexualism moves farther and farther away from categories concerned with sex and sexuality—and therefore away from consideration as a sexual perversion or paraphilia—and toward other disorders whose etiological pictures (supposedly) more closely mirror its own.[87] This is part of the normalization of transsexualism as a psychiatric disorder.[88]

Homosexuals and transvestites also were actively involved in transforming their position in the discourses of psychiatric medicine. Homosexuals worked politically to get themselves out of the DSM series, succeeding in 1973.[89] Heterosexual male transvestites were instrumental in producing and maintaining a clinical definition that differentiated them from homosexual men who also dressed as women.[90] The difference between homosexual and transvestite activists and their transsexual counterparts, however, is that the former attempted (and continue to attempt) to throw off medical regulation, while transsexuals needed medical regulation and therefore sought to obtain (and manage) it. Homosexuals and transvestites were (and in some cases, continue to be) subject to physiological medical regulation—in the 1950s male homosexuals were subject to hormone therapies and both groups subject to aversion therapies using electric shocks and nausea-inducing drugs. These technologies were engaged, however, to *alleviate* or *get rid of* what were considered perverse behavioral patterns. The technologies involved in transsexualism, on the other hand, were (and are) engaged in order to *facilitate* the transsexuals' desires—to alleviate their suffering, yes, but through accommodation of their demands.[91]

The technologies engaged in the 1950s in treatments for homosexuality and transvestism were completely in keeping with the idea of physiology as "nature." Since homosexual and transvestic behaviors were thought to go against the conventional relations of sexual orientation to physiology, the behaviors were targeted for change. Transsexuals, on the other hand, exploited the established classifications of psychiatric sexology by utilizing diagnostic categories like transvestism but displacing their behavioral focus through a demand for immediate, technological intervention that transformed the body's original sex. Transsexuals were able to invert the conventional perception of physiology as "nature" by getting doctors to target not their behaviors, but their bodies, for technological intervention. One concomitant of this transgression and its diagnostic codification has been a subtle shift from physiology to psychology in the idea of the "nature" of sex—a shift initiated in the instantiation of the intersexual treatment protocols in the 1950s, but reaching its final expression in the institution of "sex reassignment" as the approved treatment for transsexualism. In sex reassignment, the congruence of physiology and behavior is still the goal (as in the treatments for homosexuality and transvestism), but anatomy and physiology are the contingent categories: it is not perceived to be good enough to *perform gender*, one's body must exhibit it as a "sex" as well.[92]

The conceptual apparatus of gender identity was not necessary for transsexuals to initiate demands for sex change, but it certainly facilitated transsexuals' attempts to distinguish themselves from transvestites and homosexuals—in the eyes of clinicians and the public both. For example, Christine Jorgensen ran into problems when her *American Weekly* series, "The Story of My Life," identified her as a transvestite. In her autobiography, published a decade and a half later, she wrote:

> When the term "transvestism" appeared . . . in the *American Weekly* articles, it created a gross misconception in the minds of many readers. . . . In the minds of an interested, but misguided public, I was immediately placed in a narrow category which led many intelligent people to believe the stories that circulated at the time: that I had been a female impersonator before going to Denmark, and in my private life as "George," I doted on wearing female clothing.[93]

She denied dressing in women's clothing "while I retained any evidence of masculinity," even though her doctors wrote otherwise.[94] But while citing Benjamin's work to define the category of the *transsexual*, Jorgensen ended her chapter with a quote from Benjamin concerning *intersexuality*. As I will discuss more fully in chapter 5, Jorgensen's reliance on a theory of intersexuality to define her condition is common among transsexual autobiographers. Yet the discussion of intersexuality in Jorgensen's autobiography did little to dispel the problems associated with the idea of transvestism. Her discussion of anatomy, genetics, and intersexuality was vague ("Disease or disturbance in this [hormone-producing] system may prevent the normal, harmonious development of the sex which nature intended, and may cause any one of the different stages of what we call 'intersexes' "), and while she was content to argue, "It was *possible*, then, that I was an individual belonging to the 'highest degree of intersexuality,' " she never fully resolved the tension between the categories transvestite, transsexual, and intersexual.[95] Christine Jorgensen, the world's first public transsexual, clearly felt stigmatized by the very terminology that, in the 1950s, enabled her transformation but which, by the mid-1960s, signified something else. By 1967, the gender identity paradigm was largely in place, although it was not strongly enough established to support a convincing narrative about *gender* gone awry.

Significantly, the introduction of gender identity disorders into the diagnostic lexicon concerned with cross-sex behaviors allowed transsexuals to claim the primacy of an identity that should take precedence over their physiology and anatomy. This facilitated the undermining of "natural sex" as the basis for "social sex" that sex change implies, since transsexuals could argue that their "aberrant" gender identity was imprinted at an early age and attempts to change it risked severe psychological hazard.[96] However, as the work of Virginia Prince demonstrates, the idea of gender identity does not have to support transsexualism and the use of medical technology for sex change.

Virginia Prince was born Charles Prince, but has lived continuously as Virginia for decades. She is one of the main advocates of transvestism in the United States, and in the 1950s began her work to educate the public about male heterosexual transvestism and related behaviors. In her 1976 publication, *Understanding Cross Dressing*, Prince included numerous articles from the periodical *Transvestia* (of which she was editor and chief writer). Prince outlined her opposition to transsexual surgeries insofar as they demonstrate the extent to which transsexual subjects confuse sex and gender in the essay "Change of Sex or Gender." For example, she wrote:

> Of all people in the world, TV's should recognize the fact that you do not have to be a female to "be" a "girl," because a great many of us definitely feel ourselves to be *girls* when we are dressed even though we are perfectly aware that we are males. If a TV looks well enough to pass on the street it should certainly be clear to her that in society she IS a girl not only to herself but to everyone who sees her or has any sort of interchange with

her. Girlness is set forth by the clothes, the hair-do, the shoes, makeup, jewelry, manner and general actions. When these are appropriate and in good taste everyone sees a GIRL and nobody pulls up her skirt to check out whether she is a female or not. Thus to herself and to the observer the TV girl in passing is expressing her feminine GENDER and her anatomical sex doesn't enter into it. This should make it perfectly evident that sex and gender are not the same thing and are not necessarily tied together.[97]

Prince continued with a discussion of a "true transsexual," one "whose maleness is non-functional" in addition to the criteria that "his masculinity should also be of a low order": "In short, the true TS could be described as a person who is inadequate, inefficient, uncomfortable, unhappy and ineffective both as a male *and* as a man (both sexually and genderally, that is)."[98] Prince insisted that if the "treatment" is to transform the subject's sexual anatomy, that anatomy must be considered defective or otherwise nonfunctional.

Prince's argument is based on the same ideas about gender identity that underlie transsexuals' demands for surgery—that "sex and gender are not the same thing," that "sex does not 'cause' gender as an automatic biological development," and that "one *learns* [gender]"—however, since she believed that transvestism was "a matter of gender identity and not sexual identity," she opposed sex change. For Prince, the theory of gender did not allow recourse to change the sexed body to fit the subject's felt gender identity. Rather, it allowed one to theorize the mistaken path of those subjects who were unable to realize that they "longed for girlishness not femaleness." The theoretical distinctions between sex and gender signified, to Virginia Prince, the *transvestite* option, the possibility of "imitating and partaking of the *gender* qualities and prerequisites of girls and women, i.e. their femininity."[99]

Prince did suggest a possible reason—other than gender identity disturbances—for the demand for sex change:

It is part of the pain of being a human being that we develop personality quirks, behavior patterns, and attitudes which are the end results of psychological and sociological traumas of one type or another occurring at various times during our lives. We can for conversational purposes lump these all together under the heading of neuroses. . . . [O]ne does not "escape" from a neurosis. One can only face it, examine it, learn its nature and causes and then seek (alone or with counselling) to remove it through destroying its usually deeply buried causes and to modify or eliminate its symptoms. Unhappily the idea of changing sex and gender appeals to some people as a sort of magic way of outwitting fate and destiny—"see, I'm not that person anymore and all those hangups and monkeys were his, don't lay them on me. I'm new and different and free."[100]

Whether or not Prince was correct to designate the desire for sex change as a desire to free oneself of ordinary human neuroses, she pointed to an interesting interpretation of the function of the discourse of gender identity in the construction of transsexualism, an interpretation that has been alluded to by another researcher, Leslie Martin Lothstein. In this interpretation, the demand for sex change that is bolstered by claims to a cross-sex gender identity covers over other forms of subjectivity that are fundamentally destabilizing.

Lothstein's *Female-to-Male Transsexualism* constitutes the first full-length study of female-to-male transsexuals. The book's purpose is to identify the disorders of personality that Lothstein believes cause the female-to-male transsexuals to seek surgery. In this text surgery is considered an effect of the disorder: Lothstein believes that surgical and hormonal technologies of "sex change" taint the etiology of female transsexualism because they allow for the consolidation of pathology around the demand for "sex change." Predictably, he advocates intense psychotherapy for female transsexuals, most of whom he believes suffer from structural defects of ego and self systems (that is, "borderline" conditions).[101] He resists the demand for sex reassignment surgery and hormonal treatments, arguing that

> [t]he view that "psychotherapy is useless to transsexuals," was uncritically accepted (especially by transsexual advocates) for several reasons: (1) patient pressure for a medical-surgical intervention; (2) the surgeon's interest in performing the surgery; (3) the conflict between psychiatry and medicine regarding the role of psychiatry in medicine; and (4) reports of transsexual "cures" with SRS.[102]

He does believe, however, that "in some cases the evaluator may conclude that the woman's gender identity and role should be consolidated as male. Indeed, there is a group of women who can only maintain object relationships when they impersonate males."[103]

One of the "myths" of female transsexualism that Lothstein debunks is that of the female-to-male transsexual's alleged psychological stability, especially compared to the clinically described instability of male-to-female transsexuals. Lothstein argues that any difference between the two groups has to do with sex differences, understood as physiological and social:

> It is not surprising that female transsexuals appear more "stable" than their male counterparts. Indeed, female lesbians appear more stable than male homosexuals; and female heterosexuals manifest significantly less sexual psychopathology and acting out than do male heterosexuals. The chief variable among the two groups is sex differences. Because of their unique hormonal milieu and radically different socialization, female behavior disorders always seem less severe than their male counterparts.[104]

This characterization of psychological sex differences diametrically opposes popular cultural stereotypes, which portray "normal" femininity as flighty, unstable, and histrionic. Female transsexuals, then, are perceived by clinical staff to be stable psychologically as "troubled" women; they must also present a stable masculinity to be convincing as "normal" men. Their psychologic stability has everything to do with clinical and popular semiotic codes, and they must learn to manipulate these expertly. Lothstein suggests, however, that a stable masculinity is one way for female transsexuals to split off from chaotic life experiences, and he cautions clinicians to be wary of a client's superficial gender presentation.[105]

Lothstein's consideration of female transsexualism suggests that in order to make a demand for surgical and hormonal sex change, men and women must take up different positions in relation to their clinicians, in order for those demands to be accepted as indicative of "real" transsexualism (that is, a true cross-sex gender identity). In other words, demanding subjectivity is split along lines of sexual difference. In making their demands, these subjects must demonstrate that they are in fact *already* the other gender. Lothstein argues that speaking from the position of "stable" masculinity is a cover for female transsexuals, whose lives can be fraught with incest, alcoholism, and violence. These are subjects for whom the development of any position as a subject is problematical. The stability of gender, in other words, covers over a chaos that threatens to annihilate the subject.[106]

The demand for sex change may then serve to consolidate gender as the stabilizing force of subjectivity for these subjects. But if transsexual subjectivity is constituted through a demand for technological intervention on the body, then the nature of demanding influences the structure of this subjectivity. In other words, it is not only the notion of technology that is significant here, but the idea of a subjectivity predicated through a demand. Lacanian psychoanalysis provides a paradigm through which to think the relation between an enunciated demand and the constitution of the subject in language.[107] In Lacanian terms, to demand something is to displace that which one wants.[108] The spoken demand necessarily reconfigures the terrain within which the speaker locates his or her "need" and knows it as such. The transformation of this "need" into a spoken demand produces desire as its supplement. Thus, demanding unsettles and displaces its subjects through the production of desire that is always unforeseen and destabilizing because it cannot be contained, accounted for, or restricted.

It is therefore in the nature of demanding to reproduce itself compulsively in the subject. In the demand for sex change, the transsexual stakes a claim for the self as a core of "needs" that determines, indeed founds, subjectivity as the "other sex." It is in the context of this structure of a demanding subjectivity that the logic of transsexualism can be understood to depend upon the claim of an internally felt gender identity as the locus of those needs which are thought of as the origin of the demand for surgical and hormonal sex change. The demand itself, however, inaugurates in the subject a desire that cannot be met through the specific surgeries and endocrinological interventions that serve to relocate him or her in the opposite sex category. What is demanded cannot compensate for the supplement (desire) produced in the process of making the request. What is left is a compulsion to repeat, to return to the demand again and again in the hopes of getting it "right." [109]

The work of transsexuals and clinicians to instantiate the demand for sex change as the central symptom of a syndrome (the origins of which remain enigmatic and socially unsettling) represents a tremendous achievement. Their success, evident in the inclusion of transsexualism in the DSM-III, depended upon the recognition by the medical institution of the reality of gender identity as the core organizing structure of sexed subjectivity and on the technological developments which made physiological sex change possible. Yet, the operation of the demand for surgical sex change as a central symptom necessary for a diagnosis of transsexualism suggests that the claim of a coherent and fixed gender identity covers over something other than the desire to change sex. After all, the idea of gender identity has been accepted in Western culture as a normative account of human development—the narrative of gender identity and its development outlined in chapter 3 work to shore up an eroding reproductive paradigm with a nonreproductive but nevertheless heterosexual paradigm of sexual normality. That gender identity is allied with such a normative, homophobic account of sexual development should be enough to warrant suspicion of its putative existence as the stabilizer of transsexual subjectivity. But there are other reasons to doubt that gender identity stands as the origin of the demand for sex change: as we have seen, the emphasis on gender identity as the core or kernel of subjectivity obscures the operations of desire that are activated by demanding sex change. In this sense, gender identity is the stabilizer of transsexual (and "normal") subjectivity only insofar as it represents the goal of the demand; transsexuals, in this scenario, demand sex change in order to achieve a position as an authentic gender.

It is possible that the concept of gender identity gone awry (that is, the conviction of being the other sex) covers over some kind of subjectivity that would more openly demonstrate the dependence of transsexualism on a demand for technological intervention—a demand, in other words, to engineer oneself as a human subject. Dallas Denny suggests as much in her article "Transsexualism at Forty: Some Uncommonly Discussed Aspects of an Increasingly Common

Phenomenon," when she writes that Christine Jorgensen "was the project manager for a bold social experiment which lasted until 1991, when she died of cancer." [110] She continues:

> Transsexual people redesign their bodies in the same way that some future bioengineer might redesign the human body for optimal functioning on a heavy gravity planet, or for underwater living. They monitor the cutting edge of medical and other knowledge and apply it to themselves, usually without the help and often without the permission of family, friends, clergy, teachers, governments, and helping professionals. They use hormones, plastic surgery, and electrolysis to fashion their bodies into a form that they find more acceptable than the ones their genes designed them for, and then they wear those bodies, venturing into society and creating a place for themselves. [111]

Denny goes on to discuss the social and psychological transformations that transsexuals must undergo, arguing that

> This human re-engineering, and not the actual genital surgery which morbidly fascinates the American populace, is the true significance of transsexual change. What is significant is not that penises and scrotums can be fashioned into vaginas or that phalluses can be made from the skin of the forearm, but that someone who is easily identifiable as a man can come to be identifiable as a woman, and vice-versa, by sheer will of self-determination (with hormonal assistance). [112]

Thus, while in this last passage Denny reneges on her earlier claims, she suggests a perspective on transsexualism rarely voiced within the transgender community, a perspective that acknowledges the role of technology in the construction of the transsexual subject, and one that suggests that to engineer oneself as a subject is as much a part of the transformation as believing oneself to really be the other sex.

The argument that gender identity is a "cover" for a desire to engineer oneself might also explain, for example, the polysurgical attitude that seems to govern transsexual women's relationships to their (newly constructed) female bodies. A significant number of transsexual women request further refinements of their feminine appearance with rhinoplastic surgery, removal of the Adam's apple, facial reconstructions, and the like. [113] Some critics argue that these additional requests for surgery indicate the extent to which transsexual women try to live up to an idealized vision of the "real" woman whose youthful femininity radiates from every pore of her body. [114] Transsexuals argue that these requests for surgery simply represent the desire of transsexual women to appear different from (and unrelated to) their former male selves. For example,

Roberta Cowell stated that she had limited facial surgery with the dual purpose of further feminizing her appearance and masking any relation to "Robert." [115]

Neither of these explanations fully accounts for the insistence with which repeated surgical interventions are demanded, however. The polysurgical attitude is, at least in part, constitutive of transsexual subjectivity insofar as the latter is organized around a demand for sex-conversion surgery. Once this surgery is achieved, this subjectivity of demand coalesces around a new surgical goal. [116] This repeated transformation and refinement of anatomy—these attempts to continually fine-tune the body's signifying of sex, to assure that the body continues to signify the right sex—reveals a compulsion to manage the semiotics of sexual difference. It also reveals the extent to which "gender identity" as a concept can never fully signify, or determine, sex in and of itself. Technological intervention must be demanded to shore up the existence of gender as identity, and it must be demanded again and again. To what extent, we may ask, is gender itself a "compulsive" concept, if in order to assure ourselves that it exists and that it operates with such power we must unceasingly demonstrate that our bodies represent it faithfully?

Gender, which has been theorized as the dominant determinant of subjectivity in transsexualism, serves to mask other divisions central to the phenomenon (as well as to the contemporary cultural formation) through a strategy of containment. The transsexual's investment in traditional gender ideologies serves as a cover for another, more radically destabilizing structure of subjectivity—a compulsive relation to technology through which the transsexual demands recognition as a subject of the other sex. Rather than its "first cause," the sex/gender system represents the goal of transsexualism. Demanding physical transformation through surgical and hormonal technologies, transsexuals seek admittance into the cultural system of gender difference as its recognizable subjects.

It seems to me that we are no closer to understanding the cause of transsexualism when we say that it represents a disorder of core gender identity than when we say that it represents a sexual deviance: we have simply shifted taxonomies. Gender, first as "role" and then as "identity," serves to shore up or support the notion of a unitary sex—and, most significantly, of unitary identity—in the face of radical destabilization. Certainly, this should be clear in the context of the medical management of intersexuality. [117] Lothstein's work suggests the ways in which forging an identity in gender works to consolidate some sense of cohesiveness for a subjectivity constantly under threat of destruction. Gender is a cover-up—for transsexuals, for those who treat transsexuals, and for the rest of us as well.

While a transsexual can become an effective representative of the other sex, an opposition between physical sexual signifiers remains as a reminder of his/

her crossing over. Genetic sex cannot be altered; other secondary sex characteristics remain. In order to maintain the form of their chosen sex, transsexuals must engage daily in material practices that counteract the operation of those physiological processes that signify their original sex. Most of these practices are not unique to transsexual subjects (hormone intake, electrolysis, make-up, hairstyling, manicure, among others), but taken together these practices take up a significant portion of the transsexual subject's life and define the experience of living in a transsexual body. These material practices serve as reminders of transsexuals' transgression of their original sexual physiology because they must be engaged routinely in order to maintain the physical signifiers of their chosen sex. While this may, in fact, be a result of the resistance of the body's "real code" to the technological regulation of its processes, it signifies that this disruption of sexual difference is contingent upon continued and accurate technical management of physiological processes.

To attend to the impact of these oppositions is to recognize the significance of the surgical and hormonal construction of the natural body to the social configuration of subjectivity. As we saw in chapter 3, the intersex researchers state as their goal the production of bodies such that intersex individuals may realize themselves in the exclusive designation of male or female. Ostensibly, these clinicians attend to the subject's sexual physiology and anatomy, yet they encourage their patients to develop an effective gender performance in order to "be" an authentic representative of their sex. Transsexuals' demands for sex change occur in the context of this reformulation of sexual difference into the product of gender performance and the technical manipulation of the body's sex.

The demand to be the other sex constructs a compulsive relation to the technological practices necessary to accommodate that demand, and is matched by the compulsory nature of gender in contemporary culture, where the punishments for aberrant gender performances are relatively severe.[118] Indeed, we might suggest that this transgression of the order of sexual physiology is a compulsive gesture, meant to erase the semiotic foundations upon which gender identity (as corresponding to the male and female sex) putatively depends. It is in this sense that transsexuals are the dupes of gender. They contain its compulsive deconstruction of sexual difference through their own compulsive relation to technology, and they produce themselves as the simulacra of sexual difference through the presentation of gender as both origin and goal of sex identity. Transsexualism is gender's alibi—seeming to prove its facticity in the demand to be recognized as the other sex, yet demonstrating the impossibility for any subject to authentically or finally "be" a sex.

5

BODY, TECHNOLOGY, AND

GENDER IN TRANSSEXUAL

AUTOBIOGRAPHIES

Thus far, my analysis has concentrated on medical discourses and practices, including the technologies that preceded and facilitated the conceptual production of "gender" as the psychological counterpart to biological sex. In this chapter, I shift gears somewhat and analyze discourses produced by transsexuals themselves about their experiences. My examination of transsexual autobiographies has two purposes: to demonstrate how "gender" discursively operates to mask the material construction of transsexuals through the technologies of medical practice and to show how transsexuals compromise the official understanding of "gender" as divorced from biological sex by their insistent reiteration of the idea that physiological intersexuality is the cause of their cross-sex identification. While the first point will allow us to see how "gender" works to contain transsexual accounts within the conceptual parameters of humanism, the second will make evident the extent to which official pronouncements of the medical establishment are not homologous to the understanding and experience of transsexuals concerning the origins and causes of their condition.

The purpose here is not to pit transsexual discourses against medical discourses in order to determine which most accurately represent the transsexual phenomenon. Rather, I am interested in marking discursive discontinuities in the context of which another story about transsexualism can be fashioned. If the story told in the first four chapters of this book is a subversive retelling of the official medical accounts concerning the emergence of transsexualism and the idea of gender, then the story told in this chapter is an attempt to subvert the official story put forth by transsexual autobiographers. Because I have thus far concentrated on the "official" history of transsexualism within medicine, here I use examples from the autobiographies of "official" transsexuals. All of the texts I examine in this chapter were published as books, many by well-established publishing houses. These texts (for the most part) do not document the stories of transients or sex workers—those marginalized sub-jects within an already marginalized subject formation—but tell the stories of celebrities or "public transsexuals" (that is, those made famous by their emer-gence as transsexuals, those who were already famous and had to account for their transformation, or those who chose to live publicly as transsexuals in order to set an example or work toward public acceptance of transsexualism).

This is not an insignificant issue, especially given the current popularity of media representations of the most marginalized transsexuals—*Paris Is Burning* comes to mind here. My decision to concentrate on the more mainstream ac-counts of transsexual experience—both within medicine and the transsexual community—is based on a desire to challenge these accounts with critical attention to their internal problematics. That is, instead of countering the offi-cial accounts of transsexualism—as well as the official accounts of gender— with evidence from more marginalized transsexual subjects (sex workers, for example), I have chosen to interrogate the official accounts themselves and demonstrate the extent to which they can be reread to tell another story. Ulti-mately, I believe, this kind of analysis will offer a more serious challenge to the hegemony of these discourses in the public sphere, where the spread of gender ideologies threatens to cover over other significant, and destabilizing, accounts of human subjectivity.[1]

The analysis of these "official" transsexual autobiographies is not unprob-lematic, however. Because most transsexuals do not write their life stories, those autobiographies authored by transsexuals cannot be taken to be rep-resentative of the "average transsexual." Yet books by transsexuals about sex change hold a significant position in contemporary transsexual culture. Mario Martino writes in *Emergence* that, as Marie, she was the first in her town to buy Christine Jorgensen's autobiography when it came out in 1967. In her autobiog-raphy, *Conundrum*, Jan Morris discusses the emotional significance of finding Lili Elbe's autobiography, *Man into Woman: An Authentic Record of a Change of Sex*, in a used-book store. Renée Richards found a copy of the same text at an important point in her life as Richard Raskind. Nancy Hunt writes in *Mirror Image*, "I can remember only once when my life has been altered by the printed word. That was upon reading an article in the *New York Times Magazine* on March 17, 1974. . . . It described the transition from man into woman of an English journalist now known as Jan Morris."[2] In addition, organizations such as the International Foundation for Gender Education (IFGE) sell all manner of books about trans-sexualism and transvestism, including transsexual autobiographies, as part of their educative outreach.

Thus, while transsexual autobiographies may not be representative of the experiences of many (or even most) transsexual subjects, they are indicative of the establishment of an official discourse (or set of discourses) regulating transsexual self-representations and, therefore, modes of transsexual subjectivity. The autobiographical texts help institute a certain discursive hegemony within a community whose members have a substantial investment in mimicking the enunciative modality of those who have been successful in achieving sex transformation. Collecting the autobiographies of successful transsexuals—either through personal contact or by print media—constitutes an important part of transsexual self-construction, self-education, and self-preparation for encounters with clinic personnel. As Sandy Stone writes in "The Empire Strikes Back: A Posttranssexual Manifesto": "[M]any transsexuals keep something they call by the argot term 'O.T.F.': The Obligatory Transsexual File. . . . Transsexuals also collect autobiographical literature."[3]

Transsexuals are a notoriously well-read patient population, primarily because their success in obtaining the medical treatments that they seek depends upon their ability to convince doctors that their personal history matches the officially sanctioned etiology.[4] In a context where telling the right story may confer legitimacy upon one's demand and the wrong story can foil one's chances for sex change, the autobiographies of those transsexuals who have successfully maneuvered within the strict protocols of the gender clinics constitute guide-books of no mean proportion. They also serve to assure would-be transsexual readers that they are members of a group and not as isolated as they may feel. This latter function helps individuals who often perceive themselves to be entirely alone and outside the cultural system to authorize themselves as deserving cultural subjects and is instrumental in their assumption of an identity as a transsexual.

All of this suggests that transsexual autobiographies serve to encourage and enable transsexual subjects to conform to the parameters of an established "transsexual personal history" in order to obtain the desired medical treatment. Certainly, I am not the first to suggest the limitations this tendency imposes on the construction of transsexual subjectivity. Sandy Stone argues that the instantiation of the "official transsexual history" necessary for approval for surgical and hormonal sex change produced a situation in which the potential "intertextuality" of transsexual subjectivity has been erased:

[I]t is difficult to generate a counterdiscourse if one is programmed to disappear. The highest purpose of the transsexual is to erase him/herself, to fade into the "normal" population as soon as possible. Part of this process is known as *constructing a plausible history*—learning to lie effectively about one's past. What is gained is acceptability in society. What is lost is the ability to authentically represent the complexities and ambiguities of lived experience. . . . Instead, authentic experience is replaced by a particular kind of story, one that supports the old constructed positions.[5]

In opposition to this tendency, she calls on transsexuals to resist passing, a behavior she claims is "the essence of transsexualism":

> I could not ask a transsexual for anything more inconceivable than to forgo passing, to be consciously "read," to read oneself aloud—and by this troubling and productive reading to begin to write oneself into the discourses by which one has been written—in effect, then, to become a (look out—dare I say it again?) a posttranssexual.[6]

Stone asks for this in order to alleviate the compromises of silence that she believes regulate transsexual subjectivity and keep an alternative, multifaceted, and potentially subversive story of gender, sex, and the body from surfacing in and through the culture at large. Stone asserts that this silence concerning the "lived experience" of transsexuals has a significant and damaging effect on their relationships with others: "Transsexuals who pass seem able to ignore the fact that by creating totalized, monistic identities, forgoing physical and subjective intertextuality, they have foreclosed the possibility of authentic relationships."[7]

"The Empire Strikes Back" is a powerful essay, representing the first attempt by a transsexual woman to argue as a lesbian-feminist and as a transsexual for the destabilizing potential of transsexualism within a cultural context that regulates the phenomenon into the relative safety of socially acceptable discourses about gender.[8] Nevertheless, Stone's argument stops short of recognizing gender as a category that might be fully deconstructed in its historical context. She claims that "the transsexual currently occupies a position which is nowhere, which is outside the binary oppositions of gendered discourse," and that consequently, "for a transsexual, as a transsexual, to generate a true, effective and representative counterdiscourse is to speak from outside the boundaries of gender, beyond the constructed oppositional nodes which have been predefined as the only positions from which discourse is possible."[9] The production of the concept of gender within research on intersexuality and transsexualism suggests, however, that the transsexual speaks fully within the cultural discourse of/on gender, not only because that discourse was produced precisely to account for intersexual and transsexual subjects' experiences, but also because the performance of transsexual subjectivity depends upon the expert manipulation of traditional gender codes. To be a transsexual is perhaps to be "in gender" more fixedly than other subjects whose gender performances are perceived to be "natural."

Stone suggests that a "true" transsexual discourse would problematize gender by destabilizing the official transsexual history of the "wrong body" and by introducing into discourse "disruptions of the old patterns of desire that the multiple dissonances of the transsexual body imply."[10] She wants to produce a more authentic history of transsexualism through a lifting of the silences necessary to secure the desired medical interventions and a destabilization of the official stories about transsexualism—in these goals she and I concur. In her discussion of transsexual autobiographies, she comments that the authors deny "mixture," what she understands as an acknowledgment of ambiguous gender: "Besides the obvious complicity of these accounts in a Western white male definition of performative gender, the authors also reinforce a binary, oppositional mode of gender identification. They go from being unambiguous men, albeit unhappy ones, to unambiguous women. There is no territory between." [11] Stone argues that in conjunction with medical discourses on transsexualism and the practices of the gender clinics, the transsexual autobiographies demonstrate these subjects' necessary capitulation to ideologies of gender difference and disambiguity.

Stone comments that while transsexuals maintain files that include autobiographical accounts, the medical gender clinics do not because "according to the Stanford gender dysphoria program . . . they consider autobiographical accounts thoroughly unreliable." [12] Indeed, a number of transsexual researchers comment on what Stone designates "constructing a plausible history," in other words, lying about one's past in order to obtain the desired medical treatment. Anthropologist Anne Bolin explains the situation in *In Search of Eve: Transsexual Rites of Passage*:

> Transsexuals have widespread networks extending nationwide. They keep tabs on what the caretakers are up to and on what their latest theories are. Transsexual lore is rich with information on manipulation and utilization of caretaker stereotypes. Transsexuals know what they can honestly reveal and what they must withhold. This lore consists of "recipes" for dealing with caretakers and the management of information that they know would discredit them in the eyes of their caretakers should it be revealed. They necessarily exploit caretakers' expectations for their own ends by presenting a transsexual identity in conformity with caretakers' conceptions of classic transsexualism. [13]

For Bolin, who advocates the depathologization of transsexualism and the equalization of power within the caretaker-patient relationship, the fact that a transsexual's lies "validate the caretakers' stereotypes about transsexuals" is a shame, given that this can "foster impressions of a homogeneous population" and lead to "a self-fulfilling prophecy and . . . a situation in which both caretakers and clients suffer." [14] Dwight Billings and Thomas Urban discuss this same issue, calling it "the con." [15]

For Robert Stoller, a psychoanalyst at the Gender Identity Clinic at the University of California, Los Angeles (which in the past has not provided surgery for transsexuals), transsexuals' lies about their personal histories have other implications. In discussing the criteria for a diagnosis of transsexualism, Stoller writes that "those of us faced with the task of diagnosing transsexualism have an additional burden these days, for most patients requesting 'sex change' are in complete command of the literature and know the answers before the questions are asked." [16] For Stoller, the discursive tangle of self-identified and self-diagnosed transsexualism is part of an overall problem in the clinical treatment of transsexual subjects, evidence of the lack of an adequate differential diagnosis. In his view, the production of the "plausible personal history" keeps clinicians from really understanding the phenomenon of transsexualism, and therefore from truly helping transsexual patients. Indeed, as Stone writes, "It took a surprisingly long time—several years—for the researchers to realize that the reason the candidates' behavioral profiles matched [Harry] Benjamin's so well was that the candidates, too, had read Benjamin's book, which was passed from hand to hand within the transsexual community, and they were only too happy to provide the behavior that led to acceptance for surgery." [17]

Is there a "true" or "authentic" history behind the autobiographical productions for the gender clinics—and behind other kinds of transsexual autobiographies? Where might we find it and of what use would it be? Sandy Stone and Anne Bolin believe that alleviating the silence around certain aspects of transsexual experience will result in a measurable change in current conceptions of transsexualism and the authenticity of transsexuals' lives. Significantly, both argue this issue with respect to transsexuals' sexual habits. Stone twice comments that a preoperative, masturbatory ritual of male-to-female transsexuals, "wringing the turkey's neck," is always excluded from transsexual self-representations, largely because the official etiology of male-to-female transsexualism denies for these subjects any kind of penile pleasure.[18] Bolin discusses the stereotype of heterosexuality that regulates the transsexual's pre- and postoperative sexual life and makes owning up to bisexuality or lesbianism (pre- or postoperatively) clinical suicide.[19] Both believe that allowing the suppressed stories to surface would be beneficial to both transsexuals and the public at large—Stone because she is interested in subverting culturally hegemonic narratives about gender, and Bolin because she wants to see transsexuals legitimated as a sexual minority rather than defined by the stigma of mental illness. Both suggest that the suppressed stories, the "truth" of the transsexual experience, are about sexuality; and both represent the power at work—the force that produces transsexual autobiography as singular and monolithic—as entirely repressive and negative, without any enabling function.[20]

Transsexual autobiographical narratives cannot merely be a part of the repressive structure of "official" transsexual experience, since they clearly enable others to identify themselves as transsexuals, thereby allowing a variety of individuals to actively construct themselves as transsexuals. This is evident in the autobiographies themselves, where the authors mention that finding texts by other transsexuals helped to authorize their own identifications. This suggests that a "true" or "authentic" transsexual experience is not necessarily repressed and excluded from the transsexual autobiographies, but rather, that transsexual experience is itself made possible by these discourses: that they involve certain necessary exclusions does not make them "inauthentic." Another way to examine these autobiographies is to use a Foucauldian model to analyze the statements made in transsexual autobiographies and thereby to examine the forms of subjectivity and experience made possible by those statements.[21] This approach would enable us to gauge the ways in which transsexual autobiographies function as enabling—and not merely repressive—narratives.

One important rhetorical strategy of transsexual autobiographers is to present arguments that resist open readings. This strategy is part of the overall structure of these autobiographies as what Judith Butler might call "constative performances." By "constative performances" she means those performances of identity that actively construct the identity they are taken to be expressions of. According to Butler, all performances that are understood as reflections of an essential identity or self are, in fact, constative performances. I call the constative performances of transsexual autobiographers "assertions" or "statements" since the latter terms suggest strategies of the written word.[22]

The statements about identity and sex that are made by the transsexual autobiographers are produced as implications of, supplements to, and corollaries for the texts' resistances to multiple interpretations. In other words, the closed nature of the texts is a central aspect of the production of discourse about transsexual personal experience. This can be linked to the kind of discursive strategies necessary for transsexuals to gain clinical treatment in the form of hormones and sex reassignment surgery. Whether the author produces a story that relies on a physiological rationale for transsexualism, or one that suggests a psychological (and therefore gender-oriented) origin of the desire to change sex, the assertions produced by the texts conform to the notion that the author was truly meant to be a member of the other sex, always has been a member of the other sex, and should be allowed to be recognized (legally and socially) as a member of the other sex.

What I find latent in these texts is not the possibility of an "authentic" account of the transsexual, nor a particularly subversive story about sexuality, but the idea of the transsexual subject as an engineered subject. The technological aspects of the transformations of "sex change" are rarely stressed in these autobiographies, and physical pain is often glossed over in favor of a quick remark concerning the "overwhelming success" of surgical and hormonal interventions. Those autobiographies that do offer representations of the plastic surgery and its aftermath suggest that the alternative narratives available in transsexual autobiography do not concern counterhegemonic discourses of gender, but rather accounts of human engineering through medical technology. The stories that detail sex conversion technologies highlight the physical pain that occurs as a result of medical intervention, and demonstrate that the "original" body exerts pressure against such change. They suggest that the demand for sex change is indicative of a desire to engineer the self as a subject without discontinuity or rupture, to produce oneself as a complete and total subject of gender. The tension between the two stories—the story of the subject as the other sex and the story of the methods used to make the subject represent the other sex—constitutes one central disjunction in transsexual autobiographical narratives.

Another disjunction occurs within the story of "gender" itself, insofar as transsexuals' claims to physiological transsexualism (a transsexualism based on intersexuality) disrupts the officially sanctioned narrative of aberrant gender identity formation (found in the entirely psychological accounts put forth by the American Psychiatric Association in the various editions of the *Diagnostic and Statistical Manual of Mental Disorders*). In some of the autobiographies, the two contradicting accounts—"transsexualism is caused by aberrant sexual physiology" and "transsexualism is caused by aberrant gender identity"—are put forth with equal stress; in others, one is privileged while the other is mentioned but not stressed. In all of the autobiographies the idea of a physiological transsexualism appears at least in the form of a passing comment.

As we saw in chapter 4, many physicians advocating "sex change" as treatment for transsexualism felt that in the future medical science would be able to find a somatic origin of cross-sex identification of the kind found in transsexual patients. A similar emphasis in the autobiographies may simply indicate a mirroring of the medical discourses as a way of legitimating autobiographical claims. However, it seems to me that something more significant is at stake in transsexuals' assertions of physiological intersexuality. These assertions, or the "clues" recounted in the autobiographies that offer hope to the writers that they may be physically akin to the other sex, reaffirm their sense that they already *are* the other sex and only need to be recognized as such. Such a belief suggests transsexuals' investment in the idea that identity resides in the body's tissues, regardless of the fact that the official medical story of transsexualism treats the body as contingent to the mind's identifications.

This is, of course, made manifest in the demand for "sex change," since demanding to be made into the other sex suggests that "being" at the level of the mind (gender) is not enough. But the claims to physiological aberration suggest as well that changing the body solely on the basis of gender identifications is not a comfortable transformation for many transsexuals—the assertion of partial physical identity as the other sex prior to sex reassignment is one way of arguing that "I was meant to be the other sex" all along. The discourses of gender, however tied to psychology and a constructionist perspective in the realm of psychiatry, maintain a connection to the idea of physiological sex through the transsexual phenomenon. As we will see, the relation between physiology and culture is both intimate and strained in the stories by transsexuals about their own "emergence."

In her "personal autobiography," Christine Jorgensen wrote:

> Neither my doctors nor I had ever advocated these procedures for other sexual breaches of Nature. Mine was a single, highly individual case and the doctors had proceeded along the lines they felt would be most benefi-cial to me alone, with my full knowledge, approval, and consent. Beyond that, I had no advice for anyone. If others had seen in me a false hope for their own problems, then surely it was "wrong" and "tragic," but help for others could only come from the acceptance and enlightenment of the public and the medical profession.[23]

Jorgensen attempted to refuse the symbolic status that she inevitably acquired as the Western world's first public transsexual by defining herself against trans-vestites and homosexuals, the two categories of sexual aberration most closely associated with transsexualism. The above statement underscores a central message of her autobiography, namely, that Christine Jorgensen's experience was unique, that her anomalous condition was in no way representative of other (sexually aberrant) individuals' experiences, that she was a model for no one but herself.

Her book, however, was (and continues to be) widely read among trans-sexuals.[24] Apparently, *Christine Jorgensen: A Personal Autobiography* was not so unique as to avoid reader identification. Mario Martino, for example, identified with Jorgensen's life story as well as Jorgensen's interpretation of her condition. As I suggested in chapter 4, Jorgensen faced a discursive difficulty in defining her case, since by the time she wrote the autobiography, the terminology used to discuss transsexualism had changed. In the autobiography, Jorgensen insisted on the (by 1967) outmoded discourse of intersexuality to identify and define her condition.[25] She herself had been enormously influenced by the "glandular thesis" presented by Paul de Kruif in his book *The Male Hormone*.[26] Jorgensen's representation of her transsexualism as a physiological condition is consis-tent with her insistence that as George her problem was not only *feeling* like a woman, but *appearing* to be a woman physically as well.[27] This is a theme that returns in many of the autobiographies.

The story, as Jorgensen related it, is of an "underdeveloped" but undoubt-edly male subject who never really felt masculine and was unable to find a place in society where he could earn a living and move up in the world. As a child, George played often with girls, especially his sister, who was relegated the responsibility of looking after him and usually let him tag along with her and her friends. He felt that a "normal" social life was denied him because of his intense insecurity about his sexuality, as well as his acute shyness. He was underweight, unhappy, and uncertain about his sexual desires for men. The decision to change sex developed over a period of time, during which George attempted to gain insight into his problems as well as to earn a living. At a certain point, it became the overwhelming focus of his life, especially while he was a student at the Manhattan Medical and Dental Assistants School and while he saved money for his trip to Denmark. In Copenhagen, he became a research subject of Christian Hamburger and members of Hamburger's endocrinology lab, in return for which Jorgensen was granted surgical and hormonal treatment resulting in sex change in 1952. When the news of her transformation was leaked to the press, Christine Jorgensen became an international celebrity and in the book claims that of necessity she decided to go into show business because she felt she would never be able to live a private life anyway.[28] The overwhelming message of the autobiography is "I was meant to be a woman—see what a good woman I turned out to be, far more successful than my male self."

In the autobiography, Jorgensen supported the physiological perspective with reported speech from her doctors. For example, according to Jorgensen, Christian Hamburger told her the following: "I think the trouble is very deeprooted in the cells of your body. Outwardly, you have many of the sex characteristics of a man. You were declared a boy at birth and you have grown up, so very unhappily, in the guise of a man. But, inwardly, it is quite possible that you are a woman. Your body chemistry and all of your body cells, including your brain cells, may be female. That is only a theory, mind you."[29] In another passage, Jorgensen claimed that "[a]lthough the term 'sex transformation' has been used by many people when referring to my case, even by me on occasion, mine was rather a process of revised sex determination, inspired by the preponderance of female characteristics."[30]

Christine Jorgensen is not the only subject whose claim to be the other sex was made almost entirely on physiological grounds—we saw a similar claim in Lili Elbe's autobiography, as well as in Michael Dillon's *Self: A Study in Ethics and Endocrinology*. Another person who underwent surgery a year before Jorgensen, Roberta Cowell, also used a physiological justification for her sex change. Indeed, Cowell was more aggressive than Jorgensen in arguing for her identity as an intersex subject, and she claimed that Jorgensen "was scientifically classified as a transvestite, a person with an irresistible urge to wear the clothing of the other sex."[31] Cowell, like Jorgensen, presented little actual physical evidence of intersexuality in her autobiography, relying instead on reported speech from her doctors and vague references to her "feminine characteristics."

A father of two, a fighter pilot during World War II, and a former race car driver, Cowell went through psychotherapy and various treatments in the post-war period until he found doctors who were struck by his "female" physical characteristics and agreed to sponsor his sex reassignment. He wrote: "In my own case, I was never either a transvestite or a homosexual. My sexual inclinations were normal until the period of hormonal imbalance began. While my body was undergoing changes, all [sexual] inclinations died. When they appeared again, they were re-oriented. But this re-orientation was normal, since I was then a woman."[32] According to Cowell, the doctors believed that there had been "an alteration in gland balance and perhaps in gland structure. The cause might possibly have been a series of emotional upsets. There seemed to be some degree of hermaphroditism present."[33]

Roberta Cowell described her physical condition by referring to stereotypes of feminine anatomy and posture. After a squash partner observed that he might want to wear a brassiere, Robert went to see a sexologist:

A few days later I was in the Harley Street consulting-room of a famous sexologist. . . .

He gave it as his considered opinion that my body showed quite prominent feminine sex characteristics: wide hips and narrow shoulders, pelvis female in type, hair distribution and skin female in type. Other female traits included the absence of laryngeal relief (no Adam's apple) and a tendency of the lower limbs to converge towards the knees.

. . . Once I realised that my femininity had a *physical* basis I did not despise myself so much.[34]

Cowell's interpretation of bodily signifiers matches her presentation of the effects of hormone treatment. After taking hormones for a period of time, Robert Cowell found that "a definite change in the functioning of my mentality began to become apparent." According to her account, Robert was transformed (by hormones) into a stereotype of femininity:

My mental processes seemed to be slightly slower, and at the same time I also showed signs of greatly heightened powers of intuition. It had been expected that the change of hormone balance might very well be manifested in changed mental processes, but I realised that it would be impossible to differentiate between the effects of mental and physical changes.

Whatever the cause, I quite definitely began to be intuitive. . . .

Sometimes when the telephone rang I would get the feeling that I knew who was calling, and I would be right.

I also developed one super-feminine quality — the ability to blush. . . .

Fiction, except for the works of P.G. Wodehouse, had rarely interested me. Now I found myself reading stories and novels of all kinds with sustained interest. . . .

In general my nature was becoming milder and less aggressive.[35]

Despite the mental transformation, however, and even after the operation "to correct the congenital absence of vagina," an operation which left him "truly a complete female," Cowell felt that her "face was still fundamentally the same." She decided to have her "face drastically altered by surgery. This would remove all residual traces of masculinity and relieve me of the fear that I would be recognised. Incidentally, I could be made better-looking." [36]

The general discussion of her progress after surgery, however, recounts both the traits of femininity Roberta had to acquire consciously, and those which she unconsciously assumed (and therefore presumed to be naturally feminine). Roberta actively learned about feminine etiquette, hair and skin care, dieting, voice pitch, vocabulary, and cooking. She suggested at times the constructedness of her new self, as when she stated, "I always had to remember that I was building a new personality, and that I would have to curb undesirable tendencies as they arose while at the same time cultivating the traits which seemed most acceptable." [37] But she stuck steadfastly to her story that "spontaneous" feminization took place before she (as Robert) sought medical help. Then again, she was insistent that one can ascertain the existence of physiological factors from rather slim visual evidence: "A normal man or woman in the clothes of the opposite sex would look quite absurd, and either appearance or demeanor would make the masquerade easy to detect. It follows logically, therefore, that when an individual is able without any effort to pass, when properly dressed, as a member of the opposite sex, there must be some physical factor at work." [38]

Like Jorgensen, Cowell included in her autobiography a discussion of the medical theories concerning transvestism, embryonic sexual development, and endocrinology. Like Michael Dillon in Self: A Study in Ethics and Endocrinology, she presented "evidence" that supported the alleged facts of her own case. For example, Cowell wrote that

Apart from legal, ethical and social considerations, a change from male to female is made more difficult by the fact that many of the male sex-characteristics are not reversible. . . . Unless the prospective patient is so feminine that he can pass for a woman before treatment commences, it is not likely that he can be helped. Presence of deep constitutional feminism is essential.[39]

She asserted, in addition, that it is easier to turn a woman into a man than a man into a woman (an assertion which has been proven false in the forty-odd years since her hormonal and surgical treatment). Indeed, "medical science believes that on the very rare occasions when an apparent man turns into a woman it is because he has been a highly virilized woman all the time."[40]

In emphasizing intersexuality as the reason for their sex change, both Jorgensen and Cowell do not only represent the prevailing theories of the period during which their surgeries took place. While presenting their sex changes as being physiologically justified, either as cases of mistaken sex assignment or of spontaneously aberrant sexual development, these authors articulate one fundamental belief of most transsexual subjects—that the sense of being the other sex is an inborn and therefore irrefutable and unchangeable aspect of the self. One way of making that statement plausible is to argue that anything inborn must perforce be physiological.

More recent transsexual autobiographies continue to make gestures toward intersexuality as a rationale for cross-sex behaviors, but few rely as heavily on this reasoning as did Jorgensen and Cowell. What we will see in the other autobiographies are more sporadic representations of intersexuality in conjunction with a developing discourse about gender identity. The result is the elaboration of a common narrative concerning the identity of the self as a sex, a narrative that insists on the idea of a constitutional (inborn) identity as the other sex. The authors may present this constitutional identity as having been encouraged by circumstances and social learning. Like Jorgensen and Cowell, the other transsexual autobiographers set out to prove that "I was really meant to be a man/woman," but unlike Jorgensen and Cowell, later transsexuals used the discourses of gender, in addition to those of intersexual physiology, to substantiate their claims.

One advantage to this strategy is that the idea of an irrevocable core gender identity relies upon the implied presence of intersexuality in the register of the psyche. Conceived as a core or kernel of identity, gender metaphorically becomes a site of psychosocial sex, the center and origin of the body's sexual signifiers. Gender identity inherits the legacy of the glandular thesis by becoming the cause of sex in the body: if "natural" sexual physiology manifests in opposition to the gender identity at the core of the body's subjectivity, then another body is said to inhabit the external one. Thus, the idea of intersexuality remains central to the experience of transsexualism through the set of statements upon which transsexuals make their case in contemporary culture: "I am a man/woman inside," "I was meant to be a man/woman," or "I really am a man/woman on the inside." In the context of gender theory, all of these suggest an actual locatability of gender identity in the body, just as in the context of intersex theory they suggested the existence of cross-sex attributes and organs in the body. These statements undergird the autobiographical narratives, where each author interprets his or her experiences as examples of the facticity of an unambiguous relation between gendered behaviors and the body.

Figure 16. My ambiguity was evident at an early age. Source: Mario Martino, *Emergence* (New York: Crown Publishers, 1977).

Emergence chronicles Marie Martino's confused youth and her journey toward sex reassignment as Mario, his organizing of a service for female-to-male transsexuals, and his two attempts at phalloplasty.[41] Like most transsexual autobiographers, Martino denies any identification as a homosexual, preferring to characterize his sexuality as "like any man's."[42] Martino insists throughout the narrative that he ought to have been born a boy and that indicators of his true sex were available throughout his life as Marie. Indeed, *Emergence* is perhaps the most aggressive of the autobiographies in its insistent assertions of the author's "true" identity as the other sex.

Marie Martino was born into a traditional Italian-American family, and all her life identified strongly with her father and older half-brother. Her sense of her maleness began very early, Martino recounts, and throughout the autobiography, he proudly presents incidents which seem to affirm the existence of this maleness. The pictures included in the autobiography are an apt example of this: see figures 16 and 17. For the author, these pictures undeniably document her childhood masculinity (as the captions confirm), yet both merely offer the reader images of a child whose sex is largely indicated by clothing. A three-year-old child with short hair is generally somewhat asexual; that is why children's, even infants', clothes are so conspicuously sex-coded. Some children maintain this sexlessness until puberty, when secondary sex characteristics can make identification of physical sex somewhat easier; others learn to produce themselves as visibly sexed subjects before puberty. But Martino

Figure 17. A boy's face in banana curls. Source: Mario Martino, *Emergence* (New York: Crown Publishers, 1977).

presents these pictures as if their meanings were absolutely unambiguous, or rather, as if the ambiguity supports his claims to maleness.

The story Martino tells is of a female subject with a male core gender identity constantly repelled by the femininity forced on it by uncaring family, friends, and colleagues. Marie Martino tried twice to become a nun, attempts that were thwarted by her inability to control her sexual feelings toward the other novitiates.[43] In the autobiography, these feelings are always represented as being heterosexual, never indicative of lesbianism. Once he had completed his first series of surgeries, Martino married the woman he had been living with for nine years, legitimating the relationship as a heterosexual union and thereby reinventing its previous (lesbian) conditions. As a result of his experiences, Martino and his wife, both nurses, created "Labyrinth Services," a counseling and referral service for female-to-male transsexuals.

The book was produced out of this same desire to aid others who share a similar plight. The rhetoric of the text, its insistence on Martino's innate "maleness," stems from this purpose. Martino wants to leave nothing uncertain so that the (transsexual) reader may identify his or her own experience with those represented in the text, and may see in them a similar indisputability. Thus, if Christine Jorgensen's "personal" autobiography attempted to limit its scope by asserting her uniqueness as an individual case, in *Emergence* Mario Martino tries to open out his experience with his readers, to encourage identification or sympathy. This is perhaps one difference between the autobiography of a "public transsexual" (Martino) and the autobiography of a transsexual celebrity (Jorgensen).

The three autobiographies discussed thus far are more or less all closed texts, ones in which the reader is interpellated only as a fixed and passive presence whose function it is to verify the narration offered by the author. Alternate interpretations are at times suggested, but immediately foreclosed by the author. In each text there are totalizing interpretations attached to acts that imply, at least to a critical reader, a number of possible readings. The effect is multiple: on the one hand, for the reader interested in verifying his or her own gender confusions, these narratives provide ample opportunity for identification and mirroring. For a critical reader, on the other hand, the reading process can be confining, especially as the author makes blanket statements concerning sex, gender, and sexuality. The purpose of the narratives is to force the reader to comply with the author's experience, to begin to interpret his or her own life along the same trajectory. To resist this interpretive insistence in the face of these monolithic narratives is exhausting. But the authors want their readers to consider themselves only in relation to the theories of gender, sex, and the body espoused in each text—not in relation to alternative scenarios that might invalidate the author's own experience. Only in this way can the author verify his or her experience, by making gender a universal category and its signification through ordinary daily experiences unilateral and unambiguous.

Martino's *Emergence* presents the best example of this kind of closed narration. At one point in her life Marie Martino became a boarder at the home of a doctor and his family:

> Baby Jenny was about four months old when I moved in. The first time I changed her diapers, I forgot the plastic pants. Learning to make Jenny's Pablum, I must've used half of the box before getting the proper consistency. Between one thing and another, I knew I would not—could not— be a mother. I was not psychologically equipped for motherhood—I lacked the fortitude.[44]

Many mothers can, of course, relate experiences similar to those represented here. Getting the right consistency to Pablum is a learned experience and not something that comes "naturally." However, Martino writes that as Marie she could never be a mother because she was not "psychologically equipped." Yet neither her inability to make Pablum nor her forgetfulness about plastic pants are psychological issues, and they are not questions of fortitude but of experience. Nevertheless, this explanation is never offered and Martino's summary "between one thing and another I *knew*" attempts to foreclose any other interpretation.

Martino relates another incident earlier in the text. Marie decided that she wanted to experience heterosexual intercourse and asked a male friend to "help" her:

> With a short grasping at my ample breasts, Bart had come to full measurement and was now thrusting, trying to penetrate my very tight vagina.
>
> "God, you are a virgin!" Perspiration was coating his body, and he was struggling.
>
> Why had there been no foreplay? It seemed funny now that I'd thought he could teach me a trick or two — why, I could teach him.
>
> No matter how high he elevated my lower torso, he could not penetrate and finally gave up. . . .
>
> That experience sealed my fate. I knew I could never live as a female, that I should never have been born one. It was all some horrendous mistake.[45]

The author suggests the possibility that Bart was simply not doing all he should to help Marie "open up," but then drops this interpretation. Sex, in this encounter, is engineered by the male partner, just as Marie would overpower her female lovers "as a man."[46] Martino's comment that the "experience sealed my fate" reveals the insistence with which this kind of incident is believed to have only one significant meaning, as well as how that significance is accepted as definitive for the subject's future. In both the passage concerning Baby Jenny and the one with Bart, the narrative ends with a statement with the operative term "I knew." The representation of experience that is immediately transformed into knowledge serves to close down interpretive options.

This element of interpretive foreclosure must be considered in relation to the clinical production of transsexualism in the dialogue between doctor and patient. There, the self-proclaimed transsexual must make clear to the doctor that there are no other diagnostic options apart from transsexualism that will make sense in his or her case. The subject's fixation on medically mediated sex change must be close to suicidal, and no other interpretive option can be made available to the doctor, who would then have just cause in denying the desired treatment. The transsexual's success in obtaining genital and hormonal sex change is therefore dependent upon his or her ability to direct the clinician's attention to specific areas of experience where the interpretation is clear and unambiguous. However, little of human experience admits of such unambiguous signification. It is therefore necessary to be able to present the interpretation in an unambiguous and assured manner, such that the interpretation becomes plausible to the doctor. The transsexual must also resist the gaze of the doctor into areas where meanings are not so clear and which might jeopardize his or her chances for sex reassignment. The autobiographies, then, mirror this function as it is forged in the clinical situation.

In the context of these autobiographies, gendered meanings are unilinear and very clear. The possibility that gender might pose a problem itself does not occur to the authors, who believe that all nontranssexual people experience gender as they do, only in the "right" bodies. This idea of the right or intended body has two sources: first, a belief that there is an organizing force to social existence, either Nature or God, and second, a belief that there is a direct connection between the body on the one hand and human behaviors, personality characteristics, and desires on the other hand. (Significantly, the "right bodies" are always considered to be heterosexual ones, in these autobiographies and in the medical literature.) In 1964 and 1968, Robert Stoller termed the latter a "biological force," which he believed to contribute substantially toward the acquisition of gender identity. He now believes this hypothesis to be questionable at best, claiming instead that clinical work overwhelmingly suggests that postnatal, cultural influences are the most significant factors in the formation of gender identity in humans.[47] Mario Martino, however, asserts a full and meaningful connection between physiology and psychology, offering a number of examples to substantiate his claims.

Martino takes whatever verification of his physiological masculinity that he can get: while working at a lab, the technicians practiced determining the 17-ketosteroid count with their own urine. Marie's turned out to be indicative of a 17-year-old male: " 'I knew it: I'm a guy!' Everyone laughed at the idea. And I laughed louder and longer than anyone. This was just one more proof of my maleness. Something very definite to hang onto."[48] Yet, in discussing Marie's use of a dildo for intercourse with her lover, Martino comments that while it is a "venerable instrument used for intercourse," he "was unhappy resorting to this device." He writes that the experience "deepened my determination that my own destiny *was not to be set by biological patterns.*"[49] And, in another twist, after reading Christine Jorgensen's autobiography, Marie considered the idea of intersexuality as it applied to herself:

> I toyed with the thought that I was an individual belonging to the highest degree of intersexuality, only my case was the reverse of Christine's since she had begun life as a boy. Then I was *not* too different! And there were tens of thousands all over the world with varying degrees of this same intersexuality.[50]

Martino's shifting reliance on the idea of biology as the basis of his transsexualism suggests a desire to have it both ways. He wants to defend the desire to change sex with the rhetoric of physiological intersexuality; he also wants to demand the construction of male sex organs. To have both, he needs to use biology and to repudiate it.

In the end, Mario Martino suggests a physiological rationale for transsexualism. While he acknowledges that "transsexuality . . . remains a rare and mystifying occurrence, its causal range as vast as the experience of life itself," he states:

> Parents often suffer guilt, wondering as to their own responsibility in this "difference." But, firm in their belief that the occurrence is inborn, many authorities discount parental practices as a factor. My own strongly held opinion is that *father and mother are not to be blamed*. We have only to look around at the number of less-than-perfect babies born every day to realize that sex disorientation is as possible, say, as a cleft palate, clubfoot, or other abnormality.[51]

None of the physical deformities he mentions, of course, entail the kind of cultural dimension apparent in the transsexual phenomenon. The equivalence Martino suggests represents his own desire to make transsexualism *like any other physical difference*, to normalize it within the recognizable limits of physiological sex.

Nancy Hunt's *Mirror Image*, unlike the autobiographies discussed above, makes no overt claims about physiology as the cause of her transsexualism. Because of this, the text aptly represents the way a story about gender—that is, the subject's psychological orientation as a sex—can depend upon the idea of an inborn physiological tendency without really stating it as such. Hunt presents the classic theories concerning transsexualism and gender identity early in the autobiography, finishing them off with the following comment: "It wasn't merely that I had cried more easily or hated fighting or thrown a ball like a girl, though these were all facts. It was a deeper difference. I wasn't like them [his male peers], and they sensed it, smelled it, and in consequence always kept me at a distance, as if I were a threat to them, as if I had been marked for punishment by the gods."[52] Poetic description of this sort pervades *Mirror Image* (as it does Jan Morris's *Conundrum*, discussed below), and serves to present only vague ideas about the causes of transsexualism. It is clear by the end of the autobiography that Hunt really doesn't care what the causes of transsexualism might be—in her opinion, "By right of suffering and endurance and the Circuit Court of Cook County, I am Nancy."[53]

Yet the autobiography does present a theoretical position about transsexualism as a disorder of gender identity, perhaps best exemplified by this statement: "Women do differ from men, quite apart from anatomy. And I always sensed which one I was—again, quite apart from anatomy. I was not a man. I was a woman. And if my anatomy did not confirm this classification, then in the final event it was going to be easier to change my anatomy than to change myself." [54] This classic statement about transsexualism was not available to either Christine Jorgensen or Roberta Cowell, and (for whatever reason) was not used by Mario Martino. It is a statement that wholeheartedly addresses the gender theories, discounting any reliance on the notion that physiological intersexuality could be the origin of transsexualism. The contours of Hunt's story—the masculine pursuits at prep school and Yale, in the army, and as a reporter for the *Chicago Tribune* are represented as "masking" the author's true feminine interior—conform to this story of an internal gender identity finally allowed authentic expression as a woman. [55]

Hunt had no illusions about her original anatomical sex: "I knew well enough that I was not a girl—I had only to look at what my body had become: five feet ten inches tall, skinny as a fence post, muscles hard, beard growing, hair sprouting on chest and stomach. Secret dreams aside, I was locked in an undoubtedly male body, and like most adolescent male bodies it was bubbling with hormones and potent as a cocked pistol." [56] Throughout the text, she discusses her desire to be a woman as a psychosocial issue, and details her growing experiences as a woman with comments like the following: "After all the scientific explanations—whether physical or psychological, there remains the inexplicable fact that the male transsexual feels altogether more comfortable as a woman in a woman's world." [57]

Yet physiological allusions appear in *Mirror Image*. In discussing her children (of which she is the father), Hunt writes: "Until I became a parent, I assumed that sex-typed behavior is acquired, but my own children convinced me that it arises spontaneously. Certainly I did not teach manliness to my son; he simply exuded it from infancy. Similarly my daughters acquired femaleness from within themselves. I marveled at their innate femininity, their grace, the delicacy of their play." [58] Later, when Hunt began to take estrogenic hormones, he claims to have begun feeling the effects on the evening after the first injection: "Already the estrogens were affecting me physically. I could feel my genitalia shrinking in a way men commonly experience when they swim in cold water." [59] This, of course, was far too soon to feel any effects from hormonal treatment. On the following page, Hunt writes, "My shoulders, which once sloped steeply down from the neck, have assumed a feminine squareness; bra and shoulder-bag straps no longer slide off." [60]

These last two quotes are interesting insofar as they exemplify the transsexual's fantasy of hormonal power: the hormones work immediately, they change the shape of the entire body. Perhaps even more interesting is the idea that *square* shoulders are feminine; Hunt's utilitarian presentation of square-shouldered femininity (bra straps and shoulder bags don't fall off) belies the historicity of this concept. In the nineteenth century, of course, it was the sloping shoulder that signaled femininity, and at the time that feature was believed to be the result of ovarian influence.

At one point Hunt mentions a conflict between her desire to become a woman and the sense that she still needed to "make her mark as a man," and this incident reveals the extent to which making a mark as a woman remained, for her, on a vastly different scale than making one's mark as a man. Hunt had been asked to become the Tribune "man in the Middle East." He did not want to go, but mused, "I was then forty-five. If I was ever going to make my mark as a man, it must be now." However, "I was more concerned with making my mark as a woman. Ellen [his second wife] and I were working on a fall suit for me: a rusty-orange plaid skirt with box pleats in front and a matching long-sleeved jacket. It was a difficult project, far beyond my own skills as a seamstress. It lay on top of the dining room sideboard, the pieces cut out but still pinned to the pattern paper. My instinct was to remain in paradise and finish my suit, but sensibly I knew that I must go to the Middle East. . . ."[61] The difference in scale here is startling. More significant, perhaps, is the way in which making a mark as a woman is presented in relation to fashion and fashioning. Hunt adheres to all the sex stereotypes of contemporary culture in her belief that to make oneself a woman is to engineer the perfect presence (or fashion the right effect), while to make one's mark as a man is to "do the right thing."

Canary: The Story of a Transsexual is reminiscent of Christine Jorgensen's autobiography, as well as Nancy Hunt's.[62] The narrative concerns Canary Conn's experiences as an "effeminate" and (as an adult) underdeveloped male (Daniel O'Connor) who grew up in the 1950s and 1960s, tried futilely to prove his masculinity throughout his adolescence, became a teenage rock music idol, married his girlfriend when she became pregnant, and eventually succeeded in obtaining sex change surgery at the age of twenty-three. The similarity to Christine Jorgensen rests largely in Conn's emphasis on other people's recognition of her effeminacy as Danny and her insistence that her male genitals were underdeveloped. These themes represent the physiological rationale that runs through the text. The autobiography is similar to Hunt's Mirror Image because of Conn's reliance on the theory of "masculinity as a mask" to explain anything that Danny did that was stereotypically masculine.

Interestingly, Canary Conn frames her account with a "medical" discussion of transsexualism: the first chapter delineates the outlines of gender identity theory, while at the end of the book she presents the possible biological aspects of the disorder. Thus, while in the first chapter she comments that "a transsexual is a person who is born one sex but who has a lifelong identity with the opposite sex. It's a problem of gender identity—genitals don't seem to match up with feelings inside," in the penultimate chapter she writes:

Although there are many different factors involved, there are also biological bases for transsexualism. Because the fetus begins as a sort of tissue which is basically feminine, there are many possible ways that the necessary male hormones which differentiate the fetus might not be present at the time they are needed, or that unneeded male hormones are added to a fetus which is female by chromosomal makeup.[63]

She goes on to make the following claim, directly in opposition to the theories of gender identity that grew out of the protocols developed by Money and colleagues in the 1950s:

"In order to illustrate," I said, "Let me ask you a question. If you, as a male, had become involved in an accident as an infant and your genitals were severed, your parents might have consulted with Dr. Lopez, or any one of the other doctors here, and decided to perform a sex change operation on you early in your life. They would then treat you as a normal female and rear you as one. How do you think you would feel? Would you feel like a boy or a girl?"

"Well—uh—that is—well, I'd feel like a boy of course. I mean, I'd have to." The audience laughed, and the man sat down suddenly.

"It stands to reason," I said, "that you would, indeed, feel as though something were wrong, at the very least. Your emotions, your physical makeup, even your sex drive toward what would be the opposite sex would all be important factors leading you to believe you were somehow in the wrong situation. . . . It's my theory that just such an accident happened to girls like myself—that we were somehow mutated in our prenatal development by drugs, diseases, etc."[64]

Conn's comments in this chapter seem to nullify her earlier claims about transsexualism as a gender identity disorder. However, in the context of these other autobiographies, all of which make some gesture toward a physiological basis for transsexualism, this position makes some sense. Transsexualism is perceived to be a gender identity disorder that (probably) has a physiological cause. What is interesting is the radical difference between this stand and that taken by Money and the Hampsons in their research on intersexuality in the 1950s, where they argued for the discontinuity between biological sex identity and a gender orientation that develops as a result of the original assignment of sex and social cues from parents and peers.[65]

It is in Jan Morris's autobiography, Conundrum, that we see the idea of transsexualism as a disorder of gender identity spun out in dazzling detail. Morris presents gender as the foremost identity of the subject, more important than sexual anatomy because it is closer to the spiritual. Morris's autobiography is the most consistently gender-oriented because in it there is almost no mention at all of physiology as a probable cause of transsexualism. Thus, while in the final chapter she states that "the transsexual urge, at least as far as I have experienced it, [is] far more than a social compulsion, but biological, imaginative, and essentially spiritual too," she never suggests elsewhere that she believes the cause of transsexualism to be rooted in the physiology of the body. Indeed, she writes, "That my conundrum actually emanated from my sexual organs did not cross my mind then [in childhood], and seems unlikely to me even now." [66]

Morris is no textbook case, however: her stint in the army, her marriage and five children, her success in the "masculine" pursuit of journalism—all of these testify to a personal history that deviates from the "official story" of total failure as a male subject. She maintains that she understood that she was "different" from an early age, that she knew at the age of three that she "had been born into the wrong body, and should really be a girl," but that she was determined to live life as a man until it became unbearable. [67] She regards her participation in all the traditional masculine activities as that of an outsider, invited in for a moment but never really accepted as "one of the boys." [68] Morris presents her decision to change sex as a decision not to continue with a false life.

Conundrum is a frustrating book to read, if only because it says so little with so many words. As a professional writer, Morris has a facility with language that makes her discourse textually more interesting as well as rhetorically more manipulative. Morris's prose is overladen with expansive descriptions, in the course of which she philosophizes on the enigma of identity and its relation to sex. For Morris, the desire to change sex was connected to the idea that the self should be unified, having only one identity and representing that identity without rupture or discontinuity:

In any case, I myself see the conundrum in another perspective, for I believe it to have some higher origin or meaning. I equate it with the idea of soul, or self, and I think of it not just as a sexual enigma, but as a quest for unity.

[Gender] is the essentialness of oneself, the psyche, the fragment of unity.

I was born with the wrong body, being feminine by gender but male by sex, and I could achieve completeness only when the one was adjusted to the other.

All I wanted was liberation, or reconciliation—to live as myself, to clothe myself in a more proper body, and achieve Identity at last.

I had reached Identity. [69]

Morris prefers the mystical to the material, and because of this, her discussion of transsexualism tends toward the indistinct. Nevertheless, some statements are made clearly enough: "I regarded sex merely as the tool of gender."[70] The vagueness of Morris's mystical spiritualism and the bluntness of her comments about gender are both the result of her refusal to think deeply about the matter: "During my years of torment, I generally found it safer . . . to approach my problem existentially, and to assume that it was altogether of itself, *sans* cause, *sans* meaning."[71] In effect, she has given herself license to say anything she wants about the matter. What she chooses to say is deeply indebted to the idea that psychology is the primary constituent of the self—thus sex can be a "tool of gender."

Besides Christine Jorgensen, Renée Richards is perhaps the most famous transsexual in the United States. She is famous largely because she fought the Women's Tennis Association in legal court in order to be allowed to play at WTA-sanctioned events as a woman. Otherwise, she might have remained as obscure as most transsexuals who attempt to "fade into the woodwork" of traditionally gendered society. Her autobiography, published in 1983, is a "play-by-play" account of her life as Richard Raskind—successful ophthalmologist, amateur tennis player, and transvestite—and her transformation into Renée—her alter ego or "feminine persona," whose subjectivity Raskind inhabited when dressed as a woman.

In a certain sense, there is much to recommend Richards's autobiography to the general reader—it is full of descriptive detail, juicy sex scenes, and hot sports cars, and contains little overt discussion of medical theory or specific ideas about the transsexual condition. There is, however, a lot of ad hoc psychologizing that Richards undoubtedly learned as his mother's son: Richards's mother was a psychiatrist and analyst. (Incidentally, this mother—as well as an older sister—are fingered as the "causes" of Richards's transsexual tendencies.) Richards provides a largely psychological narrative of her original inclinations to cross-dress and its development into transsexualism, and while her story does not coincide with all the aspects of the officially sanctioned medical history of transsexuality (she enjoyed too much heterosexual sex as Dick to be convincing as a failed man), it is a story largely about gender identifications gone awry. In this sense, *Second Serve: The Renée Richards Story* is an account aligned with the current medical conceptualization of transsexualism.

How interesting, then, to find the following comment at the beginning of the second chapter of the book (the first is dedicated to the story of Dick Raskind's birth, a harrowing tale of maternal courage as well as stubbornness, told with the edge of bitterness that accompanies all of Richards's recollections of her maternal parent):

Another reason why [my childhood] remembrances are unsettling is that they seem so contrived. If I sat down to write a case history of an imaginary transsexual, I could not come up with a more provocative set of circumstances than that of my childhood. *The peculiar thing about this is that the cause of transsexualism may someday be proven to be biochemical.* If this happens, I can only conclude that fate has a sense of humor because my early life is strewn with unsubtle touches that beg to be seen as reasons for my sexual confusion. *If they aren't the true cause they ought to be.*[72]

The "unsubtle touches" referred to here include enforced cross-dressing, early morning closeness to the mother's body, competition with a tomboy sister, an absent and ineffectual father, an early association between voluntary cross-dressing and the lessening of anxiety, and the creation of an alternate female persona (Renée) who embodies all the femininity Dick excludes from his own behavior. In many ways, Richards's account presents her as a classic *transvestite* who becomes convinced that sex change was the only way to live out the contradictions of Dick's "sexual confusion."[73]

Richards's suggestion that transsexualism may well in the future be found to have a "biochemical" basis is the only reference to the possibility of a physiological cause of transsexualism in her book. Other than this brief mention, she sticks to the psychological account. There are clues in the text, however, that this account has been constructed specifically in relation to "official" medical discourses concerning transsexual etiology. For example, Richards relates her initial discussion (as Dick) with Harry Benjamin as follows:

As [Dr. Benjamin] listened to me reviewing my history, he tilted his head first one way and then another, sometimes nodding agreeably. Occasionally, when I would grope for words, he would supply them so casually that I didn't notice at first. *Then I began to realize that this old man really did understand, so much so that he could probably have told the story without my help.* The childish exploits, the futile years of psychotherapy, the driving compulsion, the skulking around—all these constituted a familiar refrain that accompanied his daily work. He listened intelligently, and he understood almost as well as I did.[74]

Read in light of Sandy Stone's comment that transsexuals were presenting "classic Benjaminian" symptoms to their clinicians *because* they had been reading Benjamin's *The Transsexual Phenomenon*, Richards's account of Dick's visit to the great doctor's office becomes significant in a way clearly unintended by the author. Benjamin's "knowledge" of Dick's story—his ability to suggest words when Dick stumbled—demonstrates his ability to construct (or at least facilitate the construction of) the self-representations of his clients, who in going to see him usually knew what they wanted and what the doctor had the power to offer (hormone treatments and access to surgical sex change).[75]

Richards's narrative, like Morris's, falls mostly within the contemporary understanding of gender as a psychological construct disconnected from physiology. Few transsexual autobiographers adhere fully to the theories of transsexualism currently offered by clinicians: as we saw in the previous chapter, the American Psychiatric Association considers transsexualism to be a disorder of gender identity that has no physiological symptoms whatsoever.[76] The insistence of most of these autobiographers that transsexualism has its origin in the physiology of the body, then, represents a disjunction between the beliefs of transsexual autobiographers and those of the psychiatrists who refer transsexual subjects for surgery. To understand this disjunction fully, we would have to examine in detail the relation between psychiatry and the other medical specialties involved in the treatment of transsexualism, a task too large for the discussion here. What this disjunction suggests in terms of the transsexual population, however, is that the idea of a gender identity fully divorced from the body and its signification of sex is only rarely accepted by transsexual subjects.[77] For if gender was thought to float entirely apart from the semiotics of physical sex, sex reassignment surgery would be unnecessary. The fact that transsexuals request sex reassignment on the basis of cross-sex gender identity demonstrates the extent to which gender is thought to bear on the body.

The transsexuals' stories about gender identity are never seamless or completely convincing — in Jan Morris's case, the assertions of cross-sex gender identity can only be offered with mystical references and vague discussions about sexless sexuality.[78] What is most consistent in transsexuals' self-representations is the oft-repeated insistence that there must be something physical, measurable, materially detectable that motivates and justifies the desire to change sex. Because of this, the transsexual autobiographers feel sure that the body he or she achieves through sex reassignment is his or her "real body," the one he or she was meant to have, the one denied by some cruel trick of Nature or God.

Understandably, then, in only one of the autobiographies discussed above are the technologies of sex change presented as fundamental to the transsexual phenomenon. To think of sex conversion technologies as fundamental to transsexualism would be to acknowledge the tremendous physical transformation involved, and to acknowledge as well the impulse of the human body to resist such change. Instead, in most of the autobiographies the technologies of sex change are presented as the means to an end, the important but theoretically inconsequential treatments through which the transsexual subject may inhabit a body more appropriate to his or her felt gender identity. Thus, if transsexual subjects depend upon a network of technologies essential for their transformation into the other sex, they also depend upon an official effacement of the significance of those technologies to their very existence. The effect this has on the autobiographies is palpable, since the discussions of the mechanics of sex change invariably reveal tensions: how can a subject truly be the other sex if such extensive technological intervention is necessary to get him or her there?

In *Emergence*, Mario Martino documents in minute detail his two surgical attempts at phalloplasty. In another autobiography, *The Man-Maid Doll*, Patricia Morgan offers detailed comments about her surgeries to construct female genitalia from male. Canary Conn discusses the problems she faced during recovery at a clinic in Tijuana. Nancy Hunt, in a move uncharacteristic of the transsexual autobiographer, opens *Mirror Image* with a detailed discussion of the surgical theater and surgical procedure of male-to-female genital sex change. Later in her autobiography, Hunt describes her own painful recovery from a first, unsuccessful vaginoplasty. And Renée Richards describes the surgical procedure in detail in *Second Serve*, even focusing on the crucial role of the anesthesiologist, and discusses as well the painful first few days of postoperative recovery. These authors vividly portray their surgical experiences as painful and psychologically draining, thereby offering the reader information about the physical transformation and psychic consequences of genital plastic surgery. The effect of these passages is to bring the reader's attention to the immediate physicality of the procedures, and to undermine the text's primary argument that the subject was really meant to be the sex which he or she must be surgically fashioned into. This undermining occurs as the reader becomes aware of the level of pain incurred through the surgical procedures, which, in these narratives, is quite strikingly represented. The existence of representations of this intense pain serves to break up or unsettle the assured narrative confidence in the story of gender.

Mario Martino's description of then contemporary phalloplastic technique comprises a litany of unsuccessful practices that is, nevertheless, concluded by these comments: "These drawbacks, serious as they are, are minor when compared to the fulfillment phalloplasty brings. Its greatest value is the psychological uplift, and this psychological stimulation can heighten the physical excitement and pleasure. The neophallus is also, of course, a safeguard against exposure."[79] This statement comes after describing a "neophallus" that, while it may be "cosmetically good," will also be subject to "accidents with zippers or radiators" (because it lacks feeling), that is either permanently soft or always erect, and that probably will not be able to carry urine. In addition, phalloplasty "cannot produce an organ rich in the sexual feeling of the natural one."[80] This argument in favor of an operation with "serious technical drawbacks," but with immense "psychological benefits," is exactly that made by the medical team of Goin and Goin in their presentation of augmentation mammaplasty (discussed in chapter 2).[81]

After describing the possibilities for phalloplasty in general, Martino presents his own experiences. A surgeon with experience in phalloplasty on men injured in battle offered to operate on Martino. In a series of two operations, a penis-like tube-within-a-tube was constructed on his thigh (this is a variant of the famous tube pedicle pioneered by Harold Gillies during World War I). Martino writes that "the tube resembled a suitcase handle." The surgery was painful, but asking himself if it was "truly worth the male picture I'd fancied for myself?" he answered, "Yes, yes! If the surgery worked it would be the realization of a dream." This first attempt ended in infection. The doctor attempted to repair the damaged pedicle flap and was willing to continue the experiment, but Martino refused since the "underpart of the tube was eaten completely through and had formed a ridge in the middle. The tube was shrivelling, curling in on itself like a small snail. Instead of the handsome phallus I had expected to grow on my thigh for later relocation, I had a disintegrating suitcase handle." He comments that "I had come out of all this pain, expense, and time with a scarred thigh and not an inch of progress toward a phallus."[82]

Martino presents the most unsettling representation of the physical and psychological effects of phalloplastic surgery as he describes his second, "mostly successful," attempt to make a penis. The skin grafts were again "excruciatingly painful." But as he returned home from the hospital and made a side trip to visit a friend, Martino positioned his new penis up against his abdomen. He comments that "the blood supply was not sufficient to reach the tip of the penis, for within the week after the trip that area turned dark, signifying death of the tissue." The remedy for this included warm baths, but even these "would not save most of the head from turning black and foul-smelling. So, nightly, I sat in the tub and, very slowly, cut away the dead tissue."[83] This horrifying image of Martino sitting in a bathtub cutting away the head of his penis so that its putrid death will not jeopardize the health of the rest of the organ is only partially alleviated by his humorous comment "Talk about castration complex!" The passage is a reminder that the construction of a penis from nongenital flesh is a partial, and contingent, event. Martino ends up with "a respectable phallus—three-fourths perfect." Again, the painfulness of its creation is deferred by his final comments which emphasize the psychological benefits of the new organ:

> Now, I can tell myself, there is a new part of me—a part I have always conceived of myself possessing. It completes outwardly a picture of myself which I have always carried in my head. By day, whether working, driving, gardening, or relaxing, I sense always the presence of this outward acknowledgment of my maleness. And, by night, my new organ—

for all its being less than perfect—is still deeply stimulating to both me and my mate, both psychologically and physically.[84]

For Martino, phalloplasty offers the female-to-male transsexual a real organ: "Whatever the technique employed, no longer must a transsexual use a *replica* at the most intimate of times."[85] The idea that the neophallus might be a replica is never considered; the penis made from the flesh of the thigh or abdomen is perceived to be the real thing, regardless of its inability to urinate or to become erect naturally. What is important is that it is of the body. Nevertheless, Martino recognizes that many female-to-male transsexuals "do not choose to have phalloplasty" due to the problems in procedure and outcome. He writes,

> They find that, after about six months on male hormones, the clitoris has usually grown too large to be contained within the protective lips or labia and now resembles a miniature penis. Resting on the outside of the labia, the clitoris is very quickly stimulated and even the feel of the dildo is sexually exciting: Any movement reminds the patient that *he has a semblance of the male organ.* So equipped and stimulated, the female-to-male transsexual realizes to some degree *the satisfaction of being male* and achieving climax. And even the artificial penetration of his mate adds to his heightened sexual drive.
>
> Many patients are very nearly content with such an arrangement. . . . The combination of enlarged clitoris and dildoe [sic] or phalloplasty seems to us *an approximation of the normal male's response.*[86]

This passage suggests that both dildos and penises constructed through phalloplastic surgery are replicas, since they can only approximate the physiology of a normal male. The passage also suggests that part of the pleasure of the transsexual man is the reminder that he is a man. Martino points out that either a dildo or neophallus can achieve this realization, although a dildo will only do so during sexual intercourse. As the passage cited previously suggests, since his phalloplasty Martino himself can experience the pleasure of this recognition twenty-four hours a day. This recognition, however, came at tremendous physical (and financial) cost.

If the destabilizing effect of the representations of physical pain and postoperative difficulties in Mario Martino's autobiography are immediately recovered by his assertions of the psychological benefits of phalloplasty, Patricia Morgan's portrayal of the corollary operations for the male-to-female transsexual are not so easily recuperated. This may be a result of the general outlines of her story, which represents her as a more marginal subject and therefore as being less subject to a normalizing narrative. Morgan portrays herself as a poor, effeminate, uneducated boy who always felt himself to be a girl and who had difficulty making a living once he left his mother's home. A male prostitute, he sought surgery partially as a way to have a more secure source of income: "[W]hen I found out that men wanted to buy my body as a woman, I said to myself, Wow! This could be even more prosperous and less hectic than running around seeking out fags."[87] After he found out about "the operation" from some other transvestite prostitutes, he began to save money. With introductions arranged by Harry Benjamin, he went to California for the surgery.

After the first surgery, Morgan writes that "I was a woman at last. But at the moment, I was just a glob of aching flesh." She continues: "Three days later, Dr. Belt returned to change my bandages. I was swathed from my waist through my crotch and around the hips. It was like being enclosed in a giant diaper. Dr. Belt took the scissors and started cutting the bandages away, throwing them on a tray on the adjoining bed. I just about got sick to my stomach at the sight and smell of all the blood and pus."[88] This first operation only removed Patricia's penis and placed her testicles in her abdomen.[89] After the operation to construct a vagina, the doctor placed a plastic form inside the new organ in order to keep it from closing:

> I just about went through the headboard when Dr. Belt and his son forced the new mole into me. I couldn't believe the pain. I grabbed the bars on the bed and gritted my teeth. The mole was tremendous. It was about nine inches long, but it felt like nine feet. They kept pushing it up and up and up inside my body. After about fifteen minutes, they finally got it in. But my body kept wanting to force it out again.
>
> I was in such pain that the nurse came in right away and gave me a shot to knock me out. I was just going under as Dr. Belt and his son started sewing the mole into my vagina.[90]

Morgan continues with the comment that for the next two weeks, the "pain remained unbearable." After being released and making another trip back to the doctor to have another mole sewn into her vagina, "I went home again and for days I was bleeding terribly." She adds that "the pain did not subside."[91]

Shortly after the second operation, while she still had a mole inside her vagina (although not one that was sewn in), Patricia Morgan was raped by a client of her prostitute roommate. She took the mole out so that the man would not discover her condition and would think that she was menstruating. Bleeding profusely, she put the mole back inside her and "tried to recover." A few days later, she and her roommate were arrested for prostitution, but she was bleeding so badly that she spent her thirty days in the prison hospital. After she got out, and subsequently underwent a third operation for an infection in her urethra, she finally engaged in voluntary sexual intercourse, during which she "bled like a red river. The bed was covered with my blood because I was still tender inside from the operation." Even after she returned to the East Coast, she "still wasn't fully recovered. There were days when I was perfectly all right and others when I ached all over."[92]

These vivid representations of genital plastic surgery are unique in the genre. For example, Christine Jorgensen writes that her penectomy "was not such a major work of surgery as it may imply. . . . Within a few days, I was resting well and had experienced little discomfort."[93] In describing her third surgical procedure, the vaginoplasty performed in the United States almost two years after her first operations in Denmark and against the clinical stance taken by her doctors in their 1953 article in the *Journal of the American Medical Association*, Jorgensen writes that the "extremely complicated operation took seven hours to perform. With skin grafts taken from the upper thighs, plastic surgery constructed a vaginal canal and external female genitalia. It was a completely successful procedure." The only problem she records were the facial burns she received due to the unforeseen need to use ether at the end of the lengthy operation.[94] While it is conceivable that her surgeries were less painful than Patricia Morgan's, and most probably more successful than Mario Martino's, all skin graft procedures entail some significant amount of pain. By not representing that pain, Jorgensen was able to deflect attention away from the actual surgical techniques that made her transformation into a woman possible; to treat them, in other words, as insignificant to the fact of her present existence as a woman.[95]

In an original and unexpected rhetorical move, Nancy Hunt begins *Mirror Image* with a description of the University of Virginia Medical Center, moving from outside to inside and finally to the operating room where "Elizabeth Johnson" is to undergo a "vaginal construction" that morning. Casually mentioning that she herself had undergone the same procedure six months before, Hunt describes the procedure, the patient's probable feelings, the attitudes of plastic surgeons, and finally, the surgery itself. From this she moves into a discussion of the possible causes of transsexualism and the reasons why psychotherapy generally fails to "cure" transsexuals of their compulsion to be the other sex ("No woman would abandon her psychological gender merely to accommodate herself to the circumstances of a biological accident. Certainly I would not. Let the biological accident be corrected, not me").[96]

This pleasant (albeit stark) introduction to transsexualism and surgical sex change does not square altogether with Hunt's own experience, which is recounted toward the end of the text. Hunt was startled by the results of her first surgical procedure (probably the castration and fashioning of the labia out of scrotal tissue; Hunt's penis would still be present): "Here was not classic mold of womanly beauty but rather a tattered mixture of the old and the new, the male and the female, the ugly and the beautiful. I was suspended halfway between two surgical procedures, neither man nor woman. I had not prepared myself for that spectacle, and I found it shocking."[97] Long after the second procedure, Hunt continued to feel pain and was told by a rather brusque gynecologist that her vagina would not be capable of heterosexual intercourse: it was too small and entered at the "wrong angle."[98] The diagnosis of the original surgical team was that there had been some stenosis, or shrinkage, during healing. Indeed, as Hunt reported her doctor saying, "When we got in there, we found a sort of pocket at the apex [of the vagina] that had been sealed off by the infection. We opened it up and did a skin graft, and you've got almost the full length of the original vagina." Another doctor was more graphic: " 'We cut in there,' he said, 'and this stuff like pus came spurting out.' " Hunt quotes from the surgeon's report: "Inspection was undertaken which revealed midline stenosis of the labia and absence of vaginal vault. The midline was sharply divided and as the stenotic vault was opened a pocket containing greenish somewhat grumous material was entered."[99]

In Canary Conn's account, her difficulties during and after her operations had to do with the ineptness of the hospital staff at the Tijuana clinic and their disdain for transsexuals. The problems she encountered demonstrate the necessity of attentive postoperative care, given the extent of the surgical intervention in sex conversion operations. After the first procedure, Conn's catheter was improperly inserted and she developed an addiction to the pain-killing drugs. The real problems came with the second procedure, which, due to Conn's financial situation, took place about two years after the first one. She reports her postoperative pain to have been excruciating, and that she did not receive medicine when she needed it. She continued to bleed, and the nursing staff did not change her sheets. Finally, bleeding profusely and fearful that no one would answer her cries, Conn recounts that she took a pair of scissors to attempt suicide. She blacked out before she was able to do anything, however, and the doctor arrived just in time to stop her bleeding.[100]

While Conn's experiences are told in a manner to heighten their dramatic impact, they exemplify some of the most significant issues in hospital social relations raised by transsexualism and sex conversion surgery. Surgical sex change is a costly and complicated procedure, necessitating intensive nursing care and the services of a team of attending physicians (surgeon, urologist, gynecologist, anesthesiologist, endocrinologist). While many writers speak of the generous and kind behavior of the staff that attended them, others like Canary Conn have less pleasant experiences. The postoperative care of the transsexual patient is part of the technology of sex conversion, and like the surgery itself, its quality and effect depend upon the human subjects who practice it. The success of the surgical procedure is, in some part, dependent on the kind of care the patient receives *after* the operation is completed. Conn's autobiography, with its account of inadequate and hostile nursing care, points out that the technologies of sex change are not limited to hormonal treatments and the specific operative procedures of genital plastic surgery; they include as well the material practices of postoperative care, much of which is undertaken by the hospital or clinic nursing staff.

For Renée Richards, the pain of postsurgical recovery was a fit ending to her life as Dick Raskind: "It [the pain] was bad, but I asked for it, embraced it. . . . it showed me that I was right in becoming Renée. If ever there was an opportunity for regret it came when I was quaking in the recovery room, yet that opportunity was not seized. At that moment I realized that I would rather have died in the attempt than live any longer in a nightmare of duality." [101] Richards provides details of the surgery and her recuperation, noting particularly the "dilator" necessary to maintain vaginal health in the absence of penile-vaginal intercourse.[102] Her narration in this section of the book is largely matter-of-fact, perhaps a consequence of her own training as a physician. At the end of this section, she writes, "By the end of my month's leave I was pretty well healed." [103] Overall, while the presentation of surgery is graphic enough in Richard's account, its significance to the rest of her story is downplayed. Surgical sex change is an experience to be gotten through, a means to an end, the techne of existence but not the stuff of it.

The discontinuity between the story of surgical sex change and the story of already being the other sex, like the discontinuity between the story of physiological intersexuality and that of gender, undermines the main assertions concerning the self as the other sex that transsexual autobiographers make and seek to maintain in these texts. Reading with attention to these discontinuities demonstrates that the statements made and supported by transsexual autobiographers concerning the primacy of gender and the innateness of the desire to become the other sex cover over other destabilizing narratives of self-construction. Reading for the subversions of technology, in other words, allows us to see how the normalizing narratives of gender work to obscure the radical discontinuities at the heart of the transsexual phenomenon.

This is not to suggest that transsexuals' accounts of their own experiences are wrong, or flawed; rather, it is to suggest that representations of transsexual experience are constructed within the parameters of a humanism that pervasively denies the existence of disruptive accounts of sex and sexuality. Feeling as if one is, truly, the other sex—all material evidence to the contrary—has been codified as a normalized sensibility within the theory of gender identity; it is no longer a culturally unintelligible narrative of subjectivity. Once we read for the discontinuities that the attention to technology and physiology affords, however, that intelligibility is compromised and can no longer sustain the story of gender as it proliferates in contemporary medical discourse and the society at large. Gender "deconstructs" because it can be shown to depend upon a relation to the body that it excludes definitionally.

Those of us who are not transsexuals may wonder what it is like to feel oneself "in the wrong body." These autobiographies reveal what it is like to want another body, understood as the other body, as a result of the subject's displacement of a radical abjection onto the body. The body, with its original sex, becomes abject through the inability of the transsexual subject to make that body signify appropriately within accepted gender codes. Reengineering the body is one way to avoid the sense of profound "outsiderness" expressed by all the transsexual autobiographers discussed above; becoming the other sex forces the body to signify according to traditional gender codes, enforcing cultural laws on the body's physiology. For these autobiographers, "sex change" makes their bodies (and experiences) intelligible at last.

It is this very intelligibility that is a problem for those who think critically about transsexualism. Sandy Stone, as discussed above, understands this intelligibility to constrain the possibility of telling the truth about transsexual experience. Yet the "true story" of transsexualism is already out, insofar as it is already at work in these autobiographies, helping to consolidate subjectivities around specifically marked parameters of behavior and narration. The official autobiography of the transsexual subject is part of the "true story" of transsexualism; without these texts we would not have the phenomenon that we have today, because within their narratives live the most important assertions—as well as the most destabilizing discontinuities—within which transsexual subjectivity is constituted. To understand transsexualism, we do not need to alleviate the suppression of an authentic story (as Sandy Stone suggests); rather, we need an analysis of the suppressive mechanisms that have constituted and continue to constitute the transsexual phenomenon in the twentieth century. And once we turn away from "gender" as the causal mechanism of transsexualism, we can recognize it as an authorizing narrative that works to ward off the disruptive antihumanism of technological self-construction.

6

SEMIOTICS OF SEX, GENDER,

AND THE BODY

Feminist theory has recently been engaged in a wide-ranging discussion concerning the relationship between "sex" and "gender" as the primary analytic categories of feminist scholarship and political practice. One of the most influential texts in this debate is Judith Butler's *Gender Trouble: Feminism and the Subversion of Identity*, a book that also circulates within Foucauldian, psychoanalytic, and deconstructionist debates concerning the constitution of the subject and the category of identity. Butler's investment in the Foucauldian paradigm has more to do with the relation of discourse to the construction of subjectivity (she argues that there is no subject "before" discourse or outside the law) than with epistemic shifts or the emergence of new subjectivities within discursive formations. In other words, Butler is interested in the philosophical and linguistic significance of Foucault's claims concerning the circulation of juridical power and the idea of the subject as enabled into being by that power. She does not seem to be as interested in the "historical Foucault."[1]

Thomas Laqueur evinces precisely the opposite tendency in his book *Making Sex: Body and Gender from the Greeks to Freud*, as he traces historical shifts in perception of "sex" from a one-sex model of the body (an ancient and early modern view) to a two-sex model (a post-Enlightenment conception), arguing that political exigencies motivated this change in scientific perception (rather than any specific scientific discovery concerning the anatomy or physiology of sex). For Laqueur, "sex" (anatomical or physiological sexual difference) is always an effect of a society's gender arrangements. Gender, as the social structure designating the proper place of subjects along an axis of differentiation, determines perceptions of the body as sexed—determines, indeed, what counts as "sex."[2] While Laqueur makes this argument through an analysis of the history of the one-sex model of the body and its transformation into a two-sex model over the course of centuries, Butler makes a similar argument in a deconstructive mode: "sex," she argues, cannot be thought of as prior to gender if gender is the law that is necessary in order to think "sex" at all. In this analysis, "sex as nature" is only the naturalized a priori that gender projects as its requisite antecedent.

Transsexualism as a phenomenon begs the question of the relation between sex and gender, and because of this I have examined the extent to which the emergence of transsexuality has contributed to—indeed produced—a dynamic relation between the two terms. To do so, I have tried to work the "seam" between a primarily historical analysis and a primarily theoretical one. The result is a text that "tells a story" about historical change, as well as a text that makes certain kinds of claims about words and their meanings. This is what I take to be the strength of the Foucauldian paradigm, insofar as it provides a model for "history" within a discursive context. Yet, in order to make sense of the changes in discourse—that is, changes in the relation between "sex" and "gender" as terms—I utilize yet another model or mode of analysis: semiotics, or specifically, Roland Barthes's semiotic model of mythology, in which he explains the production of "mythic signs" through recourse to an analysis of the relation of myth to history.

Barthes's work in cultural semiotics, as exemplified by *Mythologies* and *The Fashion System*,[3] makes possible a method of reading the body as a sign system whose signifiers are both part of a "real code" beyond the discursive capacity of language to appropriate and part of a terminological or descriptive system produced by science to bring the body into language and therefore into epistemology and ideology. This kind of semiotic analysis facilitates the mediation between history and theory that sutures this book, since it enables me to examine the material and discursive effects of new scientific discoveries in medicine—that is, not only what these discoveries allow doctors to do, but also what doctors know, and based on this knowledge, what they become willing to do. Ways of seeing the body, ways of encoding anatomy and physiology into the language of medicine, have a significant impact on imagined and imaginable forms of subjectivity.

Barthes's semiotics of mythology thus allows me to "work the join" between Laqueur's and Butler's two appropriations of Foucault, to make theoretical claims via a historical analysis and to use history to understand the problematical discursive relationship between sex and gender. It is important to remember, however, that as Elizabeth Grosz suggests, "[a] model is a heuristic device which facilitates a certain understanding, highlighting certain features while diminishing the significance of others; it is the selective rewriting of a situation whose complexity entails the possibility of other, alternative models, models which highlight different features, presenting different emphases."[4] I am not aiming for a totalizing theory here—rather, I want to insert into the discussion a perspective that has heretofore been overlooked and without which the conversation has been impoverished.

In chapter 1 of Gender Trouble, "Subjects of Sex/Gender/Desire," Butler examines the naturalized relation between gender, sex, and desire that produces the idea of identity in the human subject. Her argument concerning the unnaturalness of gender and its presumptive regulation of sex is made through a very precise analysis of the linguistic and philosophical logic that maintains sex as the origin of gender by obscuring how gender serves to produce sex as "the natural" condition of its existence as an identity. Butler uses philosophical and political discourses as the stage of her analysis, relying heavily on readings of Michel Foucault, Monique Wittig, Simone de Beauvoir, Luce Irigaray, and Jacques Lacan to substantiate her claims. Butler's purpose in writing Gender Trouble is to unsettle the premises of both feminist politics and theory insofar as each relies on the idea of an identity that precedes the subject of feminism. That is, Butler's argument against "gender" is one whose real target is the politics of identity that have supported feminist theorizing and political action in recent years.

The arguments of my study are made with a distinctly different set of source materials and with another purpose in mind. I use a theoretical analysis of the historical production of the term "gender" to further elucidate a particular phenomenon—transsexualism—in its relation to technological "progress" and the demand for a culturally coherent subjectivity. Those readers of this text who have also read Butler's will see how the materials I discuss support the analysis she offers (and vice versa). However, because I ground my analysis in the idea that the term gender, as a codification of the "cultural construction of sex," was produced at a particular point in history and with particular theoretical effects, I hope to offer a critique of Butler's project. I do not wish to say that my project, as a specific instance or realization of the theoretical arguments elaborated by Butler, should either verify or make immaterial those arguments. Rather, I am suggesting that my conclusions concerning the problematical relation between sex and gender should illuminate some residual difficulties apparent in Gender Trouble.

The first line of the preface to Gender Trouble claims that "contemporary feminist debates over the meanings of gender lead time and again to a certain sense of trouble, as if the indeterminacy of gender might eventually culminate in the failure of feminism."[5] While feminist theorists such as Teresa de Lauretis attempt to alleviate that trouble through further specifications of the category "gender,"[6] Butler proceeds in the opposite direction, attempting to unsettle its signifying power and thus reorient its position as a signifier in feminist theory and action. She demonstrates that rather than being the expression of sex, or the cultural production of sex, the idea of gender in fact regulates the notion that sex is the natural condition of the human body. Butler makes this claim as part of a broader demonstration of Foucault's work on "juridical systems of power [that] *produce* the subjects they subsequently come to represent."[7] She analyzes the relation of sex and gender in order to show that what is thought to be the primary condition (sex) is actually an idea mediated by what poses as its secondary effect (gender).

Butler takes her analysis further by arguing that the (fictive) category of gender identity is actually constituted by the performative acts that it is thought to produce as its "expression." She establishes that gender identity is not a "descriptive feature of experience" but a normative ideal.[8] As such, it operates in a regulatory fashion, producing subjects who fit its requirements for "harmony" between sex, gender, and sexuality and punishing those for whom the categories are in disarray. Indeed, she argues that "the very notion of 'the person' is called into question by the cultural emergence of those 'incoherent' or 'discontinuous' gendered beings who appear to be persons but who fail to conform to the gendered norms of cultural intelligibility by which persons are defined."[9] Gender becomes intelligible through the "heterosexual matrix," which she defines as "that grid of cultural intelligibility through which bodies, genders, and desires are naturalized." It is characterized by "a hegemonic discursive/epistemic model of gender intelligibility that assumes that for bodies to cohere and make sense there must be a stable sex expressed through a stable gender . . . that is oppositionally and hierarchically defined through the compulsory practice of heterosexuality."[10]

Butler's arguments (and my own) work to demonstrate the problematic conceptual position of gender in the field of its operations. There are significant points of difference between us, however, especially concerning the conclusions we make at the end of these investigations. Ultimately, Butler argues for the "redeployment" of gender performances—those behaviors and activities that produce gender in everyday life and constitute as men and women the subjects who engage them—through subversive, parodic repetitions. These parodic acts would unsettle received notions concerning the naturalness of gender as the core of identity by highlighting the artificial relation of gender to bodies and sexualities. Butler suggests that drag performances are one example of this parodic replaying of gender in order to subvert its meanings in contemporary culture. She implies that these acts reveal "the performative status of the natural" and argues that the "task is not whether to repeat, but how to repeat or, indeed, to repeat and, through a radical proliferation of gender, *to displace* the very gender norms that enable the repetition itself."[11] Once identities are no longer considered the basis for political action, but are understood to be performatively constituted through such action, and once those actions are engaged in the process of deconstruction Butler designates "subversive repetition," "cultural configurations of sex and gender might then proliferate or, rather, their present proliferation might then become articulable within the discourses that establish intelligible cultural life, confounding the very binarism of sex, and exposing its fundamental unnaturalness." [12]

The "proliferations" Butler envisions inaugurate the subversion of these terms, which represent the two discursive categories available. Butler would argue that we cannot wish ourselves outside of the existing ideological field in which sex and gender are understood as separate but linked phenomena. The presentation of these two terms—"sex" and "gender"—as the inevitable categories in play, however, is possible only because Butler disregards the historical production of the idea of gender *as* identity. Her lack of historical analysis results in the presentation of these two terms as inevitable; subversion must engage them because they are (always already) what is (and has been) available. If, however, it is acknowledged that "gender" was produced at a specific historical moment in response to particular circumstances, and that its introduction into medical and popular discourses had measurable effects in the conceptualization of sexed subjectivity, then it would be possible to investigate what were perceived as the articulations of sex prior to the introduction of "gender" and to examine the possibility of returning to and "redeploying" sex—not as the natural body, but as a conceptual apparatus designating the body and representing it in medical and other discourses.

To this, Butler might argue that since sex is mediated by gender—that is, gender is the foundational category that regulates sex as sexual difference in a binary opposition—to redeploy gender and proliferate its meanings would be to reconfigure the possibilities of sex. What I am arguing is that while cultural perceptions regulate the articulation of "sex" historically, influencing and producing particular representations of sex as the natural, original condition of the body in sexual difference, the specific conditions of "gender" have not—until the latter half of the twentieth century. It is possible to rethink sex as a category of representation that refers to both body and culture, and in so doing, to expose the contemporary notion of "gender" as a specific kind of regulation of the category sex. In this sense, I am privileging a deconstructive, semiotic critique of the discourses of science, in order to reposition scientific representations of sex as their ideological regulation shifts historically. [13]

To disrupt the currently problematic theoretical relation between sex and gender, it is not enough to specify, problematize, or proliferate definitions and deployments of gender. It would be more profitable, because more unsettling, to attack the category "sex," to investigate how it operated as a concept before the current articulations of "gender," and to reconceive the scientific discourses that mandate its unitary "nature." This critical "attack on sex" would be possible because the discourses of science include counterdiscursive tendencies, positions that are conceived of and then lost, or overwhelmed by the mandates of ideological thinking. (The discussion in chapter 1 concerning the synecdochal relation between sex hormones and male and female bodies—and certain scientists' resistance to that relation—demonstrates the way in which potentially subversive scientific narratives are subsumed within prior ideological systems.) There are alternative scenarios of "sex" available in scientific literature that we can "redeploy" in the service of deconstructing it as a category of analysis; that is, in the service of its proliferation as representation.

I prefer the proliferations of sex to those of gender because the former category is more closely connected to the body than the latter—and by "the body" I mean that structure represented in discourse, but nevertheless meant to stand in for that "real" body that can never be captured as a code. "The body," of course, holds an ambivalent position in feminist theory, characterized by some as the root of women's oppressions and heralded by others as the source and meaning of femininity. Still other feminists reject "the body" as a ground or basis for feminist theorizing. However, I argue that theoretical revisions of the conceptual relation between sex and gender should take explicit account of the body because it is through claims made in its name that specific oppressions are enacted, as well as "experienced." In addition, interpretations of the body represent the very stake of the debates concerning the relation of "sex" to "gender." Reconceptualizing "sex" in the discourses of medicine would inevitably entail rethinking what it is we are talking about when we refer to "the body."

Clearly, this is one goal of Judith Butler's more recent book, *Bodies That Matter: On the Discursive Limits of "Sex."* [14] Here there is a shift in attention from "gender" to "sex," and an attempt to recapitulate, recharacterize, and renegotiate some of the central claims and categories of *Gender Trouble* through a sustained consideration of the materiality of sex. However, Butler is more interested in materiality than the material, more committed to investigating the normativity of sex than its specific signifiers, and has no explicit interest at all in the way in which the body, as a code outside of and resistant to discourse, can resist its inevitable encoding within medicine, science, and philosophy.

The strength of the text lies in its insistent revisions of what Butler understands as the most insidious misreadings of *Gender Trouble*: that performativity implies volitional choice, that the proliferation of gender performances implies subversion at every turn, and that the hegemony of heterosexuality is constraining only insofar as subjects do not understand their own performative potential to undermine its powerful articulation as "the norm." As always, Butler asks immensely significant questions: "Through what regulatory norms is sex itself materialized?" [15] "How does [the] materialization of the norm in bodily formation produce a domain of abjected bodies, a field of deformation, which, in failing to qualify as the fully human, fortifies those regulatory norms?" [16] "To what extent is 'sex' a constrained production, a forcible effect, one which sets limits to what will qualify as a body by regulating the terms by which bodies are and are not sustained?"[17] These and other questions throughout *Bodies That Matter* resonate with the analysis that I provide in this book.

Yet Butler's questions seem to return consistently in the same form(s), and the answers to these questions always concern the "outside" that is necessarily prior to the "inside," the excluded and abject nonsubject that is required for the conception of the subject to cohere, or the constraining regulations that produce those objects they are said to discipline and describe. Butler uses the questions to move the theory along in a predictable deconstruction of the relations between sex and gender, body and matter, race and gender, sexuality and race, and so on. Every category ends up being intelligible precisely because of what it excludes from it as the abject or the undesirable. This is not to say that Butler is *wrong* in her formulations. It is to suggest, however, that what motivates this book is a certain theoretical project within the discursive realm of philosophical and political inquiry, and not the category of "the body" at all.

Bodies are not, of course, the "simple objects of thought" that Butler suggests in the preface. This phrase, I think, belies her desire to present "the body" as opaque, "simple," uncomplicated: How could it ever sustain the kind of inquiring scrutiny she serves on the other categories in this text? It is telling, too, that one leitmotif of the text, a recurring idea that Butler presents herself as consistently having to respond to, concerns violence against (female) bodies: "If everything is a text, what about violence and bodily injury?"[18] The reiterations suggest that this is the only problem with poststructuralist notions of the constructed body; that violence is the only experience that can wrest the body back from discourse into the real and therefore into true materiality. This may only indicate that this was a consistent question asked of Butler in the aftermath of *Gender Trouble's* momentous impact on the scene of feminist theory—a question that seemed in need of a sustained answer. However, I read its repetition also as indicating the extent to which Butler herself has *accepted* the question of bodily violence as *the question* that may unsettle her claims, and thus the extent to which other questions that would point us back toward the body in less extreme circumstances are obscured or overlooked.

Those who read *Gender Trouble* with interest and enthusiasm will read *Bodies That Matter* similarly, and certainly, the reformulations Butler provides in the latter text are valuable reconsiderations of problematic moments of the former. What I am suggesting is that *Bodies That Matter* does not effectively deal with the residual difficulties in *Gender Trouble* that I remarked upon earlier and, indeed, *Bodies That Matter* suggests a new range of problems all by itself. I am left with the feeling that "sex" is still outside of Butler's analysis because of her insistence on remaining within the realm of philosophy and theory to argue through the matter of the body. What is needed in order to address the body is a set of materials or documents for which the material of the body is precisely a *material* problem, because it is in these contexts that we can see in striking detail how the practitioners who must deal with the body's material constraints (what tissue will do and not do given the current state of technology) perceive, justify, and theorize their practices. These are precisely those theoretical constraints that produce the body as a normativized construction whose very materiality depends upon discourse. Within this context, we can be very precise about how the perception of the body as always already sexed is in fact a normalizing regulation of matter that is necessary to produce the idea of a body at all.

Thomas Laqueur's work, in its historical examination of "sex" as a concept, does provide something close to this material consideration, as he analyzes directly representations of the body in medical literature, considering both what was objectively "known" about the body and how that knowledge was portrayed in medical illustration and discourse. The basic argument of *Making Sex* is that from classical antiquity through the early modern period, there was one sex. This one sex was made manifest in male and female bodies; the female body was an imperfect version of the male body and a woman's "sex" was but an imperfect inversion into her body of male genitalia (which on male bodies presented themselves externally). "Gender," what Laqueur understands as the social ordering of subjects according to cultural laws of status and stratification, regulated the body's articulations, insofar as there was, really, only one body with more or less perfected versions of "sex" exhibited on its flesh. In the eighteenth century, he argues, "sex as we know it was invented" — that is, the body became "the foundation of incommensurable difference." [19]

Thus, the "natural body" — two sexes each with its requisite body — became "a new foundation for gender" and "the cultural work that had in the one-flesh model been done by gender devolved now onto sex." [20] That is, the ideas about social hierarchy that used to support interpretations of the body, the actual perception of the body as sexed, came to be supported by the idea of sex (of two distinct sexes) as the "natural" condition of the body. In Laqueur's analysis, the body *became* foundational to ideas of cultural order — it hadn't always been so — and therefore sex *became* the basis for gender distinctions (rather than the other way around). In addition, perceptions of the body's real condition as a sex changed: "[V]agina" and equivalent words "to designate the sheath or hollow organ into which its *opposite*, the penis, fits . . . only entered European vernaculars around 1700"; and "[o]rgans that had been common to both sexes — the testicles — came as a result of the discovery of sperm and egg to have each its own name and to stand in synecdochal relationship to its respective sex." [21]

This last comment conveys a somewhat different meaning than the overall thrust of Laqueur's claim, which is that the shift from a one-sex to a two-sex model of the body (and the concomitant change in the relation between sex and gender) did not occur as the result of specific discoveries or theoretical progress in medical/scientific knowledge, but rather as a result of political exigency and historical contingency. That is, Laqueur argues that medical and scientific perceptions of the body and its "sex" have more to do with the social situation within which they emerge than with any kind of objective appreciation of the body's material technology. Laqueur claims throughout *Making Sex* that *social* imperatives drive scientific representations of the body.

What is significant about Laqueur's claims, especially in the context of Butler's discussion, is that "sex" was not always the conceptual ground (the biological "original") of gender (the cultural "copy"). If Laqueur is correct, then Butler's analysis needs historical grounding, because its universalism is misleading. *Gender Trouble* implies that gender's regulation of sex as a foundational category is not bounded by historical considerations. However, Laqueur claims that it is only recently that "sex," and therefore the body, has been perceived to be the foundation and basis of culture. This claim unsettles the underlying assumptions of Butler's ahistoricity.

Laqueur's argument also suggests that the shifts I am trying to describe—how something called "gender identity" comes into being as a concept and how it comes to determine "sex," to be primary to "sex"—is a return of an older paradigm, although with a difference. This difference has to do with the explicit theorization of "gender" within medical, psychological, and sexological discourses that occurs subsequent to its introduction as a term designating the social and psychological components of sexed identity. If I have any problems with Laqueur's analysis, it has do to with this point. He uses "gender" as it is used today, to designate the social articulation of (as well as regulation of) sex, that is, to specify those social codes and structures that govern cultural life and that can be posed against the idea of biological sex (or the body). However, this usage of the term is quite new: as I mentioned in the introduction and detailed in chapter 3, John Money and colleagues introduced the word "gender" to denote the social aspect of sexed identity in the 1950s, in the context of research on intersexuality.

"Gender," in this sense and usage, is a concept linked to contemporary psychosociological conceptions of "role" and "identity"—and as such was unthinkable for pre-twentieth-century subjects. While it may be useful to think through the category gender in order to understand previous formulations of "sex"—and Laqueur's book is nothing if not a testimony to this point—one must recognize the limits of applying current notions of "gender" to the past. For example, Laqueur writes (concerning a number of cases where individuals seemed to "change sex" spontaneously, or where they came to be defined juridically as the sex other than the one in which they had been living):

It seemed to matter little in any of these cases what sex the protagonists felt themselves to be, *what they were inside*. One of the disconcerting and poignant aspects of cases like Marie de Marcis' is how little regard was paid, in the accounts themselves and in the final determination of sex, to what we would call gender identity, the sense that infants acquire very early on of whether they are girls or boys. No one probed what gender a person thought herself or himself to be before a change occurred or an accusation was made (*I use the words "sex" and "gender" interchangeably here, precisely because the distinction has now broken down*). As long as sign and status lined up, all was well. Or, conversely, gender as a social category was made to correspond to the sign of sex without reference to personhood. . . . Subjects were assumed to change from being socially defined girls to being socially defined boys with no difficulty or turmoil.[22]

In this passage, Laqueur seems surprised, or at least somewhat taken aback, at this lack of attention to what he does acknowledge is a current category of understanding the self: gender identity. But that this should even be a question is itself surprising: not only was there not a linguistic or semantic distinction between "sex" and "gender" during the period he is discussing, but the idea of identity as an *internally felt* sense of self separate from community and family—but nonetheless "integrated" within the individual as a coherent "personality"—was foreign to this period as well.[23] And his comment that "sex" and "gender" have become interchangeable by this point obscures the fact that there were not two conceptually distinct categories to become interchangeable—it is only in the hindsight of analysis that we can see that in these cases cultural conceptions of status were indecipherable from perceptions of the physiological body.

What does it mean to suggest that "gender" as we use it today is a historical concept, that its discursive circulations are regulated—at least in part—by the conditions of its original introduction into medical discourse? To begin to answer this question, I will move into a discussion of Barthes's "mythological" approach to the study of signs, as a way of integrating theory and history in yet another approach to the analysis of cultural forms. As should become clear, Barthes's "mythology" offers a way to think about why "gender" seems not to have a history as a signifier, and why it is so important to reclaim that history.

In this book I have argued that "gender" as a term was part of a new discourse on sex made possible by technological advances in medicine. The new technologies were responsible for the production of alternate descriptions of physiological processes, as well as the introduction of innovative treatment practices, both of which led to changes in conceptions of the conventional relation between the body and its sex (that is, what Laqueur would call the two-sex model of the body and its sex—as noted, a relatively recent model). Gender, as a concept, came to mediate this relation in the discourses of psychiatric sexology and the medical management of intersexuality after the mid-twentieth century.

In *Mythologies*, Roland Barthes described the two orders of signification that make up myth, "a peculiar system, in that it is constructed from a semiological chain which existed before it: it is a second-order semiological system."[24] The second-order signifying chain uses the sign of its first-order counterpart as its signifier, thereby linking the two systems in an apparent homology. The second-order signification negates the first-order semiotics on which it depends, however, and constitutes itself as myth, the transcendent sign that comes to ground the first-order system.

For example, in *Mythologies* Barthes offers the example of the black man saluting a flag. He writes, "I am at the barber's, and a copy of *Paris-Match* is offered to me. On the cover, a young Negro in military uniform is saluting, with his eyes uplifted, probably fixed on a folded tricolour. All this is the *meaning* of the picture."[25] The "meaning" is the signification resulting from the first semiotic chain. Barthes continues, "But . . . I see very well what it signifies to me: that France is a great Empire, that all her sons, without any colour discrimination, faithfully serve under her flag, and that there is no better answer to the detractors of an alleged colonialism than the zeal shown by this Negro serving his so-called oppressors."[26] This myth, produced by the picture insofar as the sign of the first semiotic chain ("a Negro is giving the French salute")[27] becomes the signifier for the second chain, overdetermines the signification of the picture. It can never only mean "a Negro is giving the French salute," but will always suggest imperialism as the very means by which the black man saluting will come to signify anything at all. His own specific racial history is denied through the signification of French imperiality as a positive sign; according to the model, the historical relation between the two semiotic chains must be effaced in order for myth to function as myth (outside of history). Thus, the signification of the second chain (the order of myth) comes to regulate the reception of the first.

In terms of "sex" and "gender," the positionality of "gender" in medical discourse depends upon a semiotic economy in which body (signifier), sex (signified), and reproductive subject (sign) constitute the first-order semiotic chain, and gender role (signifier), gender identity (signified), and the heterosexual subject (sign) constitute its second-order counterpart. We can graph the relation as Barthes does (figure 18). To understand the constitution of gender as a myth that both depends on and erases the signifying relation between body and sex, denying the impact of medical technologies through the production of a new semiotics of gender, we need to examine this model further.

Barthes describes myth as depoliticized speech. For him, myth represents

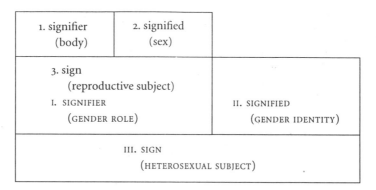

Figure 18. The Constitution of Gender as Myth. Source: Barthes, *Mythologies*, trans. Annette Lavers (New York: Hill and Wang, 1972), p. 115. This figure is not precisely the same as the graph in Barthes's text, in that he does not include the specific designations of sex, body, gender, etc., that I use here.

a hollowing out of history and the naturalization of a historically contingent concept. He writes that "myth is constituted by the loss of the historical quality of things: in it, things lose the memory that they once were made." In addition, myth "organizes a world which is without contradictions because it is without depth, a world wide open and wallowing in the evident, it establishes a blissful clarity: things appear to mean something by themselves." Myths are also motivated signs, although they work by naturalizing that motivation: "Myth is experienced as innocent [descriptive, objective] speech: not because its intentions are hidden—if they were, they would not be efficacious—but because they are naturalized."[28] In this sense, the loss of history in myth is connected to myth's naturalized status: that which is "natural" does not need history to explain its existence.

Gender, in Western culture, is an effect of this mythic form of signification. Through its signification, the body ceases to be the signifier of sex; instead, the sign of the reproductive subject—the result or completion of the first semiotic chain—becomes what Barthes calls the "form" of the second chain: in this case, gender role. A role, of course, is "empty," a form, a set of behaviors that suggests a "content" that comes to be defined as gender identity. And as myth is a motivated system, according to Barthes, this content, or signified, will be seen to motivate or determine the signifier—to be, in other words, its necessary antecedent. Taken together, the signification of the myth of gender is the heterosexual subject, whose body is only a contingent factor in the acting out of sexuality, whose body, we will later see, is actually motivated by gender itself.

In loosening itself from its former history, the mythic sign makes the second-order signification seem primary and original. Barthes writes that "semiology has taught us that myth has the task of giving an historical intention a natural justification, and making contingency appear eternal." As the sign shifts from one order to the other, becoming a signifier and shedding its history as a sign, it accedes to the level of ideology: "The relation which unifies the concept of the myth to its meaning is essentially a relation of *deformation.*" It is in the context of this movement, from signified to signifier, from sign to its transposed counterpart, that the second-order signifier is able to leave behind its history, the specific conditions of its production as a sign of the first order signification, and appear as natural ("innocent") and unmotivated. Myth "transforms history into nature. . . . [W]hat causes mythical speech to be uttered is perfectly explicit, but it is immediately frozen into something natural; it is not read as a motive but as a reason." [29]

As I demonstrated in chapter 3, gender was first produced as a concept in 1955 to describe how an intersex child came to establish particular behaviors that would indicate its assigned sex: in its first usages, gender was modified by the words "role" or "orientation." [30] The idea of a gender orientation or role was later understood as the behavioral or performative counterpart of a "gender identity" thought to motivate the subject's actions. [31] Subsequently, in the context of research on transsexualism, the idea of gender identity came to signify appropriate bodily sex: that is, what sex the subject should be allowed to have. Placing this history in the context of Barthes's model, we see that in the first semiotic chain, the body was the signifier for sex: this is what Laqueur understands as the two-sex model of the body, where the "sex" is taken to be the basis for cultural formations. As clinical researchers recognized that the body for intersexual subjects could not signify sex unequivocally (and the subject could not enter culture as man or woman), specific behaviors (such as toy choice, taste in clothing, gestural tendencies, and sexual object choice, among others) that identified the subject within a reproductive paradigm—regardless of the subject's ability or inability to reproduce—became the signifiers for gender identity, an internally felt sense of oneself as a male or female person.

The reproductive subject, sign of the semiotic relation between the body and its sex, index of the subject's bodily sex in the social realm, was redefined as "gender role" as researchers perceived the body to be an unreliable signifier of sex and therefore an unreliable foundation for the social. Theoretically, the researchers replaced the physiological object of the body as a signifier with the idea of sexed "behaviors" (gender role) and drained the ambiguously physical *and* psychosexual signified "sex" of its physical aspect by transforming it into "gender identity." In other words, they dealt with the instability of the body's significations (the fact that the body has numerous sites of "sex" within its tissue) by superseding the conventional relation between physiological signifiers

and sex status. Being a man or a woman could be signified by an adequate performance of gendered behaviors—clearly this was imperative for intersexual
subjects unable to authenticate a singular physiological sex identity. But this
step involved the production of gender identity as the *source* of one's sex, its
origin and cause, as well as the production of the heterosexual subject as the
signification of the gender myth.

This heterosexual subject is one divorced from the reproductive practices
that define the "gender role" on which it is based. The heterosexual subject
must position him- or herself in relation to reproduction—whether or not
reproduction is a physiological possibility for this subject—in order to be perceived as an authentic representative of gender, but actual reproduction is no
longer required to authenticate one's social position as a sexed subject. The
heterosexual subject does, however, need a body to ground its signifying practices. Yet the body as ground of signification is precisely what was destabilized
by the advancements in medical technology in the first half of the twentieth
century; this destabilization motivated the production of gender on the order
of myth. Gender came back to the body as its "original" signifier through the
intervention of the demand of transsexuals who affirmed the inconsequence
of the body's natural sex. That is, gender could only come back to the body as
the latter's a priori condition.[32]

This was the result, in part, of transsexuals' demands for sex change. The
gender researchers recoded the performative or external gender role (the signifier on the order of myth) so that it would signify an internal gender "identity." The internalness of gender identity still relied on a metaphoric reference
to a *psychic* space, however, and not to a (real) physical one. Gender was not
yet "in" the body because as gender identity it referred to psychology and not
physiology.[33] Gender achieved a simulated physicality when it was taken to be
a signifier for the body and its sex. This occurred through the demand of the
transsexual for sex change, a demand made through claims to the priority of
gender identity as an index of proper sex assignment. Through this movement,
gender returned to a body that had obtained a stability by being divested of
its unsettling polysemy. Appropriate sex (as gender) became a reflection of a
psychological attitude of the subject toward the body and culture. What remained the same were the social expectations concerning the body's coherence
as a sign of and for sex and the idea of an appropriate binary relation between
sex and sexual orientation.

Most significantly, the signifier/signified relation body/sex was subsumed
within another: gender role/gender identity. The appropriation of sex by gender, demonstrating gender's ability to dominate the signifying economy of
sex, characterizes the transsexual phenomenon perfectly. The transsexual body
is transformed to accommodate the apparent fixity of gender identity as a sig-

nified—the "content" of gender role—that, we can now recognize, grounds itself and then demands the production of the body it seeks to inhabit. As Baudrillard has said: "We too live in a universe everywhere strangely similar to the original—*here things are duplicated by their own scenario.*" [34]

Thus, the "scenario of gender," first produced to describe the experience of intersexual subjects in a sexual economy dependent upon a binary structure, reduplicates itself in the phenomenon of transsexualism. In other words, gender was originally produced as a theoretical concept to guide clinicians treating intersexual subjects whose physiological sex transgressed the expected binary opposition between male and female. The identification of a gender role aided the clinician in designating a correct sex in which to assign the patient. But gender role itself was eventually taken to signify an internal, gender identity that inheres in every individual. Transsexuals picked up on this semiotic relation, and, claiming the production of an aberrant gender identity, demanded the appropriately "matched" body/sex. Thus gender, a descriptive term, the sign of a first-order signifying system, theoretically came to ground the making of new bodies in a process that simulates the scenario of its original unfolding.

In *The Fashion System*, Roland Barthes extends and complicates the semiotic model he developed for *Mythologies*. He describes three levels of the semiotics of "written fashion": the real code, the terminological system, and the rhetorical system. In the context of fashion, the real code refers to the clothing as produced and worn; it is real in the sense that it participates in a semiotic economy of texture, form, and materiality apart from its significations in language. In the context of medical discourse, the human body constitutes the real code. The body participates in a physiological semiotics that operates outside of the languages in which it is described. Medical practice basically comprises attempts to bring a discursive system to bear on the real code of the body; that is, to appropriate the body into a discourse said to describe its functions.

Barthes calls this descriptive discourse a terminological system, which he further defines as a metalanguage. Metalanguages are understood to be "*operations, they form the majority of scientific languages, whose role is to provide a real system, grasped as signified, out of an ensemble of original signifiers, of a descriptive nature.*" He defines metalanguages in opposition to what he calls connotations: "As opposed to metalanguages, connotations pervade languages which are primarily social, in which a first, literal message serves as a support for a second meaning, of a generally affective or ideological order." [35] Connotations are part of the rhetorical system. The relation between metalanguages and connotations, or the terminological system and the rhetorical system, is the same as the relation between the first-order signifying chain and its second-order counterpart (that is, myth) in figure 18.

The value of thinking the relation of sex and gender through the cate-

gories developed in *The Fashion System* is that the idea of a terminological system
overlaid by a rhetorical system enables the critic to distinguish among different amounts or levels of ideological appropriation. For example, both endocrinology and cosmetic surgery function as medical practices in accord with
descriptive discourses concerning the body's physiological processes: in this
sense, they operate as terminological codes. Both are also governed by ideological systems of meaning concerning the form, function, and operation of
sexual difference: in this sense, they operate as rhetorical codes. Yet endocrinology is more connected to its terminological "mode" than is cosmetic surgery, whose main purpose is to change the human body, not to describe its
functions. Thus, the latter medical specialty is more subject to ideological appropriation.

This is not to say that cultural expectations and beliefs about proper behavior, appearance, and performance as a sex do not influence endocrinology as a
discourse and practice. There is no sense in which a terminological code is not
already in the social world of ideology. Yet the terminological codes of medical discourse do have an investment in describing the body as it seems to be
given — and the body, insofar as it can resist its captation by discourse, provides the real limit of the descriptive system of medical knowledge. This is why
a true acknowledgment of the "naturalness" of intersexuality may prove to be
a powerful subversive wedge in current medical conceptions of sexual difference, because intersexuality subverts the paradigm of normative sex — that is,
it disrupts the primary appropriation of the body's signs by the terminological code of binary sex.[36] Thus, to attend to the body's construction as a "sex,"
rather than the appropriation of the idea of sexual difference by the rhetoric
of "gender," will allow us to return to the body in a powerful critique of normalizing scientific narratives that ignore the body's resistance to appropriation
within descriptive systems.

Yet the rhetoric of the "gender system" has so overtaken our contemporary
conceptualizations of "sex" that we cannot see sexual difference except as it
is regulated by the specific ideological requisites of "gender." We cannot, in
other words, separate the semiotics of body/sex from those of gender; cannot
distinguish between the workings of the terminological code and its rhetorical counterpart. Using the word "gender" has become a way to speak of sex,
to signify even the biological events or signs that sex is supposed to indicate.
This is a result of the fact that as a myth, gender depends upon a history that is
erased in the process of signification and a meaning that is naturalized in the
moment of its elaboration. Judith Butler writes of gender identity as a "literal-
izing fantasy" that is "established through a refusal of loss that encrypts itself in
the body and that determines, in effect, the living versus the dead body." [37] For
Barthes, the construction of myth involves a similar opposition between life

and death: "Myth, on the other hand, is a language which does not want to die: it wrests from the meanings which give it its sustenance an insidious, degraded survival, it provokes in them an artificial reprieve in which it settles comfortably, it turns them into speaking corpses."[38] If gender is a fantasy that literalizes on the body signs of pleasure that ward off the death threatened by the loss of the (desired or loved) object, it is only as a living corpse that the subject can maintain itself in the myth of gender—as an empty shell, or an impersonation.

For Baudrillard the order of simulation signifies a kind of death of the real, or its "liquidation." Death is present in simulation through the absence of any real to dissimulate. In Butler's schema concerning melancholia, simulation might be understood as a melancholic incorporation of what is already gone; that is, a refusal of the death of the real, whose passing is established in the very gesture of incorporation. V. N. Volosinov suggests that it is in the nature of ideological systems to stifle the vitality of the sign, to squash its multivocality, to deaden its signifying capacity. In *Marxism and the Philosophy of Language*, he writes:

> The ruling class strives to impart a supra class, eternal character to the ideological sign, to extinguish or drive inward the struggle between the social value judgments which occurs in it, to make the sign uniaccentual. . . . In the ordinary conditions of life, the contradiction embedded in every ideological sign cannot emerge fully because the ideological sign in an established, dominant ideology is always somewhat reactionary and tries, as it were, to stabilize the preceding factor in the dialectical flux of the social, generative process, so accentuating yesterday's truth as to make it appear today's.[39]

This describes the living death of the mythic sign through its attempts to consolidate the past and naturalize it as the truth of the present. In this sense we can see how gender was produced in the mid-1950s to represent a concept developing in medical research on intersexuality that was not yet codified. As soon as it was introduced into the discourse on sex and the body, gender became a way to maintain the old social relationships through a new terminology and, most significantly, a newly developed technological practice.

In the context of transsexualism, medical technology enacts what is known as sex change, although the official terminology—sex conversion, sex reassignment, or, more recently, gender reassignment—underscores the contingency of the procedures through reference to an original condition that is changed. The organs produced or reconfigured are only simulations of the "real thing," which is itself made uncertain through the advent of these procedures: as Baudrillard remarks, "it is now impossible to isolate the process of the real, or to prove the real."[40] Plastic surgeons are able to make female genitalia that fool even the most expert of gynecologists,[41] although the successes of phalloplasty are more measured. As I demonstrated in greater depth in chapter 2, the power of the ideal is very strong in the discourses of plastic surgery. The manufactured organs correspond to fantasies of the "real thing." All of anatomical and physiological sex is thrown into the realm of simulation: the surgically and hormonally treated version seems more real through its approximation of the ideal. After all, why settle for the natural organ if the medically constructed counterpart is more desirable because it is more convincingly real?[42]

The technologies of plastic surgery and endocrinology produce simulated genital and secondary sexual organs that rival their real counterparts in terms of "authenticity." While these technological practices facilitate the disappearance of the idea of sexual difference as a natural or original human condition, it is the idea of a "core gender identity" that truly deconstructs sexual difference.[43] While it is part of a semiotic economy in which sexual difference remains an operative concept, and while it depends on the idea of sexual difference for its signifying capacity, the idea of gender identity disrupts the binary opposition understood as given in nature. As the body can be made to signify in opposition to its original designation as male or female, the clinical opinion that an individual has a cross-sex core gender identity usually signifies a decision to go ahead with surgical and hormonal treatments to effect sex change.[44] In this scenario, the binary opposition between the sexes turns on the determination of gender; that is, sexual difference is undone by the idea of identity.

This means that the signified of the second-order semiotics (gender identity) transgresses the basis on which the first-order semiotic chain depends (the two-body model of sexual difference). The two orders are not homologous: this is how the myth is constructed, through a difference that is never acknowledged. We can understand the second-order process as a semiotic simulation, that is, a second-order semiotic chain that pretends to subject itself to the law of its first-order counterpart but which in fact breaks that law while engaging in a cover-up. Transsexuals engage the semiotics of gender, on the order of simulation, in order to transgress the law of sexual difference that would mandate that they accept and accommodate themselves to the sexual meanings of their natural bodies. They demonstrate the disjunction between the two semiotic orders through the demand for sex change, which is a demand for a simulated body. The demand is made on the basis of gender identity, which is hypernatural—that is, beyond the natural, beyond the male/female opposition, a simulacrum of the idea of sexual difference that undergirds the semiotics of body/sex. Because the disjunction between the two orders (body/sex and gender) is obscured by the apparent homology between them, the demand made on the basis of gender identity, a simulation, can make things happen in the real, on the body, thereby disrupting the order of sexual difference.

Transsexualism demonstrates the incongruity of a semiotic logic that will intervene at the level of the physical signifier to accommodate a cultural fantasy of stable identity. And while this is perhaps the paradigmatic example of simulation in Baudrillard's sense, transsexuals' discourse resists this interpretation. Transsexuals stake their claim in terms of illusion: according to the protocols set forth by the Harry Benjamin International Gender Dysphoria Association, would-be transsexuals must live in their gender role of choice for at least six months prior to admission to surgery. They are experts at the arts of impersonation, although they claim that the illusion is only contingent, a historical accident, a mistake of nature. The illusion, in their representations, is over once transsexuals are able to present the "real thing" (that is, signify their true gender identity) courtesy of surgical and hormonal treatments.

Still, the staging of illusion, as Baudrillard suggests, depends upon a logic of the real; it is dissimulation, the masking of what exists in order to present an alternative interpretation, an interested lie. Simulation, on the other hand, masks nothing.[45] Transsexuals' discourse attempts to prop up the real through an assertion of a semiotics of illusion. They claim to be dissimulating—engaging illusion as a strategy of representation—in order to shore up the idea that gender really exists and that the body is its double. In this way, they evade the most disturbing implications of their practices—the accession of sex to the order of simulation, the production of gender as the real of sex.

In the flip-flopping of signifiers in the semiotics of sex, the body becomes that-which-can-be-transformed to accommodate the cultural category gender. The body, which once signified sex, can now be made to signify a gender opposed to its original configuration. The practices that achieve this transformation are technically difficult, decidedly interventionist, and cause intense pain for the subject involved. These practices are engaged in the service of gender identity and its maintenance as a reasonable signifier for the body's "intended sex." To advocate their use one must accede to the facticity of gender and its status as the master signifier of sex. In other words, one must believe in the simulation as real.

Gender, like the phallus, is a master signifier that everyone lacks, the personification of which everyone hopes to achieve. It has taken the place of "sex," which as a term has come to signify the merely "natural" facts of human reproductive physiology and anatomy. Transsexuals seek to become the true representatives of a gender, and perhaps they come closer than most, because at least they know they have done all that is technically possible to make the signifiers line up in the "correct relation" mandated by culture. However, like the phallus, gender does not "exist," or exists only as that which constitutes the nothing it allegedly designates. It is, at times, useful to engage strategically, but it cannot be articulated against the persistence of its historic affiliations. In addition, as it is currently deployed, gender is a concept meaningful only within heterosexuality and in advocacy of heterosexuality—after all, its signification is the heterosexual subject.[46] It masquerades as the ground for what is ungroundable (the body) and it pretends a fixity and stability that are conferred by a cultural system desperate to maintain a "body" as its natural counterpart.

EPILOGUE

One major objection to the claims made in this book will be that in recent years some transsexuals have worked against the medical regulation of transsexualism, attempting to depathologize its definition as well as to guarantee access to necessary procedures without stigmatizing transsexuals as mental misfits. This objection would seem to suggest that transsexuals themselves are not invested in establishing and maintaining a relation to the medical institution, as I have argued throughout this text, but work in opposition to it, gaining access to the requisite medical treatments despite a fundamental antipathy to the regulatory mode of medical surveillance. In this scenario, the transsexual subject who demands medical treatment in the form of technological interventions to change sex resents the medicalization of transsexualism as a "gender disorder" and contacts the medical establishment only because medical doctors are the stewards of such treatment and therefore regulate its use.

Another question that will arise as a result of my research concerns the status of "transgenderism," a relatively new term that describes either the cross-gender community as a whole, or, more specifically, those subjects who choose partial technological "sex change," or those who cross-live without the technological mediation of medical intervention (although other technological mediations might be engaged). This question challenges my understanding of transsexualism insofar as the existence of the second two transgender options, with their emphasis on partiality—of sex change, of gender performances—suggests that there are subjects whose desire to be the other sex also involves an implicit repudiation of the binary "gender system." In this sense, transgenderism is understood to transgress the order of gender by flaunting disobedience to the idea that "sex," "gender," and "sexuality" must be intelligible within a bipolar, heterosexual framework. Kate Bornstein, for example, suggests that the word "transgendered" should be used to signify "transgressively gendered."[1] Transsexualism, in this scenario, might be understood as a necessary precursor to the "real" gender challenge — transgenderism — and therefore a phenomenon forced into a more conservative articulation by the medical profession. In my concluding remarks, I would like to comment upon these two possible challenges to the preceding discussion.

In arguing that transsexualism must be conceptualized in relation to medical discourses and medical technologies, I have tried to demonstrate that transsexuality cannot be defined solely through recourse to the narratives of "gender" in contemporary Western culture. In addition, I have argued that it is through an analysis of the emergence of transsexualism in relation to the developing medical technologies of "sex change" that we can trace the introduction of "gender" as a term referring to the social articulations of sexed identity. As I discussed in chapter 6, biological sex and cultural gender are analytically distinguished yet materially linked through the practices of "sex change" enacted by the medical profession, as well as through the conventional wisdom concerning the development of "gender identity" from "natural sex." Examining transsexualism allows us to critique gender's domination of the signifying field of sex, and can encourage us to reconsider the usefulness of an analytic paradigm that separates physical sex from gender in order to liberate men, women, and others from the strictures of contemporary gender narratives. Indeed, I have argued that proliferating and re-presenting "gender" as a plural geography of difference that does not reference the body is a problematic move, given that the body then drops out of the picture as a cultural code and comes to signify "biological sex." To truly destabilize bipolar gender schema, we must question and unsettle the scientific representations of the body as verifying a two-sex system upholding heterosexuality as the human (and animal) norm.

It is hard to resist calls to "open up" the gender system to proliferating representations and identity formations. This is perhaps why Judith Butler's *Gender Trouble* was so insistently read to advocate a sort of willful gender pluralism (much to the dismay of the author) — what was at most an argument for limited room to maneuver within social/discursive constraints was read by many as a manifesto for voluntarist gender fashioning.[2] Anne Bolin's recent essay, "Transcending and Transgendering," suggests that while traditional transsexualism reiterated the Western equation of gender with genitalia (that is, the coincidence of gender with biological sexual signifiers), transgenderism has the potential to transcend and therefore deform the gender system by refusing the connection between the visibly sexed body and performances of gender.[3] To a certain extent, this latter claim is true: to promote transgenderism is to suggest that individuals of either sex can inhabit roles associated with the "other sex" and thereby unsettle the connections between biology and society upon which the gender system putatively depends.

At this writing, Kate Bornstein is perhaps the latest voice in a growing movement to proliferate "gender" out of its containment within the heterosexist binary and thereby unsettle its hold on cultural representation. Her book, *Gender Outlaw: On Men, Women, and the Rest of Us*, is an extended plea to recognize and celebrate a multiplicity of gender performances, the repression of which (she argues) stifles human creativity and threatens the very existence of the "differently gendered." The contradictions that emerge from her arguments, however, demonstrate the extent to which the transgender movement bases its claims within the conventional parameters of the gender identity paradigm— rather than transgressing that paradigm, as it claims to do.

For example, the desire to celebrate and proliferate individual gender performances as a way to destabilize "gender" at large is based on liberal humanist assumptions of self-determination. Bornstein argues that the transgender movement involves a "struggle for freedom of expression" and she suggests that gender should become a "consensual" form of play and identification.[4] While Bornstein asserts that gender should be questioned and "deconstructed," she also wants to maintain the possibility of gender identity as a necessary retreat from the incoherences of nonidentity: "I love the idea of being without an identity, it gives me a lot of room to play around; but it makes me dizzy, having nowhere to hang my hat. When I get too tired of not having an identity, I take one on."[5] In this passage, the "I" makes a decision to be identitiless or to conform to a "recognizable" identity—it is an "I" prior to identity, where "identity" is understood as fashion.[6] Gender identity here is a choice, a decision made on the part of the subject; it is voluntaristic and willed. And while much of *Gender Outlaw* attempts to describe the rigidities and enforced aspects of the Western gender system, Bornstein's consistent, "transgressive" response is to call for people to recognize and be more genders than they accommodate, or perform, today.

There is a logical inconsistency between doing away with gender and making more genders. It is never clear how proliferating gender performances will undo (or "deconstruct," in Bornstein's words) the gender system, since the proliferation always relates back to the binary. As Janice Raymond argues in the introduction to the 1994 edition of *The Transsexual Empire*, transgenderism is basically a movement within the logic of gender, and one that is "more style than substance." In this sense, political resistance to societal constraints has devolved into "an expressive individualism" that replaces "collective political challenges to power," and the new "gender outlaws" are just newer versions of the old "gender conformists." Even as Raymond recognizes that many transgenderists do more than simply switch gender performances, she suggests that even "gender-bending" is just another incidence of the same old thing: "The transgenderist assumes the posture of rebellion, but only as restricted by the sex role scene, and going only as far as a melding of both roles."[7] In Raymond's argument—and my own—one cannot "escape" gender by switching roles or performances and thereby confuse the binary logic, because that logic defines the possibility of the switching in the first place. "Transcending" gender (Raymond's words) involves a more critical project, as well as the possibility of unsettling the stability of those who see themselves as "normally sexed."

For Bornstein, everything is gender; "sex" refers to sexual relations, (or "fucking," as she puts it).[8] "Biological sex" is really "biological gender," and she understands its primacy in gender signification to indicate a "belief in the supremacy of the body in the determination of identity."[9] While she does include a section in the beginning of her book concerning her sex reassignment surgery, providing for the reader explicit details of the procedures, the body is not really a significant player in the story she tells in *Gender Outlaw*. Indeed, this absence of the body's significance is central to use of the phrase "biological gender," because in Bornstein's scenario, all gender should be voluntary. Hence her statement "I am a transsexual by choice, not by pathology."[10] Everyone should be able to have access to another body: "Each of us needs to name and attain our own point of comfort. Insurance-based coverage for genital surgery should, I believe, be made available for those who can't afford it, and for whom the comfort point would require that surgery." Clearly, that "comfort" is important to Kate Bornstein, self-described "gender outlaw": "I had my genital surgery partially as a result of cultural pressure. . . . Knowing what I know now, I'm real glad I had my surgery, and I'd do it again, just for the comfort I now feel with a constructed vagina. I *like* that thang [sic]!"[11]

One logical conclusion of Bornstein's argument about gender and its relationship to genitals—for example, subjects with penises should be allowed to be "women" if they so choose—would be that sex reassignment surgery is part of the culture's gender mandate. Transsexuals, in this argument, succumb to the gender system in order to accommodate their difference within the recognizable parameters of gender identity. At points in *Gender Outlaw*, Bornstein does suggest that transsexualism is not transgressive of the gender system. Yet her insistence that sex change is a viable choice for certain "differently gendered" subjects and her defense of her own sex change contradict this view by allowing that people deserve the right to demand genitalia to match their gender experiences. In other words, Bornstein argues that people should be allowed to demand technological interventions to be the other sex.

What distinguishes that argument from those we have seen in the transsexual autobiographies is that Bornstein wants transsexuals to identify *as transsexuals* rather than as the men or women they have become. This call—similar to the one made by Sandy Stone in "The *Empire* Strikes Back" for transsexuals to give up passing[12]—defines the difference between traditional transsexualism and transgender transsexualism. Those who, like Bornstein, take up positions as public transsexuals in order to question binary gender and the cultural imperative that we all be either men or women see themselves as transgressing binary gender. The question is, are subjects who change their sex in order to make their bodies "match" some kind of internal experience of the self defined as gender really able to question the "system" that so clearly demarcates their choices? Can changing the body be viewed as only a contingent factor in the being of gender? Is voluntaristic gender play, including technologically mediated changes in physical sex characteristics, an effective way to reconfigure "gender" as a system of disciplinary regulation?

As I have argued throughout this book, we can chart another kind of resistance to "gender" through examining the body and its relation to "gender performances." If there are subjects willing to live with partial sex change (usually hormonal, without surgery), this may be an indication that the attempts at technological sex change do not achieve the changes desired. This would be precisely because the body does not accommodate all of the procedures of "sex change"; the body, in other words, resists making "gender" real.

There are those who argue that it is the medical profession that "medicalized" transsexualism, and that transgenderism is an attempt to redefine transsexual subjectivity outside of the purview of clinical treatment. Indeed, many of the documents I discuss in chapter 4 can be read as indicating physicians' overwhelming desire to medicalize (and therefore pathologize) their patients' dis-ease in sex categories. However, to interpret them in that way discounts the involvement of the transsexual subjects themselves in encouraging a medico-therapeutic response on the part of their clinicians. In other words, it seems problematic to me to construe transsexuals solely as the victims of the medical establishment, when the evidence suggests as well that transsexuals actively confronted the medical establishment by seeking specific medical procedures and, in so doing, created with their practitioners a new category of "being" in sex. What we can see in current calls to demedicalize and depathologize transsexualism is a desire to continue to allow transsexuals access to "sex change" technologies without the stigma associated with psychiatric diagnosis.[13]

Removing the psychiatric diagnosis from transsexualism yet continuing to provide medical "treatment" for subjects who exhibit its symptoms is unthinkable in the current circumstances of medicine in the West. Transsexualism depends upon the connection between psychology and the body that is made manifest by the use of physical treatment for a psychological "disorder." The paradox of transsexuality is that medical treatment and technological intervention are necessary to realize the being of the transsexual subject, who nevertheless subscribes to the opinion that he or she was simply "born into the wrong body"—that is, that the "treatment" is not an intervention but the rectification of an unnatural situation. Transgenderism, even with limited technological intervention, usually involves hormone treatment, and taking hormones, even in small doses, is risky.[14] Taking hormones in the dosages necessary to maintain the opposite sex's morphology is not something that should be done without proper medical treatment and supervision. To ignore these facts is to discount the significance of technological intervention on the body's tissue and functions, which is precisely one goal of the transsexual—to forget or dismiss the technological intervention necessary to maintain his or her chosen sex. While the transgenderist might highlight the technological intervention as part of the performance of a constructed (and not natural) self, his/her ingestion of hormones, or participation in other procedures such as plastic surgery, merit medical attention because of the inherent dangers of reconfiguring the body's tissues. Medical surveillance of cross-sex behaviors is extremely problematic, but so is the proposed deregulation of the treatments and practices of "sex change."

What we must do is rethink the body as the site for sexual signification. Theorizing the body means taking it seriously as a material structure that exceeds the power of language to inscribe its functions. This does not mean, however, that we must concede any and all ability to examine it. Rather, we need to account for those points at which discourse cannot describe or regulate the body's significations, to understand how theory cannot appropriate the body as its signifier. This is why I think that studying medical practice and medical discourse is so important for radical critiques of the "gender system"—not because it is within medicine that "gender" overdetermines perceptions of physical "sex," but because medicine encounters and tries to account for the body in its materiality, and because medical discourse and practice consistently fail in their attempts to make the body conform to their parameters. The body is the horizon of medicine, as it represents both the object of medical practice and the impossibility of realizing a total discursive captation of the material. In this sense, we can read the body's resistance to "gender"— legible, for instance, in plastic surgeons' continuing difficulty in constructing penises and in the medical silence surrounding problems with vaginoplasty or the long-term effect of using massive doses of sex hormones—as suggesting that in a critical return to "sex" we may find a way to destabilize "gender" as a normalizing narrative in the twentieth century.

NOTES

Introduction

1   "Agnes" is the pseudonym given by Harold Garfinkel ("Passing and the Managed Achieve-
    ment of Sex Status in an 'Intersexual' Person," in *Studies in Ethnomethodology*, by Harold
    Garfinkel [New York: Prentice-Hall, 1967], 116–85, 285–88).
2   "Hermaphroditism" is the older term for what is now clinically defined as "intersexu-
    ality." The word "hermaphrodite" usually implies a mingling or coexistence of the two
    sexes, while "intersexuality" suggests a stage between the two sexes. "Intersexuality"
    was introduced into the medical lexicon in the first half of the twentieth century. The
    significance of shifting from one term to the other will be discussed at greater length
    in chapter 3.
3   Garfinkel, *Studies in Ethnomethodology*, 119; Robert Stoller, Harold Garfinkel, and Alexander
    Rosen, "Passing and the Maintenance of Sexual Identification in an Intersexed Patient,"
    Archives of General Psychiatry 2 (1960): 379–80; Robert Stoller, "A Contribution to the Study
    of Gender Identity," *Journal of the American Medical Association* 45 (1964): 225; Stoller, "A Fur-
    ther Contribution to the Study of Gender Identity," *International Journal of Psycho-Analysis* 49
    (1968): 365; and Stoller, *Sex and Gender: On the Development of Masculinity and Femininity* (New
    York: Science House, 1968), 133–140.
4   Stoller, Garfinkel, and Rosen, "Passing," 380.
5   As the title of Garfinkel's chapter indicates, the researchers were interested in part in
    Agnes's "passing" strategies, which they understood as those strategies that allowed her
    to move from the category of "normal male" to that of "normal female," as well as
    those strategies that enabled her to live as a woman. Garfinkel defines "passing" in the
    following manner: "The work of achieving and making secure their rights to live in the
    elected sex status while providing for the possibility of detection and ruin carried out
    within the socially structured conditions in which this work occurred" (118). "Passing"
    thus suggests both the movement from one category to another *and* the achievement of
    legitimacy in the second category.
6   Stoller, "Further Contribution," 365.
7   Stoller, "Contribution," 225.
8   Garfinkel, *Studies in Ethnomethodology*, 152–55n.
9   Stoller, *Sex and Gender*, 135.
10 Stoller, "Further Contribution," 366.

11   American Psychiatric Association, *Diagnostic and Statistical Manual of Mental Disorders*, 3d ed. rev. (Washington, D.C.: American Psychiatric Association, 1987), 74. Vern Bullough and Bonnie Bullough put the current incidence of transsexualism for both men and women at 1 in 50,000 in their *Crossdressing, Sex, and Gender* (Philadelphia: University of Pennsylvania Press, 1993), 314.

12   The medical profession as a whole has not accepted transsexualism as a legitimate disorder requiring the surgical and hormonal treatment of "sex reassignment" (SRS). Indeed, it is probable that only a small minority of physicians believe transsexualism to indicate SRS. Yet transsexualism has been codified by the American Psychiatric Association as a "gender identity disorder," and SRS is available at a number (albeit a small number) of U.S. hospitals and clinics. Thus, while the legitimacy of transsexuality continues to be debated within the medical profession, there is enough support within the profession to make SRS available to at least a portion of those subjects demanding sex change. See American Psychiatric Association, *Diagnostic and Statistical Manual of Mental Disorders*, 3d ed. rev., 71–78, esp. 74–76.

13   For examples of these approaches, see Richard Green, *Sexual Identity Conflict in Children and Adults* (New York: Basic Books, 1974), 3–13; Green, "Mythological, Historical, and Cross Cultural Aspects of Transsexualism," in *Transsexualism and Sex Reassignment*, ed. Richard Green and John Money (Baltimore: Johns Hopkins University Press, 1969), 13–22; Vern Bullough, "Transsexualism in History," *Archives of Sexual Behavior* 4 (1975): 561–71; Richard F. Docter, *Transvestites and Transsexuals: Toward a Theory of Cross-Gender Behavior* (New York: Plenum Press, 1988). For a broader perspective on sexological and historical analyses of a "third sex," see Gilbert Herdt, ed., *Third Sex, Third Gender: Beyond Sexual Dimorphism in Culture and History* (New York: Zone Books, 1994). Catherine Millot suggests that there is a transhistorical desire to be the other sex that is transformed in the twentieth century through the possibility of a material response to that desire (*Horsexe: Essay on Transsexuality*, trans. Kenneth Hylton [New York: Autonomedia, 1990]). Vern Bullough and Bonnie Bullough do address this issue in their recent book *Crossdressing, Sex, and Gender*, 253.

14   See Bullough, "Transsexualism in History." See also Vern Bullough's commentary in the *Journal of the History of Sexuality* 4, no. 2 (October 1993): 288–90.

15   The obvious text to cite here is Michel Foucault, *The History of Sexuality: An Introduction*, vol. 1, trans. Robert Hurley (New York: Vintage, 1978). Much of recent gay and lesbian historiography follows—or takes issue with—Foucault's work.

16   Some influential and important texts include: John D'Emilio, *Sexual Politics, Sexual Communities: The Making of a Homosexual Minority in the United States, 1940–1970* (Chicago: University of Chicago Press, 1983); D'Emilio, *Making Trouble: Essays on Gay History, Politics, and the University* (New York: Routledge, 1992), esp. 57–73, 96–113, and 138–154; Jeffrey Weeks, *Sexuality and Its Discontents: Meanings, Myths, and Modern Sexualities* (London: Routledge and Kegan Paul, 1985); John Boswell, "Revolutions, Universals, and Sexual Categories," in *Hidden from History: Reclaiming the Gay and Lesbian Past*, ed. Martin Bauml Duberman, Martha Vicinus, and George Chauncey Jr. (New York: New American Library, 1989), 17–36; David M. Halperin, "Sex before Sexuality: Pederasty, Politics, and Power in Classical Athens," in *Hidden from History*, 37–53; George Chauncey Jr., "From Sexual Inversion to Homosexuality: Medicine and the Changing Conceptualization of Female Deviance," *Salmagundi* 58–59 (Fall 1982–Winter 1983): 114–146; and Eve Kosofsky Sedgwick, *Epistemology of the Closet* (Berkeley: University of California Press, 1990), esp. 1–90. This is, of course, not a complete list of all the interesting and pertinent texts in gay and lesbian studies.

17   See Gayle Rubin, "Thinking Sex: Notes for a Radical Theory of the Politics of Sexuality,"

in *Pleasure and Danger: Exploring Female Sexuality*, ed. Carol Vance (Boston: Routledge and Kegan Paul, 1984), 267–319, for one example of an argument linking transsexuals with homosexuals and others as a sexual minority. Rubin's position is especially odd given that she argues for a theory of sexuality that is divorced from theories of gender. Whenever she mentions transsexuals, it is in the context of a list of other sexual minorities — transvestites, fetishists, homosexuals, sadomasochists, intergenerationalists — that reduces all the groups to equivalent status. The fact that transsexuals do not constitute a group stigmatized for their *sexual practices*, but rather for their *gender performances*, does not enter into her analysis, even though she clearly states that "it is essential to separate gender and sexuality analytically to more accurately reflect their separate social existence" (308). In addition, Rubin consistently argues that psychiatry has increasingly brought "sexual deviations" within its purview and defined them as pathologies (e.g., 280); this analysis ignores the extent to which transsexuals *necessarily* seek the attention of physicians and psychiatrists. In fact, as I discuss in this introduction and throughout the book, much of the medical attention to transsexualism as it emerged in the 1950s and 1960s involved the agency of transsexual subjects who sought specific interventionary medical procedures to alleviate what they felt to be a congenital anomaly — being born into the wrong sex.

18   For an important compilation of the transsexual's legal status in the United States, see Sr. Mary Elizabeth, *Legal Aspects of Transsexualism*, Educational Resources Publication (Wayland, Mass.: International Foundation for Gender Education, 1990).

19   American Psychiatric Association, *Diagnostic and Statistical Manual of Mental Disorders*, 3d ed. (Washington, D.C.: American Psychiatric Association, 1980), 261–64. My research led me to believe that homosexuality was removed from the DSM series at the same time that transsexualism was included (in the DSM-III, 1980). However, Holly Devor has informed me that homosexuality was removed from the DSM-II at its seventh printing, after being voted out by the American Psychiatric Association in December 1973. She suggests that the textual change may have occurred in 1974. (Holly Devor, personal communication through electronic mail, February 19, 1995.)

20   I was reminded of this by Chad Heap. See also Chauncey, "From Sexual Inversion to Homosexuality."

21   See, for example, Christine Jorgensen, *Christine Jorgensen: A Personal Autobiography* (New York: Paul Eriksson, 1967).

22   Stoller, Garfinkel, and Rosen, "Passing," 380. Emphasis added.

23   Garfinkel, *Studies in Ethnomethodology*, 160.

24   I am here considering fellatio a form of sexual intercourse, insofar as the penis is inserted into the orifice of the mouth.

25   Garfinkel, *Studies in Ethnomethodology*, 121, 160.

26   Ibid., 157.

27   Ibid., 163.

28   Stoller, *Sex and Gender*, 148.

29   At the International Foundation for Gender Education's annual "Coming Together/ Working Together" convention in Denver, April 1991, the public discourses (that is, those discourses generated for the public and not for those attending the convention) were extremely homophobic. The IFGE convention has as its primary clientele crossdressing heterosexual men, although a substantial number of transsexuals and transgenderists are involved in the running of the organization and the convention. While discourses internal to the convention — those that circulated among registered attendees only — were quite inclusive in their characterizations of a continuum of cross-dressing,

gender-transgressing, and gay-associated behaviors, those discourses produced exclusively for the meetings open to the public were rife with normalizing, heterosexist
commentary: "We are really very normal, middle-class folks. . . . We have lots of law-
yers, doctors, accountants, insurance executives (etc.) in our organization. We are just
like you, except that we like to dress in women's clothing" is the statement (although
not an exact quote) central to those public discourses meant to legitimate transvestites
and transsexuals as "regular people."

30   J. A. H. Murray, ed., Oxford English Dictionary, vol. 4 (Oxford: Clarendon Press, 1933), 100.

31   J. A. Simpson and E. S. C. Weiner, eds., Oxford English Dictionary, 2d ed., vol. 6 (Oxford:
Clarendon Press, 1989), 428.

32   Julia Epstein includes the following note in her article "Either/Or—Neither/Both:
Sexual Ambiguity and the Ideology of Gender," Genders 7 (Spring 1980): 99–142: "Robert
Edgerton cites a statistic of 2 to 3 percent in 'Pokot Intersexuality: An East African Example of the Resolution of Sexual Incongruity,' American Anthropologist 66 (1964): 1289.
Dr. Iraj Resvani of St. Christopher's Hospital for Children in Philadelphia believes this
estimate to be too high, while John Money asserts that the incidence of gender disorders approaches 4 percent" (131, n. 6). Anne Fausto-Sterling asserts that Money now
denies the 4 percent figure because he believes it is too high. Based on the research of
some of her students, Fausto-Sterling believes that the "figure hovers somewhere in the
1% range. Depending on how you finagle the stats it could really be 0.5% or 2%, but
probably not higher except in some small interbreeding populations where there is a
high frequency of a gene causing pseudohermaphroditism" (personal communication
through electronic mail, December 9, 1993).

33   For example, see Gayle Rubin, "The Traffic in Women: Notes toward a Political Economy of Sex," in Toward an Anthropology of Women, ed. Rayna R. Reiter (New York: Monthly
Review Press, 1975), 157–210.

34   Elizabeth Grosz, Volatile Bodies: Toward a Corporeal Feminism (Bloomington: Indiana University Press, 1994), 17.

35   Texts that come to mind include Ruth Bleier, Science and Gender: A Critique of Biology and Its
Theories on Women, Athene Series (New York: Pergamon, 1984), esp. chap. 4; Anne Fausto-
Sterling, Myths of Gender: Biological Theories about Women and Men (New York: Basic Books,
1985); Ruth Hubbard, The Politics of Women's Biology (New Brunswick, N.J.: Rutgers Uni-
versity Press, 1990); Donna Haraway, Primate Visions (New York: Routledge, 1989); and
Haraway, Simians, Cyborgs, and Women: The Reinvention of Nature (New York: Routledge, 1992).

36   Donna Haraway, "Gender for a Marxist Dictionary: The Sexual Politics of a Word," in
Simians, Cyborgs, and Women, 138.

37   Ibid., 133. Haraway's final comment is incorrect, as the first sex change surgeries occurred at least a decade earlier, and, as we shall see, already involved an incipient "gender identity paradigm."

38   Ibid., 133–34.

39   This phrase was made popular by Harry Benjamin in The Transsexual Phenomenon (New
York: Julian Press, 1966). See also chapter 4.

40   For more extensive definitions of cultural feminism, see Alice Echols, "The New Femi-
nism of Yin and Yang," in Powers of Desire, ed. Ann Snitow, Christine Stansell, and Sharon
Thompson (New York: Monthly Review Press, 1983), 439–59; and Echols, Daring to Be Bad:
Radical Feminism in America, 1967–1975, (Minneapolis: University of Minnesota Press, 1989).

41   Janice Raymond, The Transsexual Empire (Boston: Beacon Press, 1979); Raymond, "Transsexualism: The Ultimate Homage to Sex-Role Power" Chrysalis 3 (1977): 11–23; Marcia

Yudkin, "Transsexualism and Women: A Critical Perspective," *Feminist Studies* 4 (October 1978): 97–106; and Margrit Eichler, "Sex Change Operations: The Last Bulwark of the Double Standard," in *Feminist Frontiers II*, ed. Laurel Richardson and Verta Taylor (New York: Random House, 1989), 281–90.

42 Rebecca West, cited in Raymond, "Transsexualism," 16 (see also p. 17); Eichler, "Sex Change Operations," 283; and Yudkin, "Transsexualism and Women," 100.

43 Raymond, "Transsexualism," 22. See also Yudkin, "Transsexualism and Women," 100.

44 Raymond, *Transsexual Empire*, 176.

45 Ibid., xxi; Yudkin, "Transsexualism and Women," 98.

46 Eichler, "Sex Change Operations," 289.

47 Raymond, "Transsexualism," 17.

48 Raymond, *Transsexual Empire*, 120–26. Dwight Billings and Thomas Urban make a similar argument in "The Socio-Medical Construction of Transsexualism: An Interpretation and Critique," *Social Problems* 29, no. 3 (February 1982): 266–82.

49 Eichler, "Sex Change Operations," 281, 289; Raymond, *Transsexual Empire*, 155, 163–65.

50 Marjorie Garber, "Spare Parts: The Surgical Construction of Gender," *Differences* 1, no. 3 (Fall 1989): 156–57. This essay was subsequently published as part of Garber's *Vested Interests: Cross-Dressing and Cultural Anxiety* (New York: Routledge, 1991). The book treats a much larger field of inquiry than this study, as transsexualism represents for Garber one instance of transvestism, which she argues is a trope central to cultural production.

51 Judith Shapiro, "Transsexualism: Reflections on the Persistence of Gender and the Mutability of Sex," in *Body Guards: The Cultural Politics of Gender Ambiguity*, ed. Julia Epstein and Kristina Straub (New York: Routledge, 1991), 248–49. Emphasis added.

52 See discussion of Marjorie Garber's position on phalloplastic surgery in chapter 2.

53 Susan Birrell and Cheryl Cole, "Double Fault: Renée Richards and the Construction and Naturalization of Difference," *Sociology of Sport Journal* 7 (1990): 2, 6.

54 Renée Richards, with John Ames, *Second Serve: The Renée Richards Story* (New York: Stein and Day, 1983), 343. Since the 1950s, intersex infants with XY chromosomes but minimal phallic development are generally raised as girls, regardless of genetic or gonadal indicators. See also Suzanne Kessler and Wendy McKenna, *Gender: An Ethnomethodological Approach* (New York: John Wiley, 1978), 53–54.

55 The International Olympic Committee introduced the buccal smear sex chromatin test for female athletes in the 1968 summer games in Mexico City. Earlier in the 1960s, female athletes were required to parade naked in front of a panel of judges, or to submit to a pelvic exam, in order to verify their sex status. The perceived need for these examinations was to prevent men from masquerading as women in athletic competitions. In a commentary published in the *Journal of the American Medical Association*, doctors involved in the International Amateur Athletic Federation Work Group on Gender Verification advised that a general "medical examination" be required of all athletes: "The primary purpose of this medical examination would be to ensure satisfactory physical status for competition and would, of course, include simple inspection of the external genitalia" (852). The doctors note that all athletes must contribute a urine sample prior to competition for drug screening, and that they are closely scrutinized to make sure that the urine comes directly from the athlete's urethra: "The likelihood of a man successfully masquerading as a woman under such circumstances seems remote in current competition" (852). The technological apparatuses used to test "sex" are central to the ideological constructions of sex in athletic competitions, as the doctors note that "the chromosomal (genetic) sex is analyzed by sex chromatin testing, not the anatomical,

psychological, or sociological status" (851). See Arne Ljungqvist and Joe Leigh Simpson, "Medical Examination for Health of All Athletes Replacing the Need for Gender Verification in International Sports: The International Amateur Athletic Federation Plan," *Journal of the American Medical Association* 267, no. 6 (February 12, 1992): 850–52. It is interesting to note, in this regard, the extent to which Eve Kosofsky Sedgwick relies upon the notion of "chromosomal sex" as her referent for "biological sex." See *The Epistemology of the Closet*, 28; and *Tendencies* (Durham, N.C.: Duke University Press, 1993), 7.

56 Carole-Anne Tyler, "The Supreme Sacrifice?: TV, 'TV,' and the Renée Richards Story," *Differences* 1, no. 3 (1989): 160–88.

57 Teresa de Lauretis, *Technologies of Gender: Essays on Theory, Film, and Fiction* (Bloomington: Indiana University Press, 1987), 1–15.

58 This is evident in an interview with "Tula" (Caroline Cossey) on the Maury Povich show ("Tula the Transsexual Model: Now She Wants to be a Mom," June 30, 1992, Journal Graphics Transcript #210 [R-#115]). In response to a question about her ability to have an orgasm, "Tula" stated, "No, it took—because the whole part of—that part of my body was totally traumatized. It took about a year that all the nerve endings and everything to sort of, come back into order" (6). In response to a question concerning hormone intake, she responded, "Yes, I took hormones when I was in my teens just to sort of, level me out and then after that, I had an endocrinologist who sort of, kept a check on everything" (7). She also briefly discussed her breast implants. However, these comments were buried within a show that concentrated on her ability to convincingly represent the female sex—her beauty, her figure, and so on—and they were clearly meant to forestall any sustained consideration of the technologies of sex change. The comment about hormone intake is also suspect, since transsexuals need a consistent supply of hormones to maintain the appearance of the sex in which they live, as do nontranssexual men and women.

59 Gender dysphoria means gender discomfort, that is discomfort or unhappiness with one's own gender. See chapter 4 for a detailed analysis of the development of the gender dysphoria perspective within psychiatry.

60 Epstein and Straub, eds., *Body Guards*, 11.

61 This problem is particularly evident in Gary Kates's essay "D'Eon Returns to France: Gender and Power in 1777," in Epstein and Straub, eds., *Body Guards*, 167–194. See my critique of Kates's essay in chapter 4.

62 De Lauretis, *Technologies of Gender*, 2. While it could be argued that cinema is also an example of "technology" in the first sense, de Lauretis does not do this, using it primarily as an example of a social technology of representation.

63 Foucault, *History of Sexuality*, 90, 118–19.

64 Judith Halberstam uses the term "technology of gender" in its scientific sense, as the technology that maintains sexed bodies in an oppositional, binary structure (male vs. female). In this way, she demonstrates how sexual dimorphism is regulated through medical technologies. See her "Automating Gender: Postmodern Feminism in the Age of the Intelligent Machine," *Feminist Studies* 17, no. 3 (Fall 1991): 439–61.

65 Niels Hoyer, ed., *Man into Woman: An Authentic Record of a Change of Sex*, trans. H. J. Stenning (London: Jarrolds, 1933), 25–27.

66 Ibid., 18, 19.

67 Ibid., 54–55. Emphasis added. It is interesting to note that in later texts, such as Jan Morris's *Conundrum*, (male) identity is associated with the penis. See Jan Morris, *Conundrum*

(New York: Harcourt Brace Jovanovich, 1974), as well as Marjorie Garber's comments on this phallic conceit in "Spare Parts," 156.

68 Hoyer, *Man into Woman*, 55.

69 Ibid., 51.

70 Ibid., 286, 283, 273. There is no indication in the text that Lili really had a uterus, and the discourse she presents about motherhood may be a cover for the less acceptable desire for sexual intercourse. Either way, she would need a vagina. As will become clear in chapter 4, early advocates of sex change surgery did not advise vaginoplasty, since "being a woman" was all the pleasure the transsexual woman desired. Lili's autobiography suggests otherwise, as do those of other transsexual women.

71 This seems to parallel George/Christine Jorgensen's experience in the late 1940s and early 1950s. See Jorgensen, *Christine Jorgensen*.

72 Hoyer, *Man into Woman*, 273.

1. Glands, Hormones, and Personality

1 Michael Dillon, *Self: A Study in Ethics and Endocrinology* (London: Heinemann, 1946), 65.

2 According to Liz Hodgkinson, until 1970, British subjects "could get their birth certificates changed if it could be shown that they belonged more to the opposite sex than to the one in which they had been born. Since 1970, however, it has been impossible for transsexuals to get their birth certificates altered unless it can be proven that a genuine mistake was made at birth" (*Michael, Née Laura* [London: Columbus Books, 1989], 63).

3 Ibid., 61. Suzanne Kessler and Wendy McKenna would describe this situation as one in which the doctors attributed to Dillon a "cultural genital," even though he lacked its physical representative (*Gender: An Ethnomethodological Approach* [New York: John Wiley, 1978], 153–56).

4 Hodgkinson, *Michael, Née Laura*, 66. Hypospadias is a congenital condition in which the urethra does not exit from the tip of the penis. In severe cases it can be accompanied by chordee (a downward bowing of the penis) and a bifid scrotum (which looks like labia). Michael Dillon may be the "Female with Male Outlook" in Harold Gillies and Ralph Millard Jr., *The Principles and Art of Plastic Surgery* (Boston: Little, Brown, 1957), 2:383–84. While some of the data on the patient's life differ from Dillon's, it is possible that Gillies was trying to protect the patient.

5 R. G. Hoskins, *The Tides of Life: Endocrine Glands in Bodily Adjustment* (New York: Norton, 1933); Louis Berman, *The Glands Regulating Personality*, 2d ed. (New York: Macmillan, 1935); William Robinson, *Our Mysterious Life Glands; And How They Affect Us* (New York: Eugenics Publishing, 1934); Edward Huntington Williams, *How We Become Personalities: The Glands of Health, Virility, and Success* (Indianapolis: Bobbs-Merrill, 1926); and Lawrence Mayers and Arthur Welton, *What We Are and Why: A Study with Illustrations, of the Relation of the Endocrine Glands to Human Conduct and Dispositional Traits, with Special Reference to the Influence of Gland Derangements on Behavior* (New York: Sears Publishing, 1933).

6 Dillon, *Self*, 4.

7 Robinson, *Our Mysterious Life Glands*, vii.

8 Mayers and Welton, *What We Are and Why*, 29–30.

9 Williams, "Introduction" to *How We Become Personalities*, n.p.

10 Diana Long Hall suggests that "the early history of sex endocrinology" (prior to 1920) was characterized by "popular enthusiasm" but "professional ridicule." I did not find

such a split between popular and medical discourses, especially in the period between 1920 and 1950 (Hall, "Biology, Sex Hormones, and Sexism in the 1920s," in *Women and Philosophy: Toward a Theory of Liberation*, ed. Carol C. Gould and Marx W. Wartofsky [New York: Putnam, 1976], 82).

11   I will discuss this particular case more extensively in chapter 2.

12   See chapter 4. Janice Irvine remarks that Benjamin's "work on hormones through the 1920s and 1930s sparked his interest in the syndrome [transsexualism], which he thought emerged from a biological substrate" (Irvine, *Disorders of Desire: Sex and Gender in Modern American Sexology* [Philadelphia: Temple University Press, 1990], 258).

13   Roland Barthes, *The Fashion System*, trans. Matthew Ward and Richard Howard (New York: Hill and Wang, 1983), 29. See chapter 6 for further discussion of Barthes's semiotics and the use of the term "terminological code."

14   Nelly Oudshoorn, "On the Making of Sex Hormones: Research Materials and the Production of Knowledge," *Social Studies of Science* 20 (1990): 25.

15   Ibid.

16   Ibid., 25–26.

17   Ibid., 23.

18   "The Gland as a Clue to the Mystery of Human Faces," *Current Opinion* 69, no. 8 (August 19, 1920): 207–9.

19   See Victor C. Medvei, *A History of Endocrinology* (Lancaster, U.K.: MTP Press, 1982), for a complete account of the history of endocrinology. See also Hall, "Biology, Sex Hormones, and Sexism." For an excellent, recent history of sex hormone research, see Nelly Oudshoorn, *Beyond the Natural Body: An Archeology of Sex Hormones* (London: Routledge, 1994).

20   Later, when testosterone had been isolated and synthetically reproduced, it was perceived to stave off the effects of aging in men. See Paul de Kruif's *The Male Hormone* (New York: Harcourt Brace, 1945) for a lengthy discussion of testosterone's alleged rejuvenating capabilities.

21   Henry Beecher, "Anesthesiology," in *Seventy-Five Years of Medical Progress, 1878–1953*, ed. Louis Bauer (Philadelphia: Lea and Febiger, 1954), 13–28.

22   Louis Berman, *The Glands Regulating Personality*, 22, 25.

23   Edward Smith, "The Reds and the Glands," *Saturday Evening Post*, August 21, 1920, pp. 6–7, 162, 165–66, 169–70; and Smith, "Your Emotions Will Get You If You Don't Watch Out," *American Magazine* (August 1925): 32–33, 72–74.

24   See Tom Lutz, *American Nervousness 1903: An Anecdotal History* (Ithaca: Cornell University Press, 1991). Edward Smith suggested that the glands themselves produce neurasthenia ("The Reds and the Glands," 6). Edward Huntington Williams wrote, "Indeed, this ability to correct various sexual deficiencies that are part of our modern civilization and apparently the result of it, is one of the real triumphs of medicine" (*How We Become Personalities*, 95).

25   See R. Keller, "The Problem of Sexual Differentiation and Hermaphroditism," *Ciba Symposia* 2, no. 3 (June 1940): 470–77; and Hugh Young, *Genital Abnormalities, Hermaphroditism, and Related Adrenal Disorders* (Baltimore, Md.: Williams and Wilkins, 1937), 50–51. Both of these texts describe Richard Goldschmidt's theory of the intersexes, which suggested that the degree of "intersexuality" of an organism depended on the time of "sex reversal" *in utero*. Young characterizes Goldschmidt's view as "genetic" versus gonadal, since Goldschmidt repudiated the gonads as the final arbiters of biological sex.

26   This is precisely what happened with Christine Jorgensen, whose doctors used her as a research subject in return for changing her sex. See Christian Hamburger, Georg K.

Stürup, and E. Dahl-Iversen, "Transvestism: Hormonal, Psychiatric, and Surgical Treatment," *Journal of the American Medical Association* 152 (1953): 391–96. See also chapter 3.

27   Sigmund Freud, *Three Essays on the Theory of Sexuality* (1905), in *The Standard Edition of the Complete Psychological Works of Sigmund Freud*, vol. 7, trans. and ed. James Strachey (London: Hogarth Press and the Institute of Psychoanalysis, 1953), 124–245; and Freud, "Analysis Terminable and Interminable" (1937), in ibid., vol. 23, 211–53. Both of these issues are central to the etiology of transsexualism as it is defined today.

28   Berman, *Glands Regulating Personality*, 21.

29   Smith, "Your Emotions," 32.

30   See, for example, ibid.

31   Edwin E. Slosson, "From Complexes to Glands," *Scientific Monthly* 15 (August 1922): 189–91. Emphasis added. See also Williams, 87–91.

32   Max G. Schlapp and Edward H. Smith, *The New Criminology: A Consideration of the Chemical Causation of Abnormal Behavior* (New York: Boni and Liveright, 1928), 24–28.

33   André Tridon, *Psychoanalysis and Gland Personalities* (New York: Brentano's, 1923), 11. See also Ivo Geike Cobb, *The Glands of Destiny (A Study of Personality)*, 2d ed. (London: Heinemann, 1936), 70–87. D. Rhodes Allison and R. G. Gordon advocated a "combined approach" for all medical practitioners, who they believed should pay attention to psychological factors in treating all physical illnesses (*Psychotherapy: Its Uses and Limitations*, Oxford Medical Publications [London: Oxford University Press, 1948], esp. 59–72).

34   Havelock Ellis, "Sexual Inversion," part 4 of *Studies in the Psychology of Sex*, vol. 1 (New York: Random House, 1942), 316; Ellis, "Analysis of the Sexual Impulse," in part 2 of ibid., 16–17; and Magnus Hirschfeld, *Sex in Human Relationships*, trans. John Rodker (London: John Lane/Bodley Head, 1935), 177–183. Arthur Weil cites Hirschfeld after the following discussion: "Homosexuality may, consequently, be caused by the presence in one person of male and female gonads, either as separate organs or as combined ovotestes. The relative proportions of male and female germ gland tissues, and the respective times of the separate optimal activities of each gland, will determine the proportionate mixtures of masculine and feminine sexual characters, both of body and mind" (*The Internal Secretions: For the Use of Students and Physicians*, trans. Jacob Gutman [New York: Macmillan, 1924], 237–38).

35   Smith, "Your Emotions"; Smith, "The Reds and the Glands"; R. G. Hoskins, "Endocrine Factors in Personality," *Scientific Monthly* 40 (June 1935): 560; Marie Beynon Ray, "Gland-Made Criminals," *World's Work* 59 (June 1930): 49–50; Alden P. Armagnac, "Gland Studies Show Why We Behave As We Do," *Popular Science Monthly* 140 (May 1942): 68, 70; Mayers and Welton, *What We Are and Why*, 71, 98–99, 121; Schlapp and Smith, *New Criminology*; and Herman H. Rubin, *Glands, Sex, and Personality* (New York: Wilfred Funk, 1952), 173. For a critical view of endocrine criminal theory, see W. H. Howell, "Crime and Disturbed Endocrine Function," *Science*, n.s. 76, supp. (October 28, 1933): 8–9.

36   Dwight Billings and Thomas Urban, "The Socio-Medical Construction of Transsexualism: An Interpretation and Critique," *Social Problems* 29, no. 3 (February 1982): 269.

37   *Ciba Symposia* 1, no. 1 (April 1939): n.p.

38   Nupercainal is still available today.

39   *Ciba Symposia* 17, no. 12 (March 1946): n.p. Emphasis added.

40   Personal communication, "Coming Together/Working Together" Conference, International Foundation for Gender Education, Denver, Colo. (April 1991).

41   At a significant point in Christine Jorgensen's life as George, he/she obtained estrogen tablets from a pharmacist; without a prescription, Jorgensen claimed to be using the estrogens in an experiment at the Manhattan Medical and Dental Assistant's School. See

Christine Jorgensen, *Christine Jorgensen: A Personal Autobiography* (New York: Paul Eriksson, 1967), 86–88.

42 The other known cessation of hormonal secretion is that of the thymus gland, which reaches its highest development at puberty and then undergoes involution (replacement by fatty and fibrous tissue).

43 Schlapp and Smith claimed that menopause can contribute to the development of kleptomania in women. See *The New Criminology*, 216–18.

44 Quoted in Weil, *Internal Secretions*, 238; also quoted in Rubin, *Glands, Sex, and Personality*, 175. Anne Fausto-Sterling uses another significant quote from Virchow as an epigraph to a chapter in her book *Myths of Gender*: "Woman is a pair of ovaries with a human being attached, whereas man is a human being furnished with a pair of testes" (*Myths of Gender: Biological Theories about Men and Women* [New York: Basic Books, 1985], 90).

45 William Berkeley, *The Principles and Practice of Endocrine Medicine* (Philadelphia: Lea and Febiger, 1926), 295. Emphasis added. See also Cobb, 78; and Chandra Chakraberty, *Endocrine Glands (In Health and Disease)* (New York: Omin, 1923), 135.

46 Rubin, *Glands, Sex, and Personality*, 163–64.

47 Weil, *Internal Secretions*, 244–45.

48 Mayers and Welton, *What We Are and Why*, 36, 313–14.

49 Berman, *Glands Regulating Personality*, 183–88; Smith, "The Reds and the Glands," 169–70; Schlapp and Smith, *New Criminology*, 134, 215–16. Schlapp and Smith contended, in addition, that "[t]housands of cases examined and investigated at Post-Graduate [hospital] have revealed that, with only the most obvious exceptions, the birth of deficient children has always been attended by emotional upheavals in the mothers during pregnancy, and it has been easy to demonstrate that gland disturbance was present" (135). Women, in their argument, merit attention as the ideal perpetrators of glandular imbalance in others, as well as being subjects of that imbalance themselves.

Evidence for woman as the ideal subject of endocrinology exists in a short film called *Endocrine Glands*, made for use in schools in the 1940s. This film uses a representation of the female body as the model for demonstrating human endocrinology, an unusual event in scientific representation, where the male body (as "norm" of the human) is usually chosen to represent the human body. See A. J. Carlson and H. G. Swann, *Endocrine Glands* (Chicago: Erpi Classroom Films, 1940).

50 Oudshoorn, "On the Making of Sex Hormones," 23. Oudshoorn mentions in a note that "[a]ndrology is usually still studied in urology departments. Moreover, there still exist vast differences in the use of gynaecological clinics and andrological clinics. The routine use of gynaecological clinics by women, including for regular Pap smears, provides clinicians with access to large numbers of women. A routine use of andrological clinics by men has not (yet?) developed, due to the lack of any regular screening programme for men (for example, for prostate cancer). So, in addition to the institutionalization of specialties, the introduction of screening programmes may also differentiate the access to research materials derived from the bodies of women and men" (32, n. 70).

51 The exact ratio has never been established, but has been suggested to be as high as 8:1 (men to women). The numbers of men and women seeking sex change are currently converging, however. See John Money and Anke Ehrhardt, *Man and Woman, Boy and Girl* (Baltimore: Johns Hopkins University Press, 1972), 147; Harry Benjamin, *The Transsexual Phenomenon* (New York: Julian Press, 1966); and Ira Pauly, "Adult Manifestations of Female Transsexualism," in *Transsexualism and Sex Reassignment*, ed. Richard Green and John Money (Baltimore: Johns Hopkins University Press, 1969), 59–61.

52   Judith Shapiro, "Transsexualism: Reflections on the Persistence of Gender and the Mutability of Sex," in *Body Guards: The Cultural Politics of Gender Ambiguity*, ed. Julia Epstein and Kristina Straub (New York: Routledge, 1991), 269. Judith Sensibar suggested to me that another reason may be men's greater access to the economic resources necessary to pay for the extensive medical procedures (Feminist Theory Workshop, University of Chicago, April 1994).

53   This is similar to the development of sex typing in the psychological research of the period. See Joseph Pleck, "The Theory of Male Sex Role Identity: Its Rise and Fall, 1936 to the Present," in *In the Shadow of the Past: Psychology Portrays the Sexes*, ed. Miriam Lewin (New York: Columbia University Press, 1984), 205–25; and Pleck, *The Myth of Masculinity* (Cambridge: MIT Press, 1981).

54   Londa Schiebinger, "Skeletons in the Closet: The First Illustrations of the Female Skeleton in Eighteenth-Century Anatomy," *Representations* 14 (Spring 1986): 42.

55   Thomas Laqueur, *Making Sex: Body and Gender from the Greeks to Freud* (Cambridge, Mass.: Harvard University Press, 1990). See also chapter 6 of this book for an extended discussion of Laqueur's thesis.

56   Cynthia Eagle Russett, *Sexual Science: The Victorian Construction of Womanhood* (Cambridge, Mass.: Harvard University Press, 1989).

57   John Money describes the early perspective on sex hormones as "univariate": "When the sex hormones were isolated in the 1920s and synthesized in the 1930s, they were named for estrus (estrogen), for the testis (testosterone), and for gestation (progesterone), thus setting the stage for an oversimplified myth of causality, relating masculinity and femininity of behavior, as well as of morphology and reproductive function, to male and female hormones, respectively. . . . [This] impeded the progress of psychoendocrinology until mid-century and beyond. . . . The hypothesis of a causal connection between hormone levels and homosexuality in men persisted, and continues to do so" (*Love and Love Sickness: The Science of Sex, Gender Difference, and Pair Bonding* [Baltimore, Md.: Johns Hopkins University Press, 1980], 189).

58   Frank Lillie, "General Biological Introduction," *Sex and Internal Secretions: A Survey of Recent Research*, 2d ed., ed. Edgar Allen (Baltimore, Md.: Williams and Wilkins, 1939), 3–4.

59   For an extended discussion of "hormonal dimorphism," see Kessler and McKenna, *Gender: An Ethnomethodological Approach*, 73–74. For another interpretation of Lillie's statement, see Hall, "Biology, Sex Hormones, and Sexism," 86–91.

60   Nelly Oudshoorn, "Endocrinologists and the Conceptualization of Sex, 1920–1940," *Journal of the History of Biology* 23, no. 2 (Summer 1990): 164, 171. See Oudshoorn, *Beyond the Natural Body*, 15–41, for a more extensive discussion of this argument.

61   See Hall, "Biology, Sex Hormones, and Sexism." Oudshoorn seems to have another perspective on the inability of researchers to give up "male" and "female" hormones as signifiers in "On the Making of Sex Hormones" (7–8). Bonnie Spanier writes that "[t]he term 'sex steroids' reflects and reproduces our dominant masculinist sex/gender system in spite of the knowledge that men and women all have both male (androgens) and female (estrogens) sex hormones, that these male and female hormones are interconverted in the body, that they affect many functions besides sex, that men and women have differing relative amounts of these hormones, and that those relative proportions change over the life cycle (so that women after menopause have lower levels of the major estrogen and progestin than do men of the same age)" (" 'Lessons' from 'Nature': Gender Ideology and Sexual Ambiguity in Biology," in *Body Guards*, ed. Epstein and Straub, 342).

62 Bernhard Zondek, *Clinical and Experimental Investigations on the Genital Functions and Their Hormonal Regulation* (Baltimore, Md.: Williams and Wilkins, 1941), x.

63 Diana Long Hall writes that the significance of the sex hormones "for sexuality is an issue that has not been resolved, as biologists have decided that female testosterone is functional—it regulates muscle nitrogen and sexual libido among other things—but that male estrogen is 'paradoxical' or a biochemical accident. Further research, however, does suggest that the female organism can protect itself against the virilizing effects of testosterone.... In sum, the old biological paradigm has undergone considerable modification; while its preoccupation with the biological issue of masculinity/femininity has not been abandoned, it has dissolved into a number of technical issues" ("Biology, Sex Hormones, and Sexism," 91).

64 Bonnie Spanier writes that "[a] feminist analysis of the formal scientific discourse of the field of molecular biology uncovers inaccurate and masculinist superimpositions of Western sex/gender systems onto organisms at the cellular and molecular levels, and explores the mutually reinforcing use of 'sex' as scientists move it back and forth between the molecular level of organization and the macro level of animal and, particularly, human behavior. My analysis . . . reveals how a masculinist ideology of a dualistic and asymmetric sex/gender system is inappropriately imprinted onto the microscopic levels of life and is then utilized to reinforce notions of natural gender dichotomy and its corollary heterosexism" ("'Lessons' from 'Nature,'" 334).

65 In relation to more recent research, Bonnie Spanier writes that in the context of "the biology of the cell and molecular levels of organization," "'natural' models exist which support a notion of gender ambiguity that challenges conventional meanings of male and female. However, I show that the paradigm of heterosexism—superimposing male and female based on a biological determinist ideology of fundamental difference—prevails, not surprisingly, and selectively overrides the use of nature as a model of alternative gender and sexual relationships" (ibid., 329–30).

66 Paradoxically, this resulted in the diffusion of "sex" itself as a signifying element in the enlarging semiotic economy of the sexed body. Sex was everything, insofar as the sex hormones could determine the most mundane details of a person's behavior. Because of this, "sex" began to lose its specific signifying capacity, until it was relegated to the strictly biological realm by the introduction of the idea of "gender" as the social articulation of sexed identity in the 1950s. See chapter 3.

67 Berman, *Glands Regulating Personality*, 177.

68 Ibid., 204. Emphasis added. Julia Epstein and Kristina Straub write that "[t]he notion of a 'natural' continuum along which sexual differentiation subtly occurs derives, then, from the earliest biomedical explanations in Western discourse [5th century B.C.E. Corpus Hippocratum]" ("Introduction: The Guarded Body," in *Body Guards*, ed. Epstein and Straub, 19–20).

69 Susan Lawrence pointed this out to me.

70 Berman, *Glands Regulating Personality*, 204–5. Emphasis added.

71 Chakraberty, *Endocrine Glands*, 140–42. Emphasis added.

72 Berman, *Glands Regulating Personality*, 88. Emphasis added.

73 Ibid.

74 Margaret Mead, "Cultural Determinants of Sexual Behavior," in *Sex and Internal Secretions*, 3d ed., ed. William Young and George Corner (Baltimore, Md.: Williams and Wilkins, 1961), 2:1476.

75 This is discussed at length in chapter 4. Some physicians and researchers believed that

contemporary technologies had provided adequate means to regulate sexual deviance. Richard Goldschmidt wrote in 1923 that "[w]e concluded then, starting once again from our intersexuality studies, that one should be able to correct homosexuality by the transplantation of normal gonads. Steinach and Lichtenstein have now actually carried out this experiment with success!" (*The Mechanism and Physiology of Sex Determination*, trans. William J. Dakin [London: Methuen, 1923], 249).

76   If it seems odd to use the work of a female-to-male transsexual to exemplify the effect of the glandular thesis on arguments for transsexualism—which I have already noted is more prevalent in the other direction, especially in the period of its emergence—that is a contradiction I cannot resolve. It is a simple fact that the one book connecting the glandular thesis to advocacy for transsexualism, a book published prior to Christine Jorgensen's famous transformation and the emergence of transsexualism into the public domain, was written by a female-to-male transsexual. It is also the case that the essay written by David O. Cauldwell that introduced the term "transsexual" was also about a woman wanting to become a man (D. O. Cauldwell, "Psychopathia Transexualis," *Sexology* 16 [December 1949]: 274–80). Nevertheless, early theories of transsexualism were almost exclusively based on male-to-female transsexualism, as will be clear in chapter 4. That some women who wished to become men in the early period of transsexualism's emergence and codification were able to use the glandular thesis to support their requests demonstrates that while endocrine discourses clearly marked "women" as exemplary endocrine subjects, "men" were not exempt from being understood as hormonally regulated as well.

77   Dillon, *Self*, 4.

78   Ibid., 98.

79   This argument identifies Dillon as a Lamarckian. Lamarck, an early nineteenth-century biologist, believed that acquired characteristics could be inherited. This theory enjoyed a resurgence with the development of Darwinian evolutionary theories in the mid-nineteenth century. Lamarck's ideas were largely disproved in the late nineteenth and early twentieth centuries, yet they informed the beliefs of a number of important thinkers, among them Lester Frank Ward and Charlotte Perkins Gilman. Dillon's Lamarckianism seems to stop, however, at the point of using education and social change to affect physiology and "innate" hormonal influence; his Lamarckianism, unlike Gilman's, is committed to changing the body and not society.

80   It might seem odd, in the context of Dillon's own experience as a female-to-male transsexual, that he would argue the traditional glandular thesis position of women's greater hormonal connection. That he does demonstrates his misogyny, commented upon by Liz Hodgkinson, his biographer, as well.

81   Dillon, *Self*, 105. The argument here concerning the "innate" nature of sex identification does not contradict Dillon's Lamarckianism as much as it might seem to. Lamarckian thinking was decidedly *hereditarian*, as it upheld the notion that characteristics were passed on through biological mechanisms of heredity. However, Dillon's staunch position against the contemporary acquisition of characteristics that might subsequently be passed on demonstrates his desire to target the body, and not society, for alteration.

82   Ibid., 39. This last claim is not substantiated earlier in the text, and represents one of Dillon's frequent rhetorical moves: to make a claim and to describe it as already having been established, when it has not been.

83   Ibid.

84   The concept of inversion is logically antithetical to that of a gradation of sexes, because

it implies an absolutism of binary categories rather than a blending of possible stages between two categorical extremes.

85   Dillon, *Self*, 49–53. Emphasis added. Lili Elbe suggested this in her autobiography as well (Neils Hoyer, ed., *Man into Woman: An Authentic Record of a Change of Sex*, trans. H. J. Stenning [London: Jarrolds, 1933]).

86   Hodgkinson, *Michael, Née Laura*.

87   Dillon, *Self*, 60–65.

88   Hamburger, Stürup, and Dahl-Iversen, "Transvestism," 392; Harry Benjamin, "Transvestism and Transsexualism," *International Journal of Sexology* 7 (1953): 13.

89   Dillon, *Self*, 122.

2. Plastic Ideologies and Plastic Transformations

1   See chapter 6 for a detailed theoretical discussion of this last point.

2   Current feminist critiques of cosmetic surgery tend to concentrate on its very recent history. In examining the discourses of cosmetic and plastic surgery from its inception during World War I through the period following World War II, I have been able to ascertain the extent to which plastic surgery *since its beginnings* has focused on transforming "normality" so as to make a place for itself as a surgical specialty. In addition, in analyzing the construction of cosmetic surgery before the widespread understanding of the self as *gendered*, I was able to examine how the creation of cosmetic surgery was central to the development of the concept of gender that we use today. This distinguishes my account from those critics who would see cosmetic surgery as one "process whereby biotechnologies are articulated with traditional and ideological beliefs about gender" (Balsamo 209; emphasis added). My work suggests that gender is a product, and not just the target, of plastic surgical discourses. See Anne Balsamo, "On the Cutting Edge: Cosmetic Surgery and the Technological Production of the Gendered Body," *Camera Obscura* 28 (January 1992): 206–37; Kathryn Pauly Morgan, "Women and the Knife: Cosmetic Surgery and the Colonization of Women's Bodies," *Hypatia* 6, no. 3 (Fall 1991): 25–53; and Naomi Wolf, *The Beauty Myth* (New York: William Morrow, 1991).

3   Jerome Webster, "Vilray Papin Blair, 1872–1955," in *The Source Book of Plastic Surgery*, ed. Frank McDowell (Baltimore, Md.: Williams and Wilkins, 1977), 487.

4   Gustave Aufricht, "The Development of Plastic Surgery in the United States," *Plastic and Reconstructive Surgery* 1 (July 1946): 21.

5   Maxwell Maltz, *Evolution of Plastic Surgery* (New York: Froben Press, 1946); Maltz, *New Faces—New Futures: Rebuilding Character with Plastic Surgery* (New York: Richard R. Smith, 1936), ix–x.

6   Reginald Pound, *Gillies: Surgeon Extraordinary* (London: Michael Joseph, 1964), 65, 72–73, 87–88, 111–12, and 122–23.

7   "Cinderella Surgery," *Reader's Digest* 35 (August 1939): 84, 85. Emphasis added.

8   "Appearance Improved by Plastic Surgery Methods," *Science Newsletter* 34 (September 17, 1938): 185.

9   "Skill of Plastic Surgeon Heals Personality Too," *Science Newsletter* 36 (November 11, 1939): 312. Emphasis added.

10   "Turning a New Face to the World," *Reader's Digest* 31 (August 1937): 30.

11   "The Case of the Ugly Thief," *Time* 53 (April 11, 1949): 69.

12   "Pretty Does As Pretty Is?" *Time* 50 (October 13, 1947): 52.

13   "Remolding Entire Lives by Surgery: Facial Operations Alter Human Characters and Capacities," *Literary Digest* 121 (May 9, 1936): 18.

14   "I'm Getting a New Face," *Good Housekeeping* 111 (October 1940): 26–27, 114–15.

15   Ruth Murrin, "A New Nose in a Week," *Good Housekeeping* 111 (November 1940): 82. Emphasis added.

16   Martin Abramson, "A New Look, A New Life," *Better Homes and Gardens* 30 (May 1952): 156, 309.

17   Maltz, *New Faces*, 72–76.

18   Elizabeth Honor, "Cosmetic Surgery," *Cosmopolitan* 141 (August 1956): 31.

19   Elizabeth Honor, "Beauty Can Be Bought," *Cosmopolitan* 144 (June 1958): 70.

20   Ibid., 73, 71.

21   Maltz, *New Faces*, 239–41.

22   Harold Gillies and Ralph Millard Jr., *The Principles and Art of Plastic Surgery* (Boston: Little, Brown, 1957), 2:385–88; Roberta Cowell, *Roberta Cowell's Story* (New York: British Book Centre, 1954), n.p. Ellipses in original.

23   Maltz, *New Faces*, 301, 260, 296, 299. Emphasis added.

24   See Georges Canguilhem, *On the Normal and the Pathological*, trans. Carolyn R. Fawcett, Studies in the History of Modern Science 3 (Dordrecht, Holland: D. Reidel, 1978), for an extended discussion of the concept of the normal and its relation to the pathological in Western medical discourses.

25   Honor, "Cosmetic Surgery," 31.

26   See "On the Cutting Edge," *People Weekly* 37, no. 3 (January 27, 1992): 60–64, 66, 68.

27   John M. Goin and Marcia Kraft Goin, *Changing the Body: Psychological Effects of Plastic Surgery* (Baltimore, Md.: Williams and Wilkins, 1981), 145.

28   Ibid., 191–92.

29   See Nicholas Regush, "Toxic Breasts," *Mother Jones* 17, no. 1 (January/February 1992): 24–31. Some of these claims are disputed in a study released to the media in June 1994.

30   Goin and Goin, *Changing the Body*, 3–6.

31   Ibid., 89–105. See also Karl Meninger, "Polysurgery and Polysurgical Addiction," *Psychoanalytic Quarterly* 3 (1934): 173–99; and Helene Deutsch, "Some Psychoanalytic Observations in Surgery," *Psychosomatic Medicine* 4, no. 1 (January 1942): 105–15.

32   Goin and Goin, *Changing the Body*, 134–35, 136, 128.

33   Ellen Berscheid, "An Overview of the Psychological Effects of Physical Attractiveness," in *Psychological Aspects of Facial Form*, ed. G. William Lucker, Katherine A. Ribbons, and James A. MacNamara Jr., Monograph 11, Craniofacial Growth Series (Ann Arbor: Center for Human Growth and Development, University of Michigan, 1980), 4, 5, 7.

34   Ronald Strauss, "Surgery, Activism, and Aesthetics: A Sociological Perspective on Treating Facial Disfigurements," in Lucker, Ribbons, and MacNamara, *Psychological Aspects*, 206–7.

35   Edmund D. Pellegrino, "The Sociocultural Impact of Twentieth-Century Therapeutics," in *The Therapeutic Revolution: Essays in the Social History of American Medicine*, ed. Morris J. Vogel and Charles E. Rosenberg (Philadelphia: University of Pennsylvania Press, 1979), 246, 264.

36   See Wolf, *The Beauty Myth*.

37   H. O. Bames, "Breast Malformation and a New Approach to the Problem of the Small Breast," *Plastic and Reconstructive Surgery* 5, no. 6 (June 1950): 504.

38   That the "norm" is defined in relation to artistic ideals of the female form encourages this response by women. See discussion of Maltz and Dürer above.

39   See Morgan, "Women and the Knife."

40   See James Reardon and Judi McMahon, *Plastic Surgery for Men: The Complete Illustrated Guide* (New York: Everest House, 1981); Eugene Courtiss, *Male Aesthetic Surgery*, 2d. ed. (St. Louis, Mo.: Mosby, 1991); and James O. Stallings, "For Men," in *A New You: How Plastic Surgery Can Change Your Life,* by James O. Stallings, with Terry Morris (New York: New American Library, 1977), 161–87.

41   W. Milton Adams, "Problems and Opportunities in the Field of Plastic Surgery," *Plastic and Reconstructive Surgery* 15 (January 1955): 1, 2. Emphasis added.

42   Thanks to Clair James for clarifying this point for me.

43   Anthony F. Wallace, *The Progress of Plastic Surgery: An Introductory History* (Oxford: Meeuws, 1982), 163.

44   John E. Hoopes, "Operative Treatment of the Female Transsexual," in *Transsexualism and Sex Reassignment*, ed. Richard Green and John Money (Baltimore: Johns Hopkins University Press, 1969), 342.

45   Maltz, *Evolution of Plastic Surgery*, 269.

46   Liz Hodgkinson, *Michael, Née Laura* (London: Columbus Books, 1989), 77.

47   Gillies and Millard, *Principles and Art of Plastic Surgery*, 2:383–85.

48   Stanley Biber, slide presentation at "Coming Together/Working Together" convention, Denver, Colo., April 13, 1991.

49   Leslie Martin Lothstein, *Female-to-Male Transsexualism: Historical, Clinical and Theoretical Issues* (Boston: Routledge and Kegan Paul, 1983), p. 299; Marjorie Garber, "Spare Parts: The Surgical Construction of Gender," *Differences* 1, no. 3 (Fall 1989): 148.

50   Biber, slide presentation.

51   Vern L. Bullough and Bonnie Bullough comment that outcomes for phalloplasty continue to be inadequate in the 1990s, causing female-to-male transsexuals to seek alternative forms of phallic morphology (*Cross Dressing, Sex, and Gender* [Philadelphia: University of Penssylvania Press, 1993], 263).

52   Wallace, *Progress of Plastic Surgery*, 79–81.

53   Basically, this means that a cavity for the vagina would be hollowed out, and then the surface would not be covered but would be left to create its own epithelial lining. Alice Dreger has pointed out to me that secondary epithelialization was a method of vaginoplasty practiced in England and France from about the 1860s onward (personal communication, June 16, 1994).

54   Heinz Gelbke, "Plastic Surgery," in *Intersexuality*, ed. Claus Overzier (1961; reprint, London: Academic Press, 1963), 490.

55   Gillies and Millard, *Principles and Art of Plastic Surgery*, 2:384–88.

56   Significantly, the medical literature only mentions the first two methods of maintaining vaginal form.

57   William Walters, Trudy Kennedy, and Michael Ross, "Results of Gender Reassignment," in *Transsexualism and Sex Reassignment*, ed. William Walters and Michael Ross (Melbourne: Oxford University Press, 1986), 149–51; Lena McEwan, Simon Ceber, and Joyce Daws, "Female-to-Male Surgical Genital Reassignment," in Walters and Ross, *Transsexualism*, 103–12.

58   Marjorie Garber, "Spare Parts," 149.

59   In addition, Garber ignores other ideological interpretations. One could argue that societies have a significant investment in reconstructing the penises of men who have lost theirs due to accident or war injury, yet though these contingencies have motivated surgical developments, they have not resulted in surgical success.

3. Managing Intersexuality and Producing Gender

1   Suzanne J. Kessler, "The Medical Construction of Gender: Case Management of Inter-sexed Infants," *Signs: Journal of Women in Culture and Society* 16, no. 1 (1990): 5, 4.

2   Ibid., 5–6.

3   Ibid., 6–7.

4   Ibid., 10.

5   Ibid., 13.

6   Ibid., 25.

7   Janice Irvine discusses this as a general trend in sexology in the twentieth century. See *Disorders of Desire: Sex and Gender in Modern American Sexology* (Philadelphia: Temple University Press, 1990), 229.

8   Suzanne J. Kessler and Wendy McKenna, *Gender: An Ethnomethodological Approach* (New York: John Wiley, 1978), 7.

9   I'd like to thank Gilbert Herdt for suggesting this language to me.

10 Julia Epstein, "Either/Or—Neither/Both: Sexual Ambiguity and the Ideology of Gen-der," *Genders* 7 (Spring 1990): 104–5.

11 Ibid., 116.

12 Ibid., 130.

13 Ibid., 105, 118, 121.

14 The development of this terminological distinction will be discussed at length later in the chapter.

15 Alice Dreger suggests that until the 1920s, in France and England there were a signifi-cant number of cases of hermaphroditism where there was no medical intervention attempted at all, and she thinks this may indicate a cultural difference concerning the willingness to use available technologies. Of course, the kind of routine interventions I discuss in this chapter only became truly routine following World War I, so more re-search would need to be done to substantiate this hypothesis (personal communication, June 16, 1994).

16 Epstein discusses the development of this notion of a "predominating sex" in "Either/Or—Neither/Both."

17 Michel Foucault, Introduction to *Herculine Barbin*, by Herculine Barbin, trans. Richard McDougal (New York: Pantheon, 1980), vii–xvii.

18 John Money, Joan Hampson, and John Hampson, "Hermaphroditism: Recommenda-tions Concerning Assignment of Sex, Change of Sex, and Psychologic Management," *Bulletin of the Johns Hopkins Hospital* 97 (1955): 284.

19 See R. Keller, "The Problem of Sexual Differentiation and Hermaphroditism," *Ciba Sym-posia* 2, no. 3 (June 1940): 470–77, for a concise, general description of Goldschmidt's theory of the intersexes. Significantly, Goldschmidt's theory depended upon the idea that in mammals the ovary had been observed to become a testis but not the other way around. Because of this, the theory postulated that "mammalian intersexes must also be genetically female" (Keller, "The Problem," 476), a fact which contradicts present knowledge. Other researchers, however, claimed that gonadal tissue is primarily tes-ticular: for example, James F. McCahey states that "in both cases [male and female de-velopment] the primary gonad is testicular. In the male it develops directly into a testis, but in the female the cortex of the ovary grows around it, compressing it into the me-dulla so that it remains vestigial under ordinary circumstances. If this primary gonad is stimulated experimentally, intersexuality may be produced in the female" (McCahey,

"Hermaphroditism: A New Conception," *Archives of Pathology* 25 [1938]: 927–28). See also McCahey, "A New Conception of Hermaphroditism," *Surgery, Gynecology, and Obstetrics* 67 (November 1938): 646–54; and Richard Goldschmidt, *The Mechanism and Physiology of Sex Determination*, trans. William J. Dakin (London: Methuen, 1923), esp. 234–54. John Money writes that "[i]n past usage, a genetic etiology was sometimes assumed for intersexuality, and a hormonal etiology for hermaphroditism, but the distinction is now known to be untenable" (*Love and Love Sickness: The Science of Sex, Gender, and Pairbonding* [Baltimore, Md.: Johns Hopkins University Press, 1980], 218).

20   See Joseph Pleck, "The Theory of Male Sex Role Identity: Its Rise and Fall, 1936 to the Present," in *In the Shadow of the Past: Psychology Portrays the Sexes*, ed. Miriam Lewin (New York: Columbia University Press, 1984): 205–25; and Lewis Terman and Catherine Miles, *Sex and Personality* (New York: McGraw-Hill, 1936).

21   Hypospadias is a condition in which the urethral opening is not at the tip of the penis but is located somewhere on the shaft or at the base of the penis. It is often accompanied by chordee, or the bowing down of the penis. According to Alice Dreger, plastic operations for hypospadias became somewhat routine in France and England in the 1890s (personal communication, June 16, 1994).

22   Hugh Young, "Preliminary Report of a Case of Mixed Sex: An Apparent Male with a Testis in Scrotum on Right Side; Ovary, Tube and Uterus in Inguinal Canal on Left Side," *Bulletin of the Johns Hopkins Hospital* 35 (June 1924): 167.

23   Hugh Young, "Operative Treatment of True Hermaphroditism: A New Technique for Curing Hypospadias," *Archives of Surgery* 41 (August 1941): 560. Emphasis added.

24   G. Cotte, "Plastic Operations for Sexual Ambiguity (Gynandrynes and Androgynes)" *Journal of the Mount Sinai Hospital* 14 (September–October 1947): 171.

25   Ibid., 172.

26   Ibid. "Cryptorchidism" is a term used to describe the failure of testes to descend into the scrotum.

27   Ibid., 173–74. Emphasis added.

28   See Jacob Finesinger, Joe Meigs, and Hirsh Sulkowitch, "Clinical, Psychiatric, and Psychoanalytic Study of a Case of Male Pseudohermaphroditism," *American Journal of Obstetrics and Gynecology* 44 (1942): 31–37; Parke Smith, James Mack, and Maynard Murray, "A Case of True Hermaphroditism," *Journal of Urology* 41 (1939): 780–800; Clinton Smith and A. Lloyd Stockwell, "Female Pseudohermaphroditism," *Journal of Urology* 43 (1940): 234–43; J. Riddle Goffe, "A Pseudohermaphrodite, in Which the Female Characteristics Predominated; Operation for the Removal of Skin Covering It for the Formation of the Vaginal Canal," *American Journal of Obstetrics* 40 (December 1903): 755–63; James Masson, "A Case of Hermaphroditism," *American Journal of Obstetrics and Gynecology* 9 (1925): 81–86; William Rubovits and William Saphir, "Intersexuality," *Journal of the American Medical Association* 110 (1938): 1823–26; Harold Hartley, "A Case of Hermaphroditism," *British Medical Journal* 2 (1928): 342–43; and William Carlisle and C. J. Geiger, "Two Cases of Intersexuality," *American Journal of Obstetrics* 36 (1938): 1047–52.

29   Francis M. Ingersoll and Jacob E. Finesinger, "A Case of Male Pseudohermaphroditism: The Importance of Psychiatry in the Surgery of This Condition," *Surgical Clinics of North America* 27 (October 1947): 1222.

30   Ibid., 1224–25.

31   Louis E. Fazen, "Female Intersex: Report of an Unusual Case," *Wisconsin Medical Journal* 48 (December 1949): 1077.

32   Ibid., 1078.

33   Albert Ellis, "The Sexual Psychology of Human Hermaphrodites," *Psychosomatic Medicine* 7 (March 1945): 119.

34   F. Guternatsch, "True Hermaphroditism: Concerning the 37 Cases Reported," *Journal of Urology* 52 (December 1944): 621.

35   Ingersoll and Finesinger, "Case of Male Pseudohermaphroditism," 1218–25.

36   Yvonne Young pointed this out to me at the annual conference for the Society for Literature and Science, Atlanta, Ga. (October 1992).

37   Leona M. Bayer, "Pseudo-Hermaphroditism: A Psychosomatic Case Study," *Psychosomatic Medicine* 9 (1947): 246–55.

38   Rita S. Finkler, "Social and Psychological Readjustment of a Pseudohermaphrodite under Endocrine Therapy," *Journal of Clinical Endocrinology* 8 (1948): 88–96.

39   Hugh Young, *Genital Abnormalities, Hermaphroditism, and Related Adrenal Diseases* (Baltimore, Md.: Williams and Wilkins, 1937).

40   Ibid., 84–86.

41   Ibid., 87.

42   Ibid., 87, 89.

43   Ibid., 91. Emphasis added.

44   Ibid., 90.

45   Ibid., 92.

46   Ibid., 142.

47   Later in the book, Young discussed two cases where the parents refused to change the sex of children, in opposition to the physicians' diagnoses. See ibid., 154–58.

48   Anne Fausto-Sterling, "The Five Sexes: Why Male and Female Are Not Enough," *The Sciences* (March/April 1993): 23.

49   Epstein, "Either/Or—Neither/Both," 130.

50   Fausto-Sterling, "The Five Sexes," 24. Emphasis added.

51   Money, Hampson, and Hampson, "Hermaphroditism"; Money, Hampson, and Hampson, "An Examination of Some Basic Sexual Concepts: The Evidence of Human Hermaphroditism," *Bulletin of the Johns Hopkins Hospital* 97, no. 4 (1955): 301–19; Money, Hampson, and Hampson, "Sexual Incongruities and Psychopathology: The Evidence of Human Hermaphroditism," *Bulletin of the Johns Hopkins Hospital*, 98, no. 1 (1956): 43–57; and Money, Hampson, and Hampson, "Imprinting and the Establishment of Gender Role," *Archives of Neurology and Psychiatry* 77 (1957): 333–36.

52   Money, Hampson, and Hampson, "Hermaphroditism," 285.

53   A 1963 *Lancet* article attempted to reinstate the reproductive principle in the case management of intersexual subjects, and thus represents an example of that position. See Ian Berg, Harold H. Nixon, and Robert MacMahon, "Change of Assigned Sex at Puberty," *Lancet* 2 (1963): 1216–17. See also C. J. Dewhurst and R. R. Gordon, "Change of Sex," *Lancet*: 2 (1963): 1213–16.

54   J. A. Simpson and E. S. C. Weiner, eds., *Oxford English Dictionary*, 2d ed., vol. 6 (Oxford: Clarendon Press, 1989), 428.

55   "Interview [with] John Money," *Omni* 8, no. 7 (April 1986): 80.

56   Janice Irvine writes: "Gender research in the 1940s and 1950s was impelled by the ongoing anxieties wrought by World War II. By the mid-1950s the sociologist Talcott Parsons had applied his conception of 'role' to the issue of gender, embedding the notion of sex role in functionalism, the dominant social theory of the decade. This ensured

the analysis of gender issues, not as power relations, but as roles and identities to be learned, accommodated, and negotiated within the context of marriage and the family" (*Disorders of Desire*, 234).

57   John Money, "The Development of Sexuality and Eroticism in Human Kind," in *Heterotypical Behaviour in Man and Animals*, ed. M. Haug, P. F. Brain, and C. Aron (London: Chapman and Hall, 1991), 131. His full treatment of this issue reads as follows: "The totality [of masculinity or femininity] includes work and play, legal status, education, manners, etiquette, and grooming. It includes, indeed, all of one's very identity and role as a boy or girl, man or woman, for male-female dimorphism perfuses an influence far beyond the narrow confines of the sex organs. The need for some term to designate this totality was recognized as imperative early in the 1950s. I tangled with the problem of writing about not only the copulatory roles but also the overall masculine and/or feminine psychology and behaviour of hermaphroditic or intersexed individuals whose social and legal sex was, in many instances, discordant singly or severally with their chromosomal, gonadal, or morphologic sex at birth. The need was met by borrowing the term 'gender' from its use in philology, to coin the expression 'gender role,' which was originally defined (Money 1955) thus: 'The term gender role is used to signify those things that a person says or does to disclose himself or herself as having the status of boy or man, girl or woman, respectively. It includes, but is not restricted to eroticism.' Eventually, it became necessary to divide gender identity from gender role, even though they are two sides of the same coin, because people proved incapable of conceptualizing their essential unity" (131–32). Further discussion in this chapter will argue against the assertion in Money's last statement.

58   Money, Hampson, and Hampson, "Hermaphroditism," 290.

59   Ibid., 289.

60   Ibid., 294. See also 289.

61   Money, Hampson, and Hampson, "Examination," 308.

62   Ibid., 309–10.

63   Ibid., 302n.

64   Money, Hampson, and Hampson, "Sexual Incongruities," 56.

65   Ibid., 49.

66   Money, Hampson, and Hampson, "Imprinting," 335, 334.

67   Anne Fausto-Sterling makes a comment concerning Money and the Hampsons' "protofeminist" antiessentialism in "How Many Sexes Are There?" History of Science Society Meeting (Santa Fe, N.M., 1993): 10–11. She adds that "Money and his colleagues, however, do not take this ball and run with it" (11).

68   Money, Hampson, and Hampson, "Hermaphroditism," 290.

69   Anne Fausto-Sterling makes the same point in "How Many Sexes Are There?" 9.

70   Ibid. The term "contained" here is derived from Elaine Tyler May's history of the 1950s, *Homeward Bound: American Families in the Cold War Era* (New York: Basic Books, 1988). In this text, May uses "containment" as a general theme for the 1950s in America, with resonance from the Cold War to marriage practices. My usage refers to her suggestion that sexuality in the 1950s was contained within heterosexual marriage. Julia Epstein makes a similar claim: "Sexual ambiguity threatens the possibility of gender contrariety as the basis for social order and thereby threatens the hegemony of heterosexuality. Its history demonstrates that this threat has been met with the heaviest artillery available to the professional discourses of medicine and jurisprudence that establish human definitions and boundaries" ("Either/Or—Neither/Both," 130).

71   McCahey, "A New Conception of Hermaphroditism," 653.

72   Ralph C. Kell, Robert Matthews, and Albert Bockman, "True Hermaphroditism: Report of a Confirmed Case," *American Journal of the Medical Sciences* 197 (1939): 830, 831. Emphasis added.

73   Ibid., 826–27. Emphasis added.

74   Ibid., 827.

75   Janice Irvine discusses at length the operation of homophobia in the "gender clinics" set up in the 1960s and 1970s to manage and cure feminine expression by males: "The literature on male homosexuality, transsexualism, and sissy boys reveals that mannerisms perceived as feminine are [when expressed by men] intolerable to researchers" (*Disorders of Desire*, 241). See also ibid., 229–78.

76   Money, Hampson, and Hampson, "Hermaphroditism," 294. Emphasis added.

77   Ibid., 295. Emphasis added.

78   This also makes sense in terms of the asymmetry of "juvenile vocabulary"—girls are expected to consolidate a heterosexual gender role around the idea of future reproduction (i.e., motherhood), while a boy's gender role need not include fatherhood as a central component. Another point seems pertinent here. Money, Hampson, and Hampson write that "a three year old girl about to be clitoridectomized . . . should be well informed that the doctors will make her look like other girls and women," but state that "[w]ith little boys, the simplest comprehensible explanation is that one day the surgeons will finish the penis so that the boy can stand up to urinate" (ibid., 295, 294). Ostensibly, that a boy look like other boys seems not to be as important as that he be able to perform like them, while the narcissism of the little girl is highlighted—she needs to feel that she will look like other girls and women. Again, the gender asymmetry of the authors' explanations fits well with the social expectations of appropriate gender role behavior and internal attitude. Anne Fausto-Sterling comments that "[Money, Hampson, and Hampson] also offer to preoperative girls that classic bit of information that while boys have a penis, girls have a vagina. Yet they know full well that these are not analogous structures (the vaginal lip/scrotum and clitoris/penis are developmental analogues)" (*Myths of Gender: Biological Theories about Women and Men* [New York: Basic Books, 1985], 138).

79   John Money and Anke Ehrhardt, *Man and Woman, Boy and Girl: The Differentiation and Dimorphism of Gender Identity from Conception to Maturity* (Baltimore: Johns Hopkins University Press, 1972), 178.

80   In his publications, Money occasionally includes a glossary within which are a number of his own neologisms. See Money, *Love and Lovesickness*, 209–25.

81   Robert J. Stoller, "A Contribution to the Study of Gender Identity," *Journal of the American Medical Association* 45 (1964): 220–26.

82   Jan Wålinder, *Transsexualism: A Study of Forty-three Cases*, trans. Helen Fry (Stockholm: Scandinavian University Books, 1967), 4.

83   Stoller, "Contribution," 220.

84   Money and Ehrhardt, *Man and Woman*, 146.

85   Stoller, "Contribution," 220.

86   Ibid. Significantly, Agnes's case is used in this article as an example of a "biological force."

87   Stoller, *Sex and Gender: On the Development of Masculinity and Femininity* (New York: Science House, 1968), 232.

88   Ibid., 92.

89 See, for example, the enormously influential text by Erving Goffman, *The Presentation of Self in Everyday Life* (Garden City, N.Y.: Doubleday, 1959).

90 Stoller, *Sex and Gender*, 39.

91 Ibid., 40.

92 Ibid., x.

93 Ibid., viii–ix.

94 Money and Ehrhardt, *Man and Woman*, 1. Emphasis added.

95 Ibid., 147.

96 This claim is related to—but in no way the same as—the observation that in the scientific literature on embryological development, female development is presented as the absence or lack of development, whereas male development is presented as the result of the active intervention of testosterone. For arguments concerning this latter view, see Anne Fausto-Sterling, "Learning about Women: Gender, Politics, and Power," *Daedalus* 116, no. 4 (Fall 1987): 61–76; and Fausto-Sterling, "Life in the xy Corral," *Women's Studies International Forum* 12, no. 3 (1989): 319–31.

97 Fausto-Sterling, *Myths of Gender*, 136. See also Ruth Bleier, *Science and Gender: A Critique of Biology and Its Theories on Women*, Athene Series (New York: Pergamon Press, 1984), 97–101; and Irvine, *Disorders of Desire*, 236–40.

98 Fausto-Sterling, "How Many Sexes Are There?" 5–6.

99 Lesley Rogers, "The Ideology of Medicine," in *Against Biological Determinism*, ed. The Dialectics of Biology Group, general ed. Stephen Rose (London: Allison and Busby, 1982), 86. The critique reads as follows: "It is important to mention that there are times when Money and his co-workers give definite credence to the cultural contribution to sex-role (e.g., the case of *penis ablatio* of an identical twin [male] subsequently raised as a girl and reported to be entirely 'feminine in behavior'). However, the cultural influence is never fully integrated with the biological. There is a very obvious contradiction between the practical side of their research and their theoretical discussion of gender identity, homosexuality, etc. In fact there is often a direct contradiction between the theory they propose and claim to have evidence to prove on one page and the data quoted several pages later. These contradictions are couched in so much medical jargon and convoluted reasoning that the reader is swept along bewildered and is hoodwinked into thinking that an integrated theory of biology and culture is being put forward" (86).

100 I don't want to suggest that these researchers' potential misuse of data is an insignificant issue, as it is clearly of profound significance within medicine, medical practice, and science research. I am only suggesting that within the confines of my research, the significance of Money and his colleagues' work involves the cultural effects that they were (and are) able to produce in the discursive realm of sex. That they may have been able to do this (as I believe) with incomplete scientific support, only confirms the cultural significance of their discursive interventions.

101 Dwight Billings and Thomas Urban, "The Socio-Medical Construction of Gender: An Interpretation and Critique," *Social Problems* 29, no. 3 (February 1982): 268.

4. Demanding Subjectivity

1 American Psychiatric Association, *Diagnostic and Statistical Manual of Mental Disorders*, 3d ed. (Washington, D.C.: American Psychiatric Association, 1980), 261–64.

2 Dwight Billings and Thomas Urban, "The Socio-Medical Construction of Transsexualism: An Interpretation and Critique," *Social Problems* 29, no. 3 (February 1982): 270.

3　For an excellent discussion of nineteenth-century sexology in terms of the theorization of homosexuality as a third sex see Gert Hekma, "'A Female Soul in a Male Body': Sexual Inversion as Gender Inversion in Nineteenth-Century Sexology," in *Third Sex, Third Gender: Beyond Sexual Dimorphism in Culture and History*, ed. Gilbert Herdt (New York: Zone Books, 1994), 213–40.

4　Richard von Krafft-Ebing, *Psychopathia Sexualis*, trans. Franklin S. Klaf (New York: Stein and Day, 1978), 188. *Psychopathia Sexualis* was originally published in 1886. Klaf's text is a translation of the 12th German edition.

5　Ibid., 30.

6　Ibid., 187–88.

7　Ibid., 222.

8　Magnus Hirschfeld, *Sexual Anomalies*, rev. ed. (New York: Emerson Books, 1956), xiii–xiv.

9　It was Hirschfeld who suggested that Eugen Steinach do experiments with the gonads of animals, which led the latter to postulate that these had an endocrinological function as well as an excretory one (producing "germ cells") (John Money and Herman Musaph, eds., *Handbook of Sexology* [Amsterdam: Elsevier/North Holland Biomedical, 1977], 56).

10　Hirschfeld, *Sexual Anomalies*, 235–56, 143.

11　Ibid., 158–60, 189–90.

12　Hirschfeld's tour-de-force on transvestism, *Des Transvestiten* was first published in 1910. It was translated into English only in 1991 (Hirschfeld, *Transvestites: The Erotic Drive to Cross Dress*, trans. Michael A. Lombardi-Nash [Buffalo, N.Y.: Prometheus Books, 1991]).

13　Havelock Ellis, "Sexual Inversion," part 4 of *Studies in the Psychology of Sex*, vol. 1 (New York: Random House, 1942), 4.

14　Ibid.

15　Ibid., 1–2.

16　Ibid., 312–16.

17　Ellis, "Eonism and Other Supplementary Studies," part 2 of *Studies in the Psychology of Sex*, vol. 2 (New York: Random House, 1942), 2.

18　Ibid., 3.

19　Gary Kates's article on the chevalier, "D'Eon Returns to France: Gender and Power in 1777" (*Body Guards: The Cultural Politics of Gender Ambiguity*, ed. Julia Epstein and Kristina Straub [New York: Routledge, 1991], 167–94), provides a useful historical account of d'Eon's experiences, as well as his notoriety in both England and France. However, while Kates's purpose in refuting contemporary claims that d'Eon was either a transsexual or a transvestite (in the modern sense of those terms) is to be applauded, he himself applies historically specific terms such as "gender identity" to understand d'Eon's experience, as well as to impute specific intentions to d'Eon's actions: "My intention here is to show that at least one eighteenth-century man at a relatively late point in his life began to think of gender identity as something to be explored and achieved" (170). Thus, while Kates states quite astutely that "it is at best anachronistic to perceive d'Eon's behavior from the viewpoint of twentieth century gender roles" (187), he does use twentieth-century categories to define and understand the chevalier's own experience of being a sex. This oversight limits the theoretical value of the essay, although its presentation of historical material is fascinating and richly suggestive.

20　Ellis, "Eonism," 36. Kates remarks that "after the Second World War, psychologists used the term 'transvestite' and then 'transsexual' to mean roughly the same kind of condition first discovered by Ellis [as Eonism]" (175).

21　Ellis, "Eonism," 28.

22   Ibid., 104–5.

23   Carroll Smith-Rosenberg, *Disorderly Conduct: Visions of Gender in Victorian America* (New York: Oxford University Press, 1985), 269.

24   "To call these hormones 'male' and 'female' overlooks the sequential nature of their synthesis: cholesterol is converted into progestin, which is converted into androgen, which is converted into estrogen. Thus, both sexes have all these hormones, although in males androgens predominate, in females progestin and estrogen" (Donald I. Mosher, "Gender," in *Human Sexuality: An Encyclopedia*, ed. Vern L. Bullough and Bonnie Bullough, Garland Reference Library of Social Science, vol. 685 [New York: Garland, 1994], 233). See also chapter 1 of this book.

25   Theories of prenatal hormonal influence on cross-sex behavior—including tomboyism, effeminacy in males, homosexuality, and transsexualism—continue to make their way into the scientific literature, although most recently interest has shifted to brain structures and the possibility of genetic determination.

26   Yet psychiatrists such as Robert Stoller continue to complain that the categories used to describe transsexualism (including the word "transsexualism" itself) are vague and almost useless (Robert J. Stoller, *Presentations of Gender* [New Haven: Yale University Press, 1985], 167.)

27   Richard Docter, *Transvestites and Transsexuals: Toward a Theory of Cross-Gender Behavior* (New York: Plenum Press, 1988), 25. See also Betty W. Steiner, Ray Blanchard, and Kenneth J. Zucker, "Introduction," *Gender Dysphoria: Development, Research, and Management*, ed. Betty W. Steiner (New York: Plenum Press, 1985), 5–6, for a dizzying use of sexual taxonomies to identify transsexual sexuality, which includes the "heterosexual transsexual" who is attracted to women preoperatively and who "may still be attracted to female sexual partners" postoperatively. They write that "it is not unknown for such a patient to establish a meaningful 'lesbian' relationship with an anatomical female" (6).

28   See Hekma, "A Female Soul." See also Hubert Kennedy, *Ulrichs: The Life and Works of Karl Heinrich Ulrichs, Pioneer of the Modern Gay Movement* (Boston: Alyson, 1988).

29   Catherine Millot, *Horsexe: Essay on Transsexuality*, trans. Kenneth Hylton (New York: Autonomedia, 1990), 17. Anne Bolin writes: "It is important to note that transsexualism, as a historical phenomenon, was defined by the development of two important medical technologies that made possible the innovative alterations of the male body: hormonal reassignment therapies and sex reassignment surgery. These treatments circumscribed the medical creation of male-to-female transsexualism. However, Vern Bullough notes that the significance of this field has been neglected in the history of transsexualism" ("Transcending and Transgendering: Male-to-Female Transsexuals, Dichotomy and Diversity," in *Third Sex, Third Gender*, ed. Herdt, 454–55).

30   Vern L. Bullough and Bonnie Bullough, *Crossdressing, Sex, and Gender* (Philadelphia: University of Pennsylvania Press, 1993), 253. This seems to be a new position for the Bulloughs.

31   In her conclusion Millot writes: "We have spoken of transsexuality before the term existed, but in a sense there was no such thing before Benjamin and Stoller invented it; there were delusions of sexual metamorphosis, but this is another thing altogether. Transsexuality involves an appeal, and especially a demand, addressed to the Other" (*Horsexe*, 141).

32   Docter, *Transvestites and Transsexuals*, 32. "Gender dysphoria" is a term designating the general condition of "gender discomfort" thought to underlie both transvestic and transsexual behaviors. I discuss its development and implications below.

33   Anne Bolin documents transsexuals' propensity to change aspects of their personal his-

tories to fit the diagnostic expectations of their health care workers in *In Search of Eve: Transsexual Rites of Passage* (South Hadley, Mass.: Bergin and Harvey, 1988).

34 Indeed, transsexuals keep up with scholarly literature on gender, transforming the meanings of that literature to match their conceptualization of gender. For example, in the 1994 publications catalogue of the International Foundation for Gender Education (IFGE), Judith Butler's *Gender Trouble: Feminism and the Subversion of Identity* (New York: Routledge, 1990) is described in the following manner: "Challenging that there is no such thing as true gender identities and natural sexes, Butler builds her own *performative theory of gender*. A challenging voice in the battle between nature and nurture as a source of the *naturalness* of gender." Butler and most of her feminist readers would argue with this characterization, which flies in the face of *Gender Trouble's* arguments and conclusions. Indeed, Butler's argument is marshalled *against* the idea of gender as "natural," even though she also argues that gender cannot be thought as the cultural copy of natural sex. IFGE's rewriting of Butler's deconstruction of the relation of sex to gender is indicative of transsexuals' active engagement with the conceptual categories understood to describe their experience, and their purposeful deformation of those discourses when they prove to be unamenable to the transsexual cause.

35 This argument would be challenged by Dallas Denny, who charges that the advent of university-affiliated gender clinics in the 1960s and 1970s led to increasingly stringent SRS criteria, which in turn left many transsexuals out in the cold concerning treatment ("The Politics of Diagnosis and a Diagnosis of Politics," *Chrysalis Quarterly* 1, no. 3 [Winter 1992]: 9–20).

36 Personal observation, "Coming Together/Working Together," IFGE convention, Denver, Colo. (April 1991). See also Denny, "The Politics of Diagnosis."

37 Docter, *Transvestites and Transsexuals*, 25.

38 Robert Stoller, *Presentations of Gender*, 167.

39 D. O. Cauldwell, "Psychopathia Transexualis," *Sexology* 16 (December 1949): 274–80. There is a controversy concerning the spelling of "transsexual," with Money and his colleagues maintaining Cauldwell's single *s* and most others, after Harry Benjamin, using two. In this book, I use "transsexual," except when quoting someone who uses the alternate spelling. Vern and Bonnie Bullough remark that the term "psychic transsexual" was first used by Magnus Hirschfeld in his 1910 publication on transvestism (*Crossdressing, Sex, and Gender*, 257). However, most researchers trace the origins of the term "transsexual" to Cauldwell.

40 I have not been able to determine David Cauldwell's medical specialty. In articles, he is listed as having both M.D. and Sc.D. degrees, but he is not mentioned in standard medical biographies. I believe that he was American, because he published out of Kansas. He published frequently on questions related to sex and sexual deviance in the 1940s and 1950s, although his work is often in the obscure journal *Sexology* (which is not indexed) or in booklet form. I conjecture that he was either an endocrinologist or, more probably, a urologist.

41 Cauldwell, "Psychopathia Transexualis," 275, 278.

42 D. O. Cauldwell, "Introduction," *Transvestism . . . Men in Female Dress*, ed. D. O. Cauldwell (New York: Sexology Corporation, 1956), 12–13.

43 Conversation with David H. Hausman, M.D., Iowa City, Ia., November 1991. Dr. Hausman is a retired pathologist who worked in a hospital where some transsexual surgeries occurred. All tissues from surgical procedures pass through the pathology laboratory. Dr. Hausman described the experience of examining healthy genital organs appearing

in the laboratory as upsetting for most of the pathologists in the lab. Transsexuals attending the IFGE convention "Coming Together/Working Together" in Denver, Colo., in April 1991 confirmed this attitude among physicians many times over. Most transsexuals have horror stories of numerous trips to doctors that ended with summary dismissal. See also Denny, "The Politics of Diagnosis."

44 The development of "gender identity" clinics which supported psychiatric, hormonal, and surgical services for transsexuals, generally as part of research projects, will be discussed later in this chapter. See Donald W. Hastings, "Inauguration of a Research Project on Transsexualism in a University Medical Center," in *Transsexualism and Sex Reassignment*, ed. Richard Green and John Money (Baltimore: Johns Hopkins University Press, 1969), 243–52; and John Money and Florence Schwartz, "Public Opinion and Social Issues in Transsexualism: A Case Study in Medical Sociology," in Green and Money, *Transsexualism*, 253–70.

45 "Ex-GI Becomes Blonde Beauty: Operations Transform Bronx Youth," *New York Daily News* (December 1, 1952): 1, 3, 28.

46 Christian Hamburger, Georg K. Stürup, and E. Dahl-Iversen, "Transvestism: Hormonal, Psychiatric, and Surgical Treatment," *Journal of the American Medical Association* 152 (1953): 391.

47 Ibid., 391; Ellis, "Eonism and Other Supplementary Studies."

48 Hamburger, Stürup, and Dahl-Iversen, "Transvestism," 393. This is a claim denied by Jorgensen in her autobiography. See discussion below and in chapter 5.

49 Christine Jorgensen, "The Story of My Life," part 5, *The American Weekly* (March 15, 1953): 13. See also Christine Jorgensen, *Christine Jorgensen: A Personal Autobiography* (New York: Paul Eriksson, 1967).

50 Hamburger, Stürup, and Dahl-Iversen, "Transvestism," 392.

51 Ibid., 393, 395, 396, 393.

52 Christian Hamburger, "The Desire for Change of Sex as Shown by Personal Letters from 465 Men and Women," *Acta Endocrinologica* 14 (1953): 361.

53 Ibid., 375.

54 Harry Benjamin, "Transvestism and Transsexualism," *International Journal of Sexology* 7 (1953): 12, 13.

55 Ibid., 13.

56 Benjamin, "Transvestism," 13–14. Emphasis added. See also Eugene de Savitsch, *Homosexuality, Transvestism and Change of Sex* (Springfield, Ill.: Charles C. Thomas, 1958), 58–60, for a discussion of the purpose of constructing a vagina in transsexual women. At the conclusion of this discussion, de Savitsch pointed out, somewhat baldly, that "no matter what technique is used and how skilfully the vagina is made, it is unlikely that the patient himself [sic] will ever be tempted to use it unless masochistically inclined: intercourse would be only painful and disagreeable. It is, in fact, only the *immense psychological benefit conferred in certain cases by its possession* that justifies the risk involved in constructing what might otherwise be regarded as a completely useless luxury" (emphasis added). Dr. Charles Wolf, in Appendix C of de Savitsch's text, agreed with the author: "Plastic surgery to provide an artificial vagina is a useless luxury; the operation involves considerable risk; if it is to remain serviceable in spite of the natural tendency for the tissues to retract, it will require constant care; even then, will it ever be used: If used, it will certainly give more pain than pleasure. For the man who has been turned into a woman, the artificial vagina will be a purely mental satisfaction" (116).

57 In the early years of the emergence of transsexualism, any suggestion on the part of the transsexual that "he" desired a vagina would have upset the increasingly institu-

tionalized etiology of the disorder, thereby risking chances for surgery. Transsexualism, unlike transvestism, was perceived to have little to do with sexual desire. Later, the lack of emphasis on sexuality was theorized as evidence that transsexualism was not really about "sex," but about gender identity. Christine Jorgensen did not have vaginoplasty as a part of her initial surgeries in Denmark (see Hamburger, Stürup, and Dahl-Iversen, "Transvestism"). She did, however, have vaginoplasty two years later in the United States. See Christine Jorgensen, *Christine Jorgensen*, 250–52.

58 Benjamin, "Transvestism," 14.

59 Harry Benjamin, "Transsexualism and Transvestism As Psycho-Somatic and Somato-Psychic Syndromes," *American Journal of Psychotherapy* 8 (1954): 220.

60 Ibid., 228–29. Emphasis added.

61 Emil A. Gutheil, "The Psychologic Background of Transsexualism and Transvestism," *American Journal of Psychotherapy* 8 (1954): 238.

62 Harry Benjamin, *The Transsexual Phenomenon* (New York: Julian Press, 1966), 22, 47.

63 Ibid., 3. That "someone" is later identified as Charles [Virginia] Prince (46).

64 Ibid., 28.

65 Ibid., 85.

66 Ibid., 91.

67 "Transsexualism" does not appear at all in the American Psychiatric Association's *Diagnostic and Statistical Manual of Mental Disorders*, 4th ed., (Washington, D.C.: American Psychiatric Association, 1994). See discussion below.

68 For Stoller's specific theory of the etiology of transsexualism, see his *Sex and Gender: On the Development of Masculinity and Femininity* (New York: Science House, 1968) and *The Transsexual Experiment*, no. 101 of the International Psychoanalytic Library, ed. M. Masud R. Khan (London: Hogarth Press and the Institute for Psycho-Analysis, 1975).

69 Betty W. Steiner, Ray Blanchard, and Kenneth J. Zucker, "Introduction," 5. Emphasis added. This category does not include intersexual subjects.

70 American Psychiatric Association, *Diagnostic and Statistical Manual of Mental Disorders*, 3d ed. (Washington, D.C.: American Psychiatric Association, 1980): 261–62.

71 In the fourth edition of the manual, gender dysphoria shows up as a possible specification in transvestic fetishism. See American Psychiatric Association, *Diagnostic and Statistical Manual*, 4th ed., 531.

72 Billings and Urban, "The Socio-Medical Construction of Transsexualism," 275.

73 Norman Fisk, "Gender Dysphoria Syndrome," *Western Journal of Medicine* 120 (May 1974): 387.

74 Ibid., 388.

75 Ibid., 387.

76 Fisk described the phenomenological approach in ibid., 390.

77 Ibid., 390. Donald Laub is featured prominently in a recent article about female-to-male transsexualism. See Amy Bloom, "The Body Lies," *New Yorker* (July 18, 1994): 38–49.

78 Billings and Urban, "The Socio-Medical Construction of Transsexualism," 275. Cf. Norman Fisk, "Gender Dysphoria Syndrome (The How, What, and Why of a Disease)," in Donald Laub and Patrick Gandy, eds. *Second International Symposium on Gender Dysphoria Syndrome* (Palo Alto: Stanford University Press, 1973), 10.

79 Billings and Urban, "The Socio-Medical Construction of Transsexualism," 276, 266.

80 Ibid., 270.

81 It is interesting to note that those clinicians involved in setting up gender clinics in the 1960s were very aware of the potential advances in surgical technologies that operating

on the transsexual population might offer. John Money and Florence Schwartz wrote: "It is fortunate that congenital absence of the penis is rare; however, its scarce occurrence limits opportunities to perfect surgical techniques for correcting those varying degrees of injury inflicted to the male organ by the more numerous hazards of daily life, including war. Surgical investigation in the treatment of transsexuals could serve the dual function of creating a more tolerable existence for the transsexual while simultaneously creating a tradition that will expand to include organ transplants, beneficial to thousands of men and women, both" (Money and Schwartz, "Public Opinion and Social Issues," 265).

82   Janice Irvine, *Disorders of Desire: Sex and Gender in Modern American Sexology* (Philadelphia: Temple University Press, 1990), 229–78.

83   Billings and Urban, "Socio-Medical Construction of Transsexualism," 275.

84   Steiner, Blanchard, and Zucker, "Introduction," 5.

85   "Transgenderism" designates at once all those subjects who cross gender boundaries (as in "the transgender community") as well as (more specifically) those subjects who undergo partial sex change, usually hormonal.

86   American Psychiatric Association, *Diagnostic and Statistical Manual for Mental Disorders*, 1st ed. (Washington, D.C.: American Psychiatric Association, 1952), 38–39; 2d ed., 44; 3d ed., 261–70; and 3d ed. rev., 71–78.

87   In the introduction to the third edition, revised (DSM-III-R) the authors write: "The approach taken in DSM-III-R is atheoretical with regard to etiology or pathophysiologic process, except with regard to disorders for which this is well established and therefore included in the definition of the disorder. . . . DSM-III-R can be said to be 'descriptive' in that the definitions of the disorders are generally limited to descriptions of the clinical features of the disorders" (xxiii). The entire classification "Disorders Usually First Evident in Infancy, Childhood, or Adolescence," however, suggests an etiological picture; it is also interesting to note that while transvestism often begins in childhood, in the DSM-III-R this category appears in the classification "Sexual Disorders" and not with those developing in childhood.

88   The fourth edition (DSM-IV) does away with the category of transsexualism and creates a new chapter, "Sexual and Gender Identity Disorders." This suggests that the psychiatric establishment is reconsidering its understanding of the relation of transsexualism to sexual behaviors. Sex reassignment surgery is not discussed in the DSM-IV as a treatment option (as is true of the DSM-III and the DSM-III-R), but it is assumed to be a possible treatment, as the description of the disorder mentions possible "postsurgical complications" (DSM-IV, 535).

89   John D'Emilio, *Sexual Politics, Sexual Communities: The Making of a Homosexual Minority in the United States, 1940–1970* (Chicago: University of Chicago Press, 1983, 238). Holly Devor suggested to me that this change appears in the DSM-II in its seventh printing. See "Introduction," note 19. It is important to note that some forms of homosexuality remain in the DSM, for example, "ego-dystonic homosexuality."

90   Clinically, transvestic fetishism is understood to be a specifically heterosexual male perversion, with some researchers continuing to insist that women, by and large, do not have a fetishistic relation to male clothing and therefore cannot be considered transvestites, at least clinically (Robert Stoller, *Presentations of Gender*, 20–21; and Stoller, *Sex and Gender*, 194–205). Virginia Prince, whose work will be discussed below, was instrumental in maintaining a clinical distinction between male heterosexual transvestites and other cross-dressers.

91   Dr. Zane Parzen refers to this as the patient "achieving her fantasy of becoming a woman," in Robert Gerner, Lewis Judd, Arnold Mandell, et al., "Male Transsexualism — Psychiatric Grand Rounds, University of California, San Diego and San Diego Veterans Administration Hospital," *Western Journal of Medicine* 120 (May 1974): 380.

92   I am grateful to Chris Looby for helping me to formulate this point.

93   Jorgensen, *Christine Jorgensen*, 173.

94   Ibid.; Hamburger, Stürup, and Dahl-Iversen, "Transvestism," 393.

95   Ibid., 172, 173.

96   See chapter 3.

97   Virginia Prince, "Change of Sex or Gender," in *Understanding Cross Dressing* (Los Angeles: Chevalier Publications, 1976), 134.

98   Ibid., 137.

99   Ibid., 143, 135, 134.

100   Ibid., 143.

101   Leslie Martin Lothstein, *Female-to-Male Transsexualism: Historical, Clinical, and Theoretical Issues* (Boston: Routledge and Kegan Paul, 1983), 303.

102   Ibid., 265.

103   Ibid., 259.

104   Ibid., 207.

105   Ibid., 98–110.

106   This is suggested as well in the work of members of the "Lacan school" on transsexualism. According to Annette Runte, Lacanian psychoanalysts theorize transsexualism as a defense against psychosis ("Das Geschlecht der Engel: Zur Theorie des Transsexualismus in der Lacan-Schule [M. Safouan, A. Faure Oppenheimer, C. Millot]" *Psyche* 39, no. 9 [1985]: 830–62). I am grateful to Mark Sandberg for indispensable help with this article. See also Millot, *Horsexe.*

107   As far as I know, the Lacan school itself has not theorized transsexualism in this particular manner, although Catherine Millot does mention the demand for surgical and hormonal sex change as central to the phenomenon of transsexualism (*Horsexe,* 17, 141). The Lacan school psychoanalysts seem to develop their theory of transsexuality in response to Stoller's work on the etiology of transsexual subjectivity (*Sex and Gender* and *The Transsexual Experiment*). Thus, they are interested in transsexualism insofar as it represents the subject's refusal to take up his/her designated position vis-à-vis the phallus as signifier of the desire of the mother and of the Name-of-the-Father (Millot, *Horsexe,* 34, 42). Millot in particular argues against Stoller's understanding of male transsexualism as arising out of a primary symbiosis with the body of the mother (*Horsexe,* 49–59) and states that for the male transsexual, "the transsexual symptom *stricto sensu* (conviction plus the demand for transformation) corresponds to an attempt to palliate the absence of the Name-of-the-Father, that is, to define an outer limit, a point of arrest, and to achieve a suspension of the phallic function" (*Horsexe,* 42; italics in original). See also Runte, "Das Geschlecht der Engel."

108   See Jacques Lacan, *The Seminar of Jacques Lacan, Book 1: Freud's Papers on Technique, 1953–1954* and *Book 2: The Ego in Freud's Theory and in the Technique of Psychoanalysis, 1954–1955,* ed. Jacques-Alain Miller, trans. John Forrester (New York: Norton, 1991). See also Jane Gallop, *The Daughter's Seduction: Feminism and Psychoanalysis* (Ithaca, N.Y.: Cornell University Press, 1982), esp. 1–14.

109   Catherine Millot writes, "The transsexual, who is formed through assignation by the other — a doctor or psychologist — finds an obdurating and even fallacious response to

the enigma of his desire when he encounters his Other in Science. The desire of the Other is no longer veiled, the verdict is pronounced: let him be operated on. The Other desires his real castration. The discovery of a solution to the enigma of desire of the Other, such that one becomes its object, provokes a certain euphoria. But there is always a residue. Transsexuals are witnesses to this" (Horsexe, 142).

110   Dallas Denny, "Transsexualism at Forty: Some Uncommonly Discussed Aspects of an Increasingly Common Phenomenon," Chrysalis Quarterly 1, no. 6 (1993): 43.

111   Ibid., 44.

112   Ibid. Emphasis added.

113   These are not to be confused with the transsexual women who return to the operating room for repair of vaginal structures that have broken down after the original surgery. Return to surgery for these purposes is common. See Billings and Urban, "Socio-Medical Construction of Transsexualism," 277, for a discussion of the literature concerning polysurgical attitudes on the part of male-to-female transsexuals.

114   This is suggested in the article by Hamburger, Stürup, and Iversen that details the specifics of the Jorgensen case, where the authors discuss the "genuine transvestite's" pursuit of an ideal of feminine perfection ("Transvestism," 392). This is also suggested by Harry Benjamin ("Transsexualism and Transvestism," 228–29).

115   Roberta Cowell, Roberta Cowell's Story (New York: British Book Centre, 1954), 136–37.

116   This point was also suggested by Harry Benjamin ("Transvestism and Transsexualism"). Polysurgical addiction is not limited, as a condition, to transsexuals. For an early psychoanalytic view of "polysurgical addiction" see Karl Meninger, "Polysurgery and Polysurgical Addiction," Psychoanalytic Quarterly 3 (1934): 173–99.

117   See chapter 3.

118   Judith Butler, "Imitation and Gender Insubordination," inside/out: Lesbian Theory, Gay Theory, ed. Diana Fuss (New York: Routledge, 1992), 24. Kate Bornstein discusses the compulsive nature of gender codes in her recent book, Gender Outlaw: On Men, Women, and the Rest of Us (New York: Routledge, 1994).

5. Body, Technology, and Gender in Transsexual Autobiographies

1   I would like to thank members of the Lesbian and Gay Studies Workshop at the University of Chicago, and especially Scott Mendel, for pointing out to me the necessity of addressing the significance of my choice to study "mainstream" discourses of transsexualism.

2   Mario Martino, Emergence: A Transsexual Autobiography, with harriet (New York: Crown Publishers, 1977), 40; Jan Morris, Conundrum (New York: Harcourt Brace Jovanovich, 1974), 45; Niels Hoyer, ed., Man into Woman: An Authentic Record of a Change of Sex, trans. H. J. Stenning (London: Jarrolds, 1933); Renée Richards, Second Serve: The Renée Richards Story, with John Ames (New York: Stein and Day, 1983), 55; Nancy Hunt, Mirror Image (New York: Holt, Rinehart, and Winston, 1978), 137. I use the gendered pronoun appropriate to the sex of the subject at the time of the event being discussed.

3   Sandy Stone, "The Empire Strikes Back: A Posttranssexual Manifesto," in Body Guards: The Cultural Politics of Gender Ambiguity, ed. Julia Epstein and Kristina Straub (New York: Routledge, 1991), 285.

4   Anne Bolin, In Search of Eve: Transsexual Rites of Passage (South Hadley, Mass.: Bergin and Harvey, 1988), 64; Richard Green, The "Sissy Boy Syndrome" and the Development of Homosexuality (New Haven: Yale University Press, 1987), 7–8.

5   Stone, "The Empire Strikes Back," 295.

6   Ibid., 299.

7   Ibid., 298.

8   Sandy Stone names herself in the essay by referring to the 1970s controversy concerning her employment at Olivia Records, an all-woman recording company, as a sound engineer. She was the subject of a vociferous debate in a number of West Coast feminist publications, and of a chapter in Janice Raymond's *The Transsexual Empire* (Boston: Beacon Press, 1979). See Stone, "The Empire Strikes Back," 283–84.

9   Stone, "The Empire Strikes Back," 295.

10 Ibid., 299.

11 Ibid., 286.

12 Ibid., 285.

13 Bolin, *In Search of Eve*, 64.

14 Ibid., 64–65.

15 Dwight Billings and Thomas Urban, "The Socio-Medical Construction of Transsexualism: An Interpretation and Critique," *Social Problems* 29, no. 3 (February 1982): 273–74.

16 Robert J. Stoller, *The Transsexual Experiment*, no. 101 of the International Psycho-Analytical Library, ed. M. Masud R. Khan (London: Hogarth Press and the Institute of Psycho-analysis, 1975), 248n.

17 Stone, "The Empire Strikes Back," 291.

18 Ibid., 289, 292.

19 Bolin, *In Search of Eve*, 61–63.

20 For a discussion of "power" as a productive and enabling force, rather than one that is solely repressive, see Michel Foucault, *The History of Sexuality: An Introduction*, vol. 1, trans. Robert Hurley (New York: Vintage, 1978).

21 For a discussion of what constitutes a statement, as well as a discursive formation, see Michel Foucault, *The Archeology of Knowledge*, trans. A. M. Sheridan Smith (New York: Pantheon, 1972).

22 Judith Butler, *Gender Trouble. Feminism and the Subversion of Identity* (New York: Routledge, 1990).

23 Christine Jorgensen, *Christine Jorgensen: A Personal Autobiography* (New York: Paul Eriksson, 1967), 206.

24 She was consistently represented as the transsexual "prototype" or model for male-to-female transsexuals—the first of her kind—at "Coming Together/Working Together," International Foundation for Gender Education convention, Denver, Colo. (April 1991).

25 According to Harry Benjamin, this perspective was not common in the United States. In *The Transsexual Phenomenon*, Benjamin wrote: "Biologically minded authors are likely to consider TVism and TSism as 'intersexual' phenomena, but those are almost exclusively European scientists. American writers . . . reserve the term 'intersexuality' exclusively for visual signs of disorders of sexual development, that is to say, for hermaphroditic and pseudo-hermaphroditic abnormalities. The Europeans, especially the Germans, use the term in a much wider sense, including not only transvestism and transsexualism as 'intersexual' but also homosexuality" (New York: Julian Press, 1966), 71. This may explain Christine Jorgensen's doctors' use of "intersexuality" to define her condition.

26 It is fascinating that Jorgensen mentioned *The Male Hormone* as having had profound influence on her, since that text concentrates almost exclusively on the curative powers of testosterone, especially for "broken" or effeminate men. De Kruif discusses these curative powers as both psychological and physiological—testosterone could mascu-

linize feminine men in both mind and body, as well as restore youthful energy to aging men. Yet Jorgensen writes that as George, she felt that she could not follow a mascu-linizing course (the one de Kruif focuses on in his book). Rather, Jorgensen became obsessed with the similarities between testosterone and estradiol (ovarian hormone): "'The chemical difference between testosterone and estradiol is four atoms of hydro-gen and one atom of carbon.'... If Dr. de Kruif's chemical ratio was correct, it would seem then that the relationship was very close. That being so, I reasoned, there must be times when one could be so close to that physical dividing line that it would be difficult to determine on which side of the male-female line he belonged" (Jorgensen, Christine Jorgensen, 84–85). See also ibid., 78–80. See Paul de Kruif, The Male Hormone (New York: Harcourt Brace, 1945).

27   For instance, Jorgensen wrote, "But the recurring questions of what to do about my effeminate appearance continued to plague me. Even if it were possible to adjust my mind and attitudes to a more male outlook, I wondered what could be done about a 'masculine' mind in a feminine body" (Christine Jorgensen, 78).

28   Ibid., 203.

29   Ibid., 101–2.

30   Ibid., 207–8.

31   Roberta Cowell, Roberta Cowell's Story (New York: British Book Centre, 1954), 165. Vern Bullough and Bonnie Bullough remark that Cowell was a genetic male, suffering from adrenogenital syndrome (also known as testicular feminization syndrome). However, if this were the case, it would be highly unlikely that Cowell would have been able to "father" two children (Vern L. Bullough and Bonnie Bullough, Crossdressing, Sex, and Gender [Philadelphia: University of Pennsylvania Press, 1993], 255).

32   Cowell, Roberta Cowell's Story, 176.

33   Ibid., 99.

34   Ibid., 99–100.

35   Ibid., 120–21.

36   Ibid., 136. Cowell conveniently neglects to mention that surgery was also necessary to remove her male genital organs.

37   Ibid., 156.

38   Ibid., 177. This is reminiscent of Michael Dillon's comments in Self: A Study in Ethics and Endocrinology (London: Heinemann, 1946). See chapter 1.

39   Cowell, Roberta Cowell's Story, 194.

40   Ibid., 193. I believe that Roberta Cowell is the "Male with Female Outlook" discussed in Harold Gillies and Ralph Millard Jr.'s Principles and Art of Plastic Surgery (Boston: Little, Brown, 1957). Cowell does not name her plastic surgeon (or any of her doctors) in the autobiography. However, she says that she went to see a surgeon who was "world-famous" and that his "kindness was proverbial, but so was his way of being remarkably outspoken when he felt so inclined" (Cowell, Roberta Cowell's Story, 129). This descrip-tion fits that offered by Reginald Pound in his biography of Gillies (Reginald Pound, Gillies, Surgeon Extraordinary [London: Michael Joseph, 1964]). Gillies believed that cos-metic surgery could lead to psychological benefit, a factor which helped to develop the possibility of sex reassignment surgeries. Finally, the discussion of the "Male with Female Outlook" in The Principles and Art of Plastic Surgery matches Cowell's autobiography almost exactly. There, Gillies quotes the endocrinologist's report of the examination of the patient's removed testes: "The general appearances are those of a postpubertal

gonadotrophic suppression. It is known that the patient received prolonged oestro-genic and progesterone therapy, just before the orchidectomy. Although there are no controls with which these sections can be compared, it is considered unlikely that hor-monal treatment alone could have caused the testicular atrophy. However, the lack of much information on the human subject means that this cannot be a dogmatic state-ment." Gillies also remarks that the patient's "nose was too big, [and] his lip abnormally long" — compare with Cowell's own comments: "The decision was to give me a new upper lip, reshape my mouth, and shorten my nose" (Gillies and Millard, *The Principles and Art of Plastic Surgery*, vol. 2, 385; and Cowell, *Roberta Cowell's Story*, 136–37).

41   The book is somewhat uncertain as to dates, although it more than makes up for that deficit in other details. Martino writes that she was in the eighth grade when the Christine Jorgensen story broke; since that story was first made public in December of 1952, that puts Marie's birth in 1939. She obtained surgical and hormonal treatments for sex change a few years after Jorgensen's autobiography was published in 1967 — that is, in her early thirties. See Martino, *Emergence*, 40.

42   Martino, *Emergence*, 131.

43   Some of the passages describing Marie's experiences as a young novice are quite tell-ing. For example, at the convent where Marie went to live during the first two years of high school, many of the nuns had men's (male saints') names: Sister Clement, Sis-ter Timothy, Sister Francis, etc. The second time Marie entered a convent, she took the name Sister Mary Dominick, after her older half-brother: "My first choice: Dom's name! It was like a new bond between my brother and me, almost placing me on par with him" (89). She became known to other nuns as "Dom," the same nickname her brother used. See Martino, *Emergence*, pp. 29–98.

44   Ibid., 121.

45   Ibid., 109–10.

46   Ibid., 130.

47   Robert Stoller, "A Contribution to the Study of Gender Identity," *Journal of the American Medical Association* 45 (1964): 220–26; Stoller, *Sex and Gender. On the Development of Masculinity and Femininity* (New York: Science House, 1968), 65–85; Stoller, *Presentations of Gender* (New Haven: Yale University Press, 1985), 65–76.

48   Martino, *Emergence*, 114.

49   Ibid., 144. Emphasis added.

50   Ibid., 163. It is interesting that Jorgensen uses this comment to identify her own singu-larity, whereas for Martino it defines a commonality with others "all over the world."

51   Ibid., 244.

52   Hunt, *Mirror Image*, 43. See also ibid., pp. 23–42.

53   Ibid., 263.

54   Ibid.

55   This same discourse about masculinity as a "mask" is utilized by Roberta Cowell.

56   Hunt, *Mirror Image*, 59.

57   Ibid., 131.

58   Ibid., 83.

59   Ibid., 141.

60   Ibid., 142.

61   Ibid., 124–25.

62   Canary Conn, *Canary: The Story of a Transsexual* (Los Angeles: Nash Publishing, 1974).

63   Ibid., 6, 320. These final comments were ostensibly made by Conn to a group of doc-
      tors, an unlikely situation, as doctors do not consider transsexuals to be reliable pur-
      veyors of medical theory.

64   Ibid., 321.

65   See chapter 3. Money has since taken a more biologistic stance, characterized by the
      book he cowrote with Anke Ehrhardt (Man and Woman, Boy and Girl: The Differentiation and
      Dimorphism of Gender Identity from Conception to Maturity [Baltimore: Johns Hopkins University
      Press, 1972]). He likes to present this as a biosocial perspective that privileges neither
      biology nor culture in the construction of gender identity, but, as I discussed in chap-
      ter 3, his language belies an emphasis on the biological.

66   Morris, Conundrum, 173, 21.

67   Ibid., 3, 40–52.

68   Ibid., 27–39.

69   Ibid., 9, 25, 26, 104, 163.

70   Ibid., 104.

71   Ibid., 169.

72   Richards, Second Serve, 5. Emphasis added.

73   In Richard Docter's terminology, this would identify Renée Richards as a secondary
      transsexual, one who came to desire sex change after a period of time as a transvestite.

74   Ibid., 164. Emphasis added.

75   There is another moment that also suggests a story created to fit the theory — Richards
      claims she discussed her transvestism with her mother in her junior year at Yale (as
      Dick): "I thought it best to start out with the academic facts as I had learned them
      in Abnormal Psych.: 'Mother, as you know there are certain mental disorders that are
      characterized by gender confusion. Somehow, the individual has feelings and impulses
      that are characteristic of the opposite sex.' I quoted a good portion of the chapter on
      transsexualism with my mother nodding in agreement" (ibid., 87). At the time (1954
      or 1955), neither "gender" nor "transsexualism" would have made it into a college text-
      book — the terminology was only then being codified into medical discourse. Clearly,
      Richards is inserting current theoretical conceptualizations back into her discussion
      with her mother.

76   American Psychiatric Association, Diagnostic and Statistical Manual of Mental Disorders, 3d ed.
      rev. (Washington, D.C.: American Psychiatric Association, 1987), 71–76. See also the
      third edition (1980), 263: "the presence of abnormal sexual structures rules out the
      diagnosis of Transsexualism."

77   If transsexuals routinely attribute their desire to change sex to the inconclusive domain
      of physiology, why is it that physicians, who have never documented any physiological
      reasons for transsexualism, accede to their demands?

78   "My more immediate physical delights were far more superficial and much easier to
      achieve. They were tactile, olfactory, visual, proximate delights — pleasures which, as
      it happened, I could handily transfer to inanimate objects too, within reason, so that
      I derived, though I tactfully kept the fact from my more intimate friends, a kindred
      sensual satisfaction from buildings, landscapes, pictures, wines, and certain sorts of
      confectionery" (Morris, Conundrum, 55).

79   Martino, Emergence, 255.

80   Ibid., 253–55.

81   John M. Goin and Marcia Kraft Goin, Changing the Body: Psychological Effects of Plastic Surgery
      (Baltimore, Md.: Williams and Wilkins, 1981), 191–92. See also chapter 2.

82   Martino, *Emergence*, 257–60.

83   Ibid., 262.

84   Ibid., 262–63.

85   Ibid., 255. Emphasis added.

86   Ibid., 264–65. Emphasis added.

87   Patricia Morgan, *The Man-Maid Doll*, as told to Paul Hoffman (Secaucus, N.J.: Lyle Stuart, n.d.), 29.

88   Ibid., 60.

89   Some physicians felt leaving the testicles might be important for male-to-female transsexual's sex drive. Harry Benjamin mentions two other reasons: "The reasons why some surgeons may wish to retain the testes is chiefly endocrine, based on the theory that the testes in transsexual men may produce more estrogen than they do normally . . . although they have as yet found no confirmation. . . . Another reason for a surgeon's wish to preserve the testes is because of a legal technicality. He cannot be accused of a (possibly illegal) castration operation" (Benjamin, *The Transsexual Phenomenon*, 100–101).

90   Morgan, *The Man-Maid Doll*, 63. The use of the term "mole" here gives us a sense of the surgical technique Dr. Belt used with Morgan. A "mole" in this context fits with the dictionary definition of "a large, powerful machine for boring through earth or rock, used in the construction of tunnels." This suggests that Dr. Belt was attempting to encourage secondary epithelialization of the vaginal canal, since with the other procedures there would be no need to bore further into a canal that had been constructed of grafted tissue. With the secondary epithelialization technique, a hole is made in the perineum and then the walls of the hollow are encouraged to form an epithelial lining similar to that of a normal vagina.

91   Ibid., 63–65.

92   Ibid., 68–72.

93   Jorgensen, *Christine Jorgensen*, 136–37.

94   Ibid., 236–37.

95   Roberta Cowell's comments about her surgery were even more reticent, as she neglected to mention at all the need to remove her male genitals, concentrating instead on the surgery done to her face. See Cowell, *Roberta Cowell's Story*, 136. Jan Morris comments in *Conundrum* that "Dr. B—'s craftsmanship, though aesthetically brilliant, was functionally incomplete, and I underwent two further sessions of surgery in an English nursing-home" (145). While she does make some limited comments about the care in Dr. B—'s Moroccan clinic, in general she says little about the surgery. Does "functionally incomplete" mean that she couldn't urinate, or that Dr. B— had not constructed a vagina, or that the vagina could not function in penile-vaginal intercourse? Did she know she would have to undergo further procedures, or did she find out after the fact? Morris does not comment.

96   Hunt, *Mirror Image*, 12.

97   Ibid., 205.

98   Ibid., 219–20.

99   Ibid., 224, 225.

100 Conn, *Canary*, 194–97, 307–19.

101 Richards, *Second Serve*, 282.

102 Ibid., 286.

103 Ibid., 287.

6. Semiotics of Sex, Gender, and the Body

1   Judith Butler, *Gender Trouble: Feminism and the Subversion of Identity* (New York: Routledge, 1990).

2   Thomas Laqueur, *Making Sex: Body and Gender from the Greeks to Freud* (Cambridge, Mass.: Harvard University Press, 1990). Laqueur's work demonstrates the problems attendant to the kind of statement David Halperin makes to introduce his article "Is There a History of Sexuality?": "Sex has no history. It is a natural fact, grounded in the functioning of the body and as such it lies outside of history and culture" (*History and Theory* 28, no. 3 [1989]:257).

3   Roland Barthes, *Mythologies*, trans. Annette Lavers (New York: Hill and Wang, 1972) and Roland Barthes, *The Fashion System*, trans. Matthew Ward and Richard Howard (New York: Hill and Wang, 1983).

4   Elizabeth Grosz, *Volatile Bodies: Toward a Corporeal Feminism* (Bloomington: Indiana University Press, 1994), 209.

5   Butler, *Gender Trouble*, ix.

6   Teresa de Lauretis, *Technologies of Gender: Essays on Theory, Film, and Fiction* (Bloomington: Indiana University Press, 1987), esp. 1–15.

7   Butler, *Gender Trouble*, 2.

8   Ibid., 16–17.

9   Ibid.

10   Ibid., 151 (n. 6).

11   Ibid., 146, 148.

12   Ibid., 149.

13   Some of this work, although in another theoretical context, is being inaugurated by molecular biologist Anne Fausto-Sterling in "The Five Sexes," *The Sciences* (March/April 1993): 20–25.

14   Judith Butler, *Bodies That Matter: On the Discursive Limits of "Sex"* (New York: Routledge, 1993).

15   Ibid., 10.

16   Ibid., 16.

17   Ibid., 23.

18   Ibid., 28.

19   Laqueur, *Making Sex*, 149. Both Alice Dreger and Anne Bartlett have expressed some reservations about Laqueur's broad historical claims (personal communications, June 16, 1994 [Dreger] and June 29, 1994 [Bartlett]).

20   Ibid., 150, 151.

21   Ibid., 159, 160–61.

22   Ibid., 138–39. Emphasis added.

23   My thanks to Mark Johnston for his input on this point.

24   Barthes, *Mythologies*, 114.

25   Ibid., 116.

26   Ibid.

27   Ibid., 117.

28   Ibid., 142–43, 131.

29   Ibid., 142, 122, 129.

30   John Money, Joan Hampson, and John Hampson, "Hermaphroditism: Recommendations Concerning Assignment of Sex, Change of Sex, and Psychologic Management," *Bulletin of the Johns Hopkins Hospital* 97, no. 4 (1955): 284–300; Money, Hampson, and Hamp-

son, "An Examination of Some Basic Sexual Concepts: The Evidence of Human Hermaphroditism," *Bulletin of the Johns Hopkins Hospital* 97, no. 4 (1955): 301–19. See also "Interview [with] John Money," *Omni* 8, no. 7 (April 1986): 79–80, 82, 84, 86, 126, 128, 130, 131.

31 Robert J. Stoller, "A Contribution to the Study of Gender Identity," *Journal of the American Medical Association* 45 (1964): 220–26; John Money and Anke Ehrhardt, *Man and Woman, Boy and Girl* (Baltimore: Johns Hopkins University Press, 1972).

32 Judith Butler argues this same point through an entirely different set of materials. See *Gender Trouble*, 6–9.

33 Clearly, I am maintaining a mind/body dichotomy that many critics would like to deconstruct. It is a useful distinction, however, in the context of the relation between sex and gender, since the opposition between the two categories is defined as that between physical sex and psychosocial gender. That is, it is an opposition between body/sex and mind/gender.

34 Jean Baudrillard, "The Precession of Simulacra," in *Art after Modernism*, ed. Brian Wallis (New York: New Museum of Contemporary Art, 1984), 261. Emphasis added.

35 Barthes, *The Fashion System*, 28.

36 This is one aspect of Anne Fausto-Sterling's argument in "The Five Sexes."

37 Butler, *Gender Trouble*, 70, 68.

38 Barthes, *The Fashion System*, 133.

39 V. N. Volosinov, *Marxism and the Philosophy of Language*, trans. Ladislav Matejka and I. R. Titunik (Cambridge, Mass.: Harvard University Press, 1986), 23–24.

40 Baudrillard, "The Precession of Simulacra," 267.

41 See discussion of Agnes in the introduction.

42 This is one way of interpreting the lower numbers of women who demand surgery to become men: the surgical procedures of phalloplasty often result in a less than satisfactory outcome. The neophallus, as it is sometimes called, does not adequately simulate the natural phallus—it comes less close to the ideal, and therefore cannot be held out as the "real thing." I discuss this at greater length in chapter 2.

43 I have shifted here to using the term "core gender identity," which was a later elaboration on "gender identity." A core gender identity is thought to be the central, irrevocable sense of oneself as a sexed being. See Robert Stoller, *Presentations of Gender* (New Haven: Yale University Press, 1985), for a more precise definition.

44 See Leslie Martin Lothstein, *Female-to-Male Transsexualism: Historical, Clinical, and Theoretical Issues* (Boston: Routledge and Kegan Paul, 1983), 12, 296.

45 Baudrillard, "The Precession of Simulacra," 266, 254–55.

46 See Butler, *Gender Trouble*, 18.

Epilogue

1 Kate Bornstein, *Gender Outlaw: On Men, Women, and the Rest of Us* (New York: Routledge, 1994), 134–35.

2 Judith Butler, *Gender Trouble: Feminism and the Subversion of Identity* (New York: Routledge, 1990), esp. 134–49; and *Bodies That Matter: On the Discursive Limits of "Sex"* (New York: Routledge, 1993), esp. ix–xii and 1–23.

3 Anne Bolin, "Transcending and Transgendering: Male-to-Female Transsexuals, Dichotomy and Diversity," in *Third Sex, Third Gender: Beyond Sexual Dimorphism in Culture and History*, ed. Gilbert Herdt (New York: Zone Books, 1994), 447–86. Gordene Olga MacKenzie's polemical *Transgender Nation* (Bowling Green, Ohio: Bowling Green State University

Popular Press, 1994) makes a similar argument, although much less convincingly. See also Martine Rothblatt, *The Apartheid of Sex: A Manifesto on the Freedom of Gender* (New York: Crown, 1995).

4 Bornstein, *Gender Outlaw*, 85, 123–25.

5 Ibid., 39.

6 See ibid., 3–4.

7 Janice G. Raymond, *The Transsexual Empire: The Making of the She-Male*, Athene Series (New York: Teachers College Press, 1994), xxxiv–xxxv.

8 Bornstein, *Gender Outlaw*, 116.

9 Ibid., 30.

10 Ibid., 118.

11 Ibid., 119–20.

12 Sandy Stone, "The *Empire* Strikes Back: A Posttranssexual Manifesto," in *Body Guards: The Cultural Politics of Gender Ambiguity*, ed. Julia Epstein and Kristina Straub (New York: Routledge, 1991), 280–304.

13 MacKenzie comments that "[r]ecent arguments to emerge from the First International Conference on Transgender Law (Houston) point out that attempts to better legislate cosmetic surgery, like being sure that doctors have surgical training, may help transsexuals obtain better care if transsexualism is de-medicalized and reclassified as a cosmetic surgery" (*Transgender Nation*, 17).

14 Continuing controversies surrounding the long-term use of birth control pills attest to this fact.

INDEX

Bernice L. Hausman is Assistant Professor of English at
Virginia Polytechnic Institute and State University in
Blacksburg, Virginia.

Library of Congress Cataloging-in-Publication Data
Hausman, Bernice Louise.
Changing sex : transsexualism, technology, and the idea of
gender / Bernice Louise Hausman.
Includes bibliographical references and index.
ISBN 0-8223-1680-3 (cl : alk. paper). — ISBN 0-8223-1692-7
(pa : alk. paper)
1. Transsexualism—Social aspects. 2. Sex change—Social
aspects. 3. Gender identity—History—20th century.
4. Transsexualism—Public opinion. 5. Hermaphroditism—Public opinion. 6. Heterosexism. I. Title.
RC560.G45H38 1995
305.3—dc20 95-17003 CIP